IMAGES
of Rail

RAILROAD DEPOTS
OF SOUTHERN INDIANA

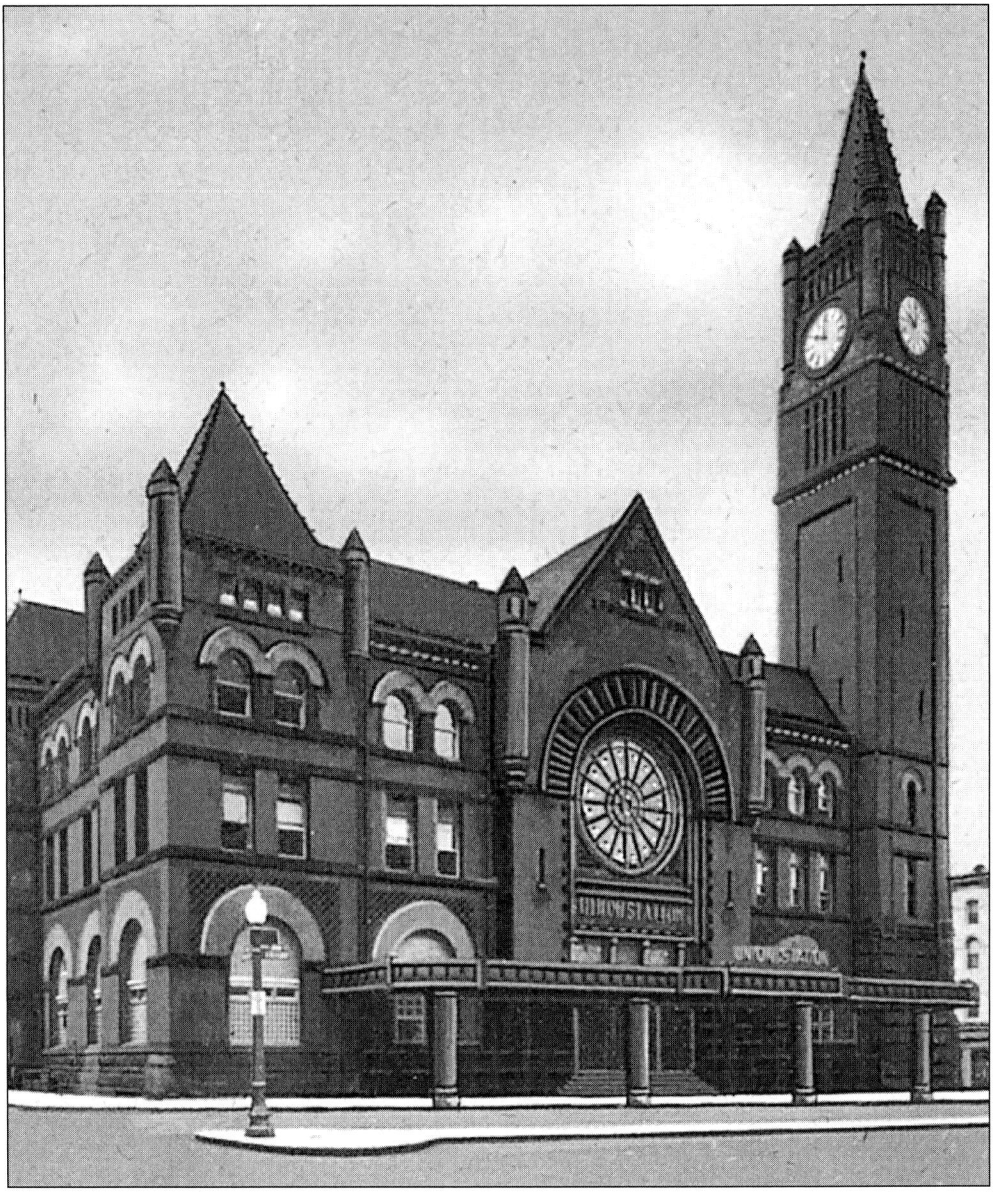

Indianapolis Union Station. The marvelous old Indianapolis Union Station is well depicted in this old postcard. However, this was not the first union station in Indianapolis. The initial structure was built in 1853 and was said to be the first union station in America; it was called Union Depot. By the 1880s, it was becoming run down and soot-covered, and it had too much business to handle. This led city leaders, railroad officials, and especially James McCrea, president of the Indianapolis Union Railway Company, to encourage the building of a new station. In 1883, a fifteenth railroad asked for accommodations at the already overcrowded old station, and the need for action in building a new station became imperative. McCrea was involved in the planning of the new structure and later oversaw its construction. The process of building a new Union Depot began in December of 1884. This new station was completed in 1887 and recently restored. This postcard depicts that second Union Station. It is currently the home of the Crowne Plaza Hotel. (Postcard by Craft Greeting Card Co.)

IMAGES
of Rail

RAILROAD DEPOTS
OF SOUTHERN INDIANA

David E. Longest

ARCADIA
PUBLISHING

ISBN 978-0-7385-3958-4

Published by Arcadia Publishing
Charleston, South Carolina

Printed in the United States of America

Library of Congress Catalog Card Number: 2005926574

For all general information contact Arcadia Publishing at:
Telephone 843-853-2070
Fax 843-853-0044
E-mail sales@arcadiapublishing.com
For customer service and orders:
Toll-Free 1-888-313-2665

Visit us on the Internet at www.arcadiapublishing.com

I dedicate this book to my father, Maxwell Longest, who always wanted to "hop an empty box car and travel across America" and to my wife, Vicky, who helped me by driving to places I would not have ventured alone. I began my photography in 1999 and worked on this labor-of-love mostly during the summers. After a moderate stroke in 2001, I found myself unable to drive for a period of time. Vicky became my eyes and gave up more than a few Saturdays in my pursuits. She's the best!

(cover) **STEAM LOCOMOTIVE #218.** This photograph shows steam locomotive #218 and several railroad workers at the Salem Monon Depot in 1909. (Courtesy the Depot Railroad Museum Collection.)

Contents

Acknowledgments

Locating and photographing old depots was certainly made easier by the website of Mark Camp. This site covers the United States and provides the seeker with the knowledge of the general location of railroad structures. Mr. Camp graciously acknowledges in his website those persons who complete individual research and share what they have discovered with him. It is a real team effort. The website covers not only depots, but also bridges, towers, car barns, office buildings, rail yards, and much more. Nevertheless, one has to wonder how many depots scattered across the state are believed to be gone, yet have been simply forgotten.

I wish to acknowledge the work of Francis H. Parker. His book, *Indiana Railroad Depots: A Threatened Heritage*, piqued my interest upon first reading. I organized my personal photograph collection as Parker did, alphabetically by county. It was my desire to update the findings of his book. Many of the dates used in my book can be attributed to Mr. Parker's fine research or to Mr. Camp's website. In these few years, I have already recorded the absence of over 40 depots that Mr. Parker listed in his text, published in 1989. Some are no longer standing, some may have been moved to other locations. I have also located 13 depots that were not in Mr. Parker's book. My initial photographic journeys were based on my desire to find as many Monon depots as I could. Later, I began combing the counties near New Albany. Mr. Parker's book was a great help as a field guide.

I also wish to acknowledge Cecil Smith, the agent/operator of The Depot, a railroad museum located in the John Hay Center in Salem. I will mention more about this fine rail museum in chapter nine. Cecil has served the history of railroading well over the years, helping local youth gain some knowledge of what the railroad meant to Salem and other communities in Washington County.

I also want to thank the Monon Railroad Historical-Technical Society for their help in allowing me to use a number of their excellent photographs. The Monon played a major role in the railroad history of Indiana. Photographs from their archives will be acknowledged as coming from the MRHTS Collection.

Other persons I thank for opportunities, information, and other help include: David Barksdale (president, Floyd County Historical Society); Eric Heidenreich (Gibson County); Jamie Harris (Lawrence County Urban Enterprise Zone); Ronald Grimes (Jefferson County Historical Society); and Alan Barnett (Indiana Railway Museum). I also received very helpful information from the office employees of the Louisville, New Albany & Corydon Railroad and workers at the chambers of commerce in the Washington and Scottsburg depots.

There were countless individuals who answered emails and telephone calls all over Indiana in response to my inquiries. I received helpful information about the status of depots from libraries, chambers of commerce, county historical societies, and railroad enthusiasts. I thank you again.

Acknowledgements for photos include: John Fuller; Robert Gibson Jr. (Gibson County); Bob McCord; the Monon Railroad Historical-Technical Society; Bob Mount; Cecil Smith; and Ron Stuckey. In addition, I wish to thank the New Albany-Floyd County Public Library for use of excerpts from these collections: 1) the Emma Carleton Collection; 2) the Reisz/Coleman Collection; and 3) the Hedden Family Collection. Photographs and images that are not otherwise credited were taken by the author or come from his personal collection.

Introduction

Depots were the front doors for many Hoosier communities served by railroads during the middle and late 1800s. They were the contact point between the local community and the outside world. A farmer could order a farm tool from Chicago and have it delivered to his town. His wife could order cookware in the same way. The depot was where we saw our military off as they ventured to foreign lands. It was depended upon by manufacturers as the means by which goods were exported. We even counted on the depot to bring us our daily news and mail.

Today, many towns that were once served by one or more railroads have none. Hundreds of miles of track have been taken up and the land returned agriculture. In some cases, the railroad has attempted to sell the roadbed to the local community at exaggerated costs—prices the towns and cities simply cannot afford to pay. In other cases, the cities have acquired the land and turned it into trails to become a part of parks and protected areas. Railroad stations that were once a vital part of the community have disappeared too. As the railroad business shifted from local deliveries to long haul, the depots were no longer needed, and many have been demolished. Fewer than 250 depots remain in Indiana today.

Many of the book's chapters are divided by regions so that you can locate, appreciate, and, if you desire, photograph these structures while in the area. Other chapters simply trace the line of a particular railroad. While I was traveling Indiana and photographing these depots, I found it simpler to create circles so that I would eventually return home to New Albany. These circles became increasingly larger and required greater amounts of time. Eventually I had to plan my trips over a couple of days to accomplish my goals.

The focus of this book is on the depots and freight houses that are still standing and in fairly good repair. I will also mention some stations that have been razed or moved and their significance to that particular region. In addition, I will discuss the function of depots and provide photographs of items related to that function. In these images, I will include other areas of railroading such as bridges, trestles, train yards, tunnels, and of course, locomotives and rolling stock.

The depots reviewed in the book will include those of Marion County and other counties that are on about the same latitude. This point of division was chosen because a majority of larger and more industrialized cities lie in the northern counties and in closer proximity to Chicago and Lake Michigan.

The final chapter deals with efforts of preservation and reclamation of railroading and depots. Depots can best be appreciated when we see the anxious people sitting on the benches, the well-dressed trainman loading the coaches with luggage, the friendly agent standing behind the window selling tickets, and the pleased ladies picking up their ordered parcels at the freight house. Those days are gone for certain, yet there is still a taste of railroading made available at some of Indiana's fine rail museums. Today's youth know very little about this part of America's past; growing an appreciation of this history in them has been made easier by the actions of these museums and their many volunteers.

The important thing is that we learn about our communities and their buildings and try to be creative in reclaiming or recycling these structures, before they are all gone. Many depots have been turned into places of business, while others are now special meeting places, and many are local museums. Yet some sit vacant, waiting for the bulldozer. Obviously there is no pat answer as to how best to use these buildings. It is more important that those who enjoy railroading and its history be active within their communities and try to protect these structures. In writing this book, I hope to remind readers that there are may be buildings in their communities worth learning about and preserving.

One

NORTH ON THE PENNSYLVANIA LINE

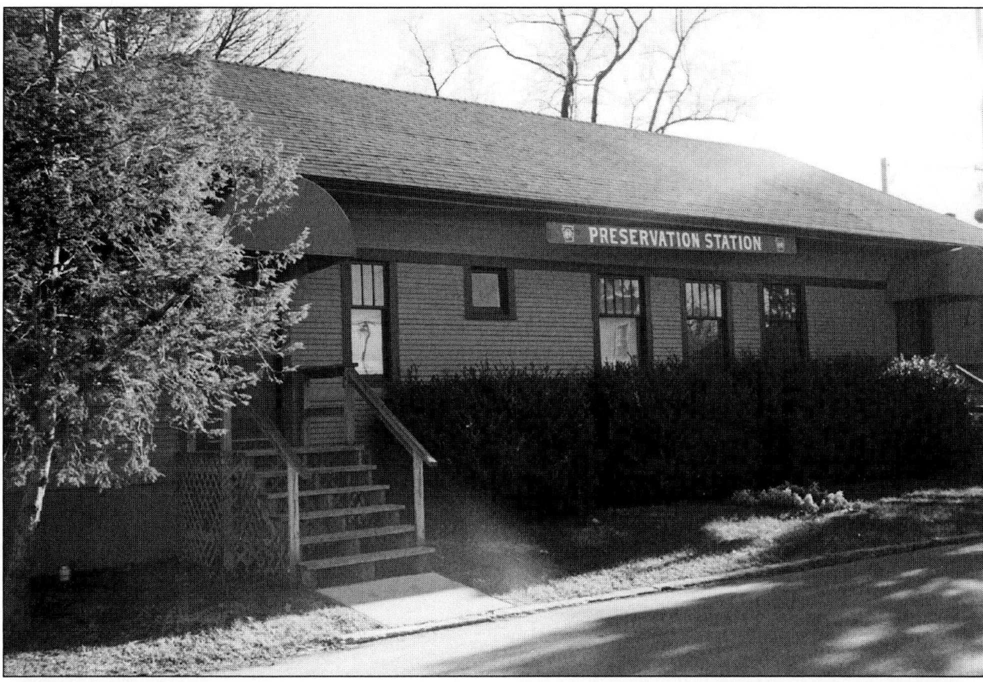

PRESERVATION STATION. Jeffersonville begins a route that shadows the old Pennsylvania (Penn Central) route. A local preservationist group in Jeffersonville was able to save the Pennsylvania passenger depot in this photo. Built in 1929, this wooden structure is now located at 100 West Court Alley. It has acquired an appropriate name, Preservation Station. The PRR depot was moved at a cost of $4,000 from Mitchell Street to its present location in 1986. It is used for special community meetings and other functions. In speaking with a representative of the preservation group, I found that only the floor of the interior remains original and that other evidences of the building's former life as a depot have been removed.

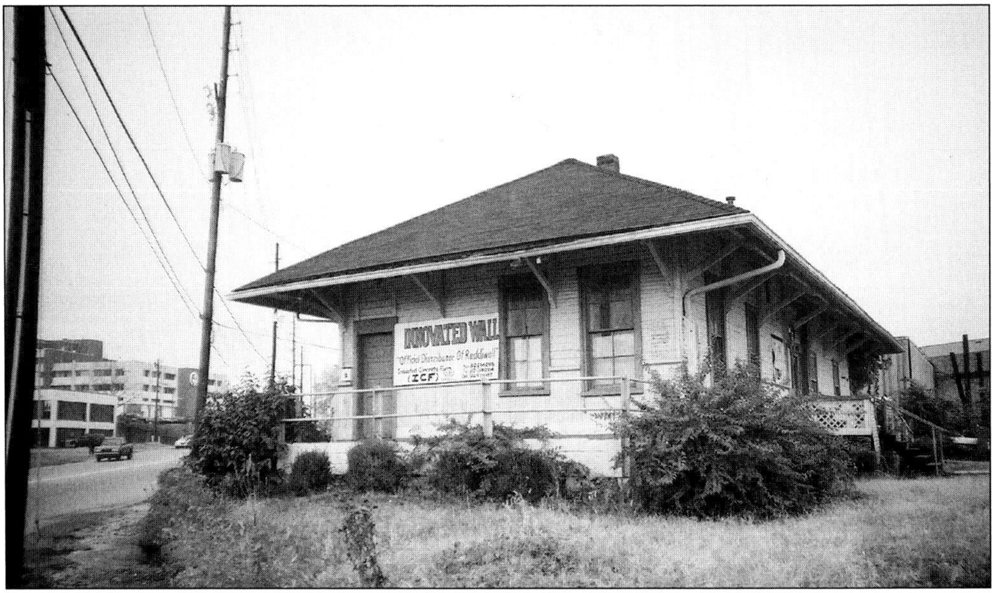

Freight Depot at Jeffersonville. A wooden Cleveland, Cincinnati, Chicago and St. Louis (CCC&StL) freight depot sits on Spring Street in downtown Jeffersonville. Currently used as a business, it is located a half block north of Tenth Street and needs a great deal of repair. The nearby tracks have recently been removed. The future of the depot is in doubt as there are plans for many changes in that area of Jeffersonville.

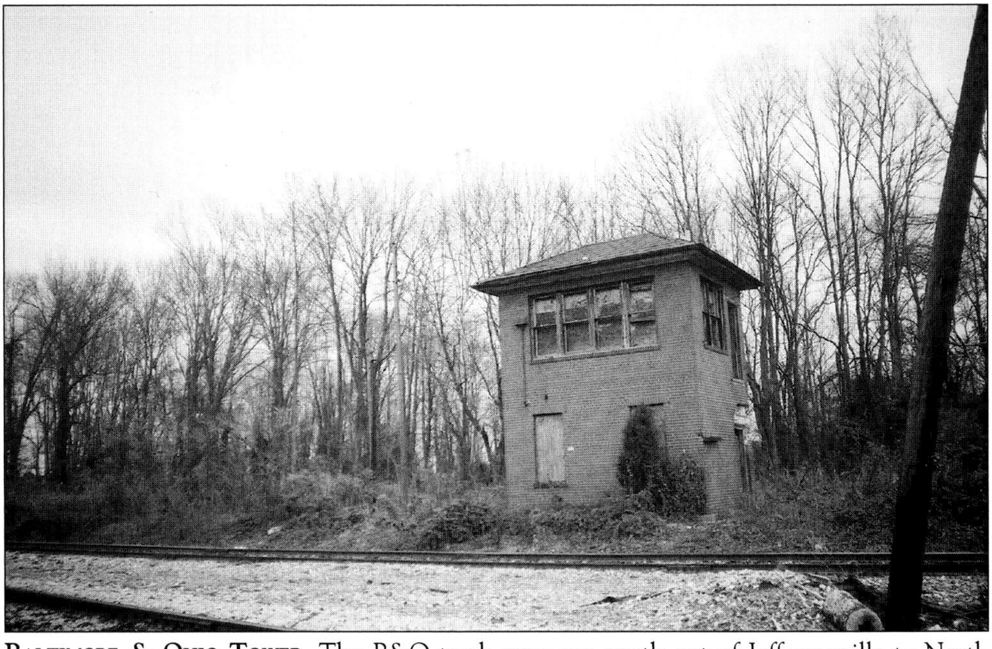

Baltimore & Ohio Tower. The B&O track once ran north out of Jeffersonville to North Vernon, where it continued east toward Cincinnati or west toward Seymour. It also ran east from Jeffersonville to Charlestown. At one time, the B&O added an extension from Watson (east of Jeffersonville) to New Albany, but it was short-lived. This B&O tower stands in the Watson area at the entrance to the yard and has been abandoned for some time.

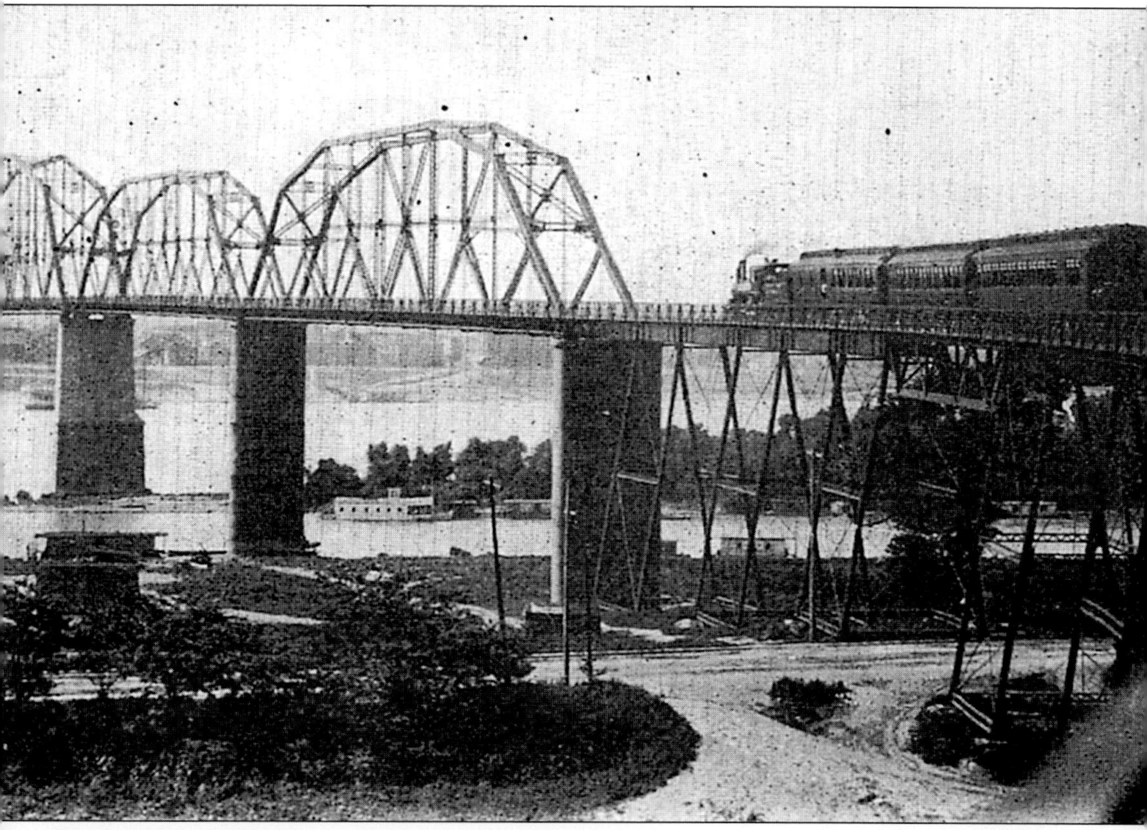

Big Four Rail Bridge. In Jeffersonville, you are quite close to the Ohio River. There are currently two rail bridges, the Big Four and the Pennsylvania. This old photograph shows a steam passenger train crossing the Big Four Bridge, which connected Louisville, Kentucky with Jeffersonville. Work on the bridge began in 1888 and was completed in September 1895. However, in 1883, on an unseasonably warm December day, construction was temporarily halted because of serious accidents. The accidents were the result of 35-mile-per-hour winds and led to the deaths of 21 men. (Courtesy New Albany-Floyd County Public Library.)

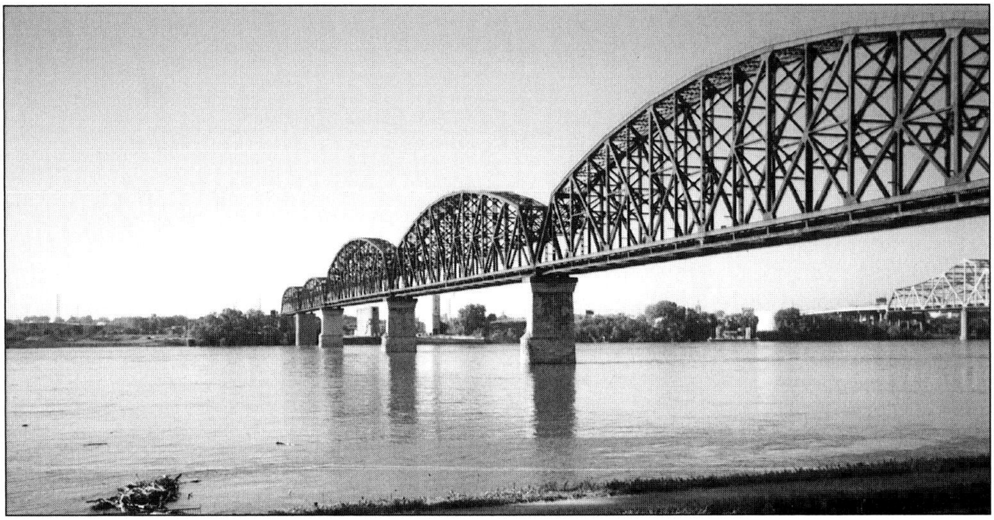

BIG FOUR RAIL BRIDGE TODAY. This bridge was renovated between 1925 and 1929, by erecting a new span within the old one. The bridge has a length of 2,525 feet. The span was declared abandoned in 1969 after a merger of the Big Four and Pennsylvania Railroads created the Penn-Central and all rail traffic was shifted to the Fourteenth Street (Pennsylvania) Bridge. The bridge's steel approaches were removed and sold for scrap soon after, although there are still huge concrete supports on some nearby properties. Plans are currently being made to include the bridge as a part of the Greenway project that will allow pedestrian traffic to cross from Jeffersonville to Louisville by walking across the Big Four Bridge.

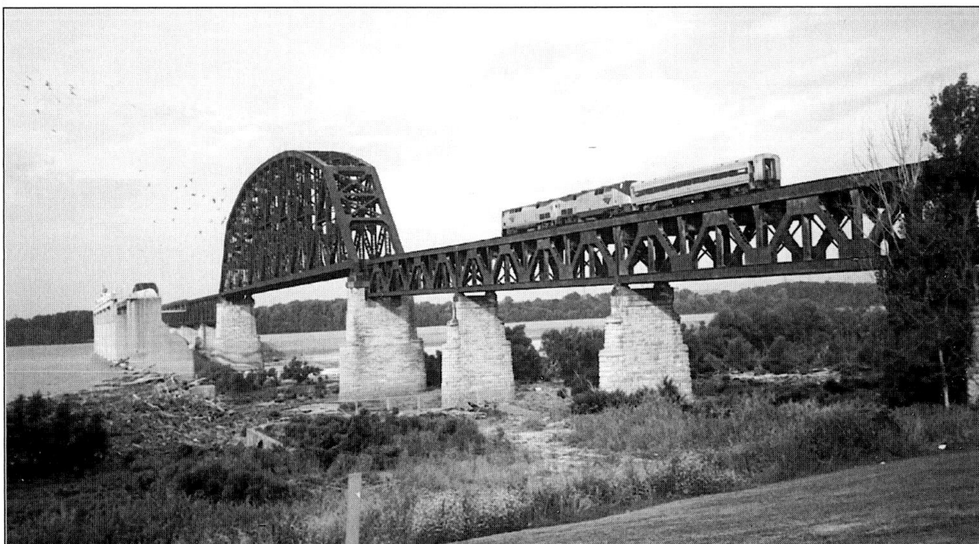

PENNSYLVANIA RAILROAD BRIDGE. The Pennsylvania Bridge is farther west, right next to the falls of the Ohio and the dam. This photograph shows the Louisville Cardinal (Amtrack) heading north on the PRR Bridge on June 27, 2002, a year before Amtrak ended the route. This bridge was built in 1918; it replaced the first bridge, constructed in 1870 as a joint project of the Pennsylvania and L&N railroads. This bridge is the oldest one to cross the Ohio at Louisville. It has a length of 5,218 feet and a lift system for use when taller river vessels go beneath the bridge and into the opening of the McAlpine Locks. It is now used by the Louisville & Indiana Railroad.

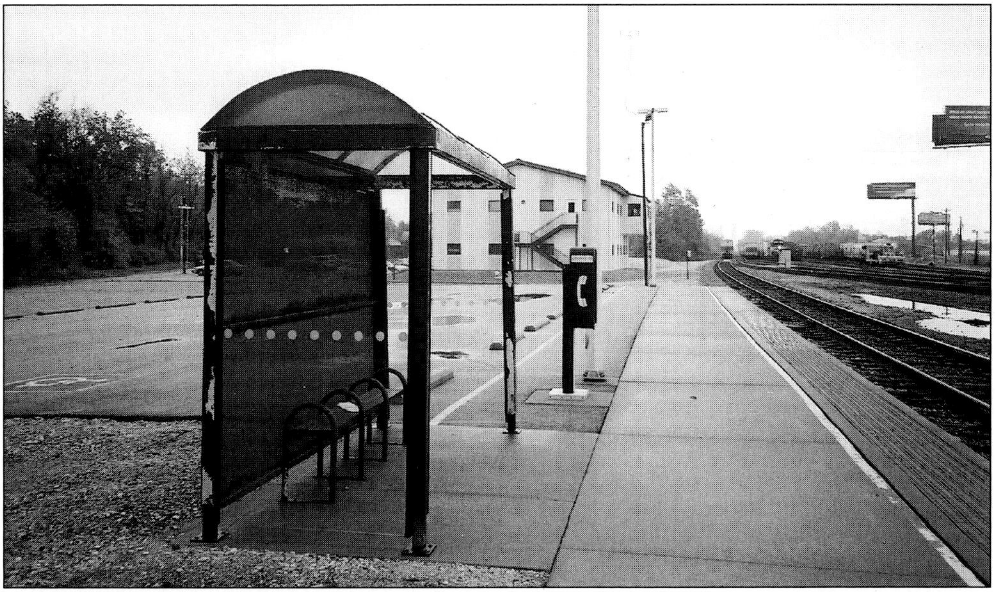

Louisville & Indiana Yard. Located just east of Interstate 65 in Jeffersonville, this is the yard of the Louisville & Indiana Railroad. This photograph shows the L&I dispatching and yard building and the now abandoned Amtrak shelter. The yard building was constructed in the year 2000. The company has about 40 employees, and the L&I owns a total of 12 locomotives. The Consolidated Grain and Barge Company, located at the Clark Maritime Centre in Jeffersonville, is one of the larger customers of the Louisville & Indiana Railroad.

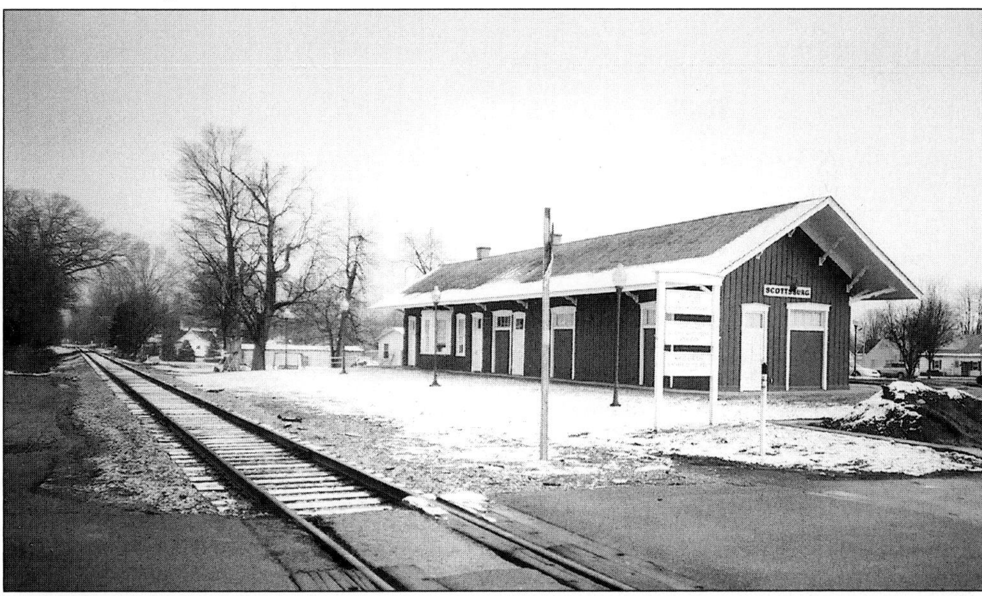

Scottsburg Pennsylvania Depot. This was the second prominent stop on the Penn Central (PC) route. It was originally a Jeffersonville, Madison & Indianapolis depot, built in 1872 and used until the 1950s. This wooden structure has board and batten siding and a wide overhanging roof. It was moved a block north of the original site several years ago, but still remains near the tracks. The tracks are still in use by CSX Railroad. The depot was listed on National Register of Historic Places in 1991.

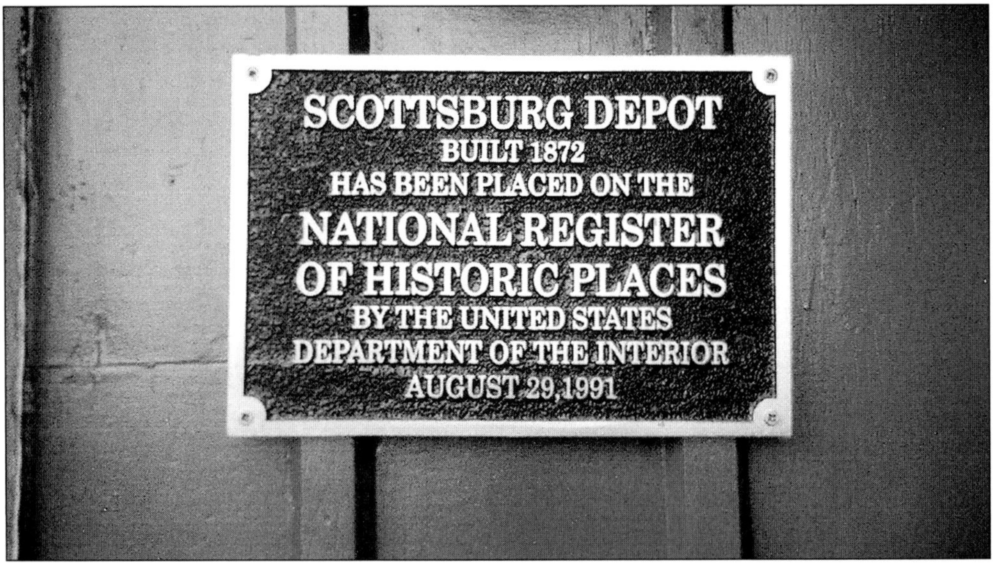

Scottsburg Marker. On the east entrance to the Scottsburg PRR depot is a marker signifying that the depot has been placed on the National Register of Historic Places. This distinguishes the depot and its place in Scottsburg's railroad history. However, a marker itself does not protect from arson or vandalism. The Monon depot in New Albany had also been placed on this register, yet in March of 1995, the New Albany depot caught fire, weakening the structure; it had to be torn down in August of that year. Recognition and acclaim are important, but they alone do not guarantee protection. We must educate the public and instill an appreciation for these historic buildings.

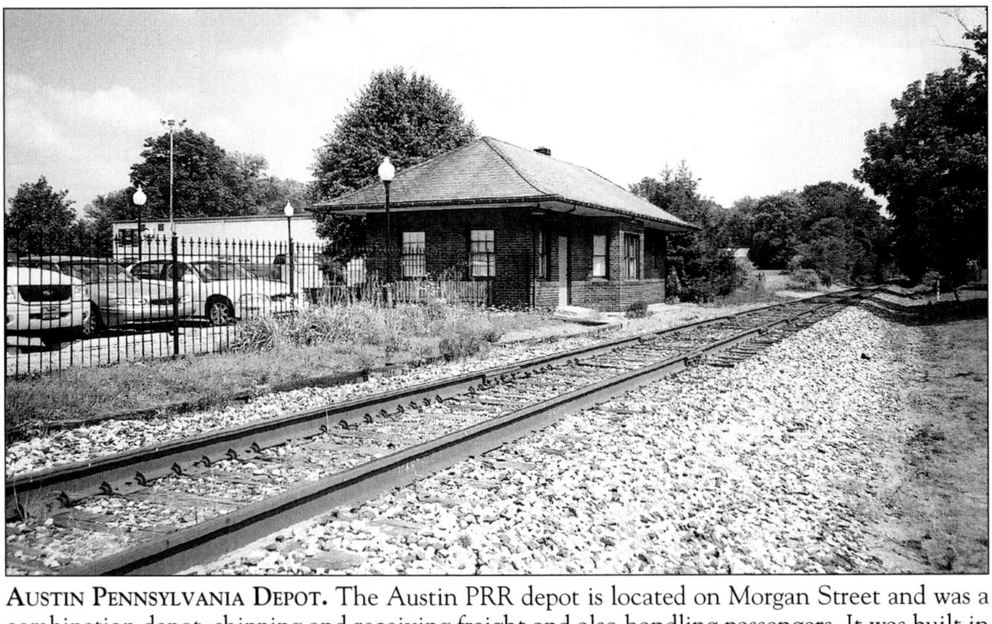

Austin Pennsylvania Depot. The Austin PRR depot is located on Morgan Street and was a combination depot, shipping and receiving freight and also handling passengers. It was built in 1934, and has a Pennsylvania caboose on the property near the brick depot to add to the rail theme. An important industry in Austin, the canning factory, used the rail line extensively in the past This depot is now used as a meeting place for the local Lion's Club.

Freight Scale. Being a combination depot, the Austin depot had to accommodate the needs of passengers and handle the receiving and shipping of small amounts of freight. Many commodities were shipped by their weight, requiring the railroad to have a scale as part of the necessary equipment. This old scale had been relegated to the outside of the Austin station.

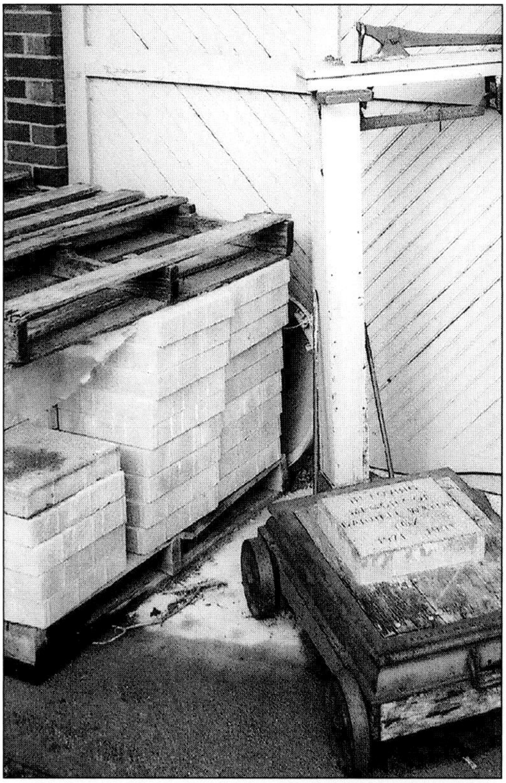

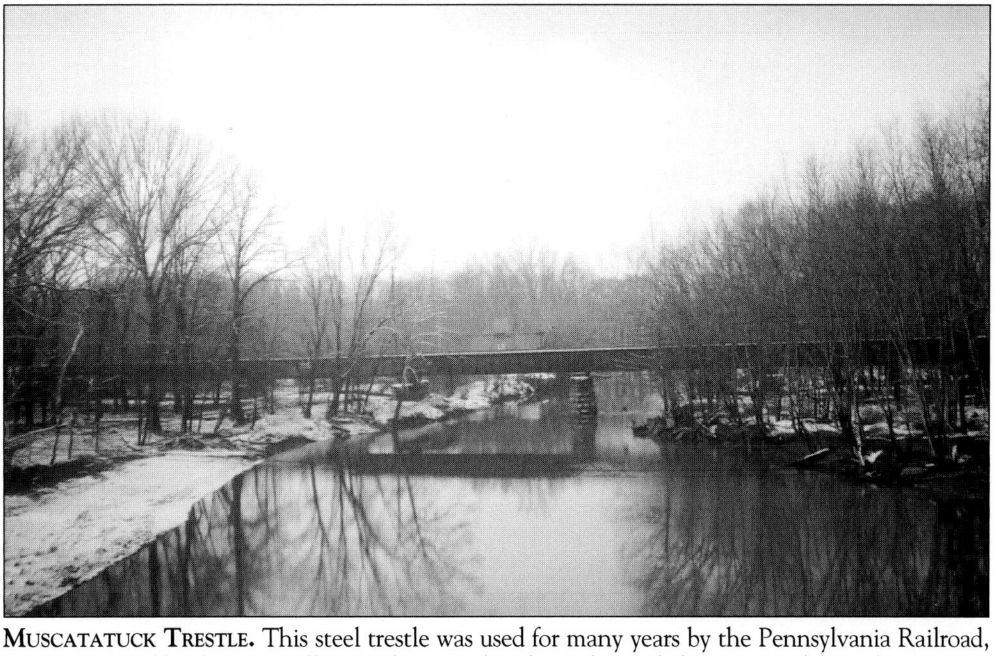

Muscatatuck Trestle. This steel trestle was used for many years by the Pennsylvania Railroad, but is now used by the Louisville & Indiana Railroad. It is located about two miles north of Austin and can be seen from U.S. Highway 31. It crosses the Muscatatuck River as the river meanders its way across southern Indiana.

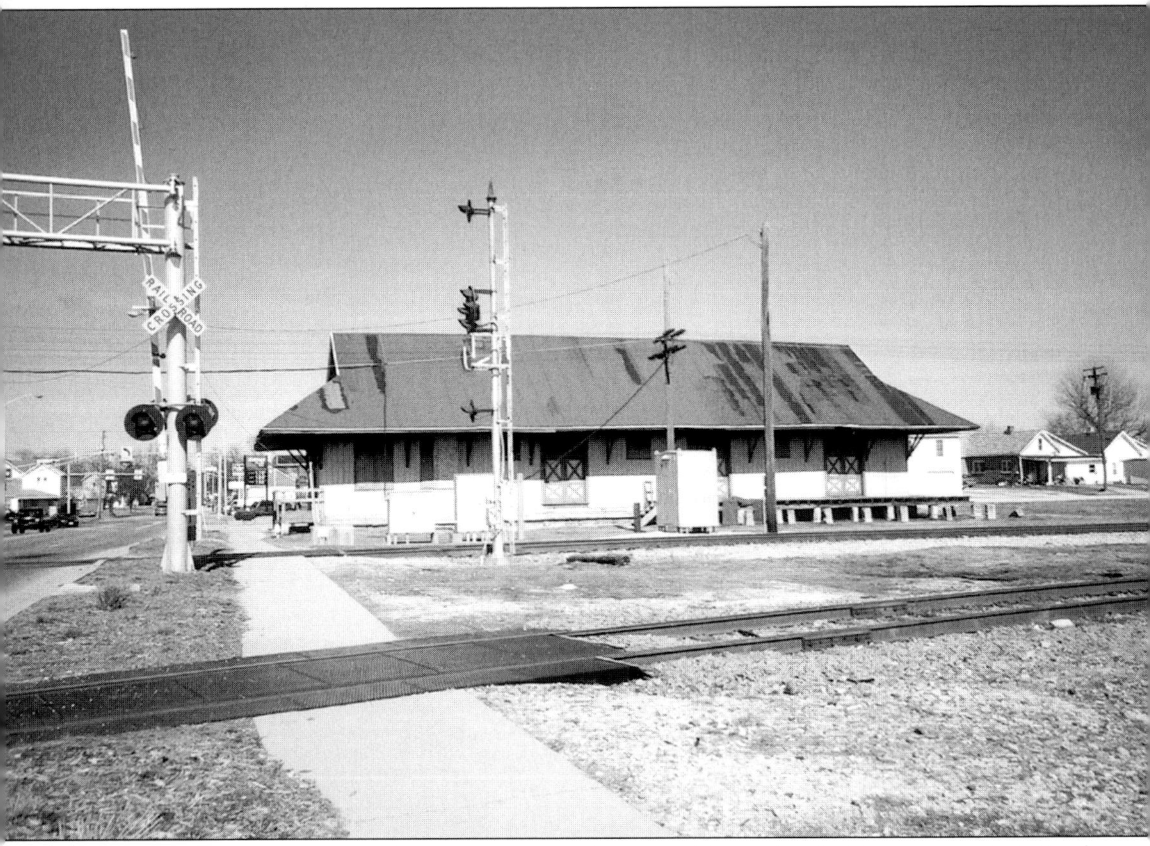

SEYMOUR FREIGHT DEPOT. This photograph shows the Milwaukee freight depot at 105 North Broadway Street The local historical society has recently acquired a grant which will be used to restore the depot. This building was constructed in 1901 by the Southern Indiana Railway and is presently vacant. The tracks are a continuation of the CSX line we have been tracing from Jeffersonville. The first train robbery in the United States was committed by the Reno brothers here in 1866. They held up the Ohio & Mississippi train as it pulled out of the Seymour depot. Their take was $15,000. The depot was added to the National Register of Historic Places in 2003.

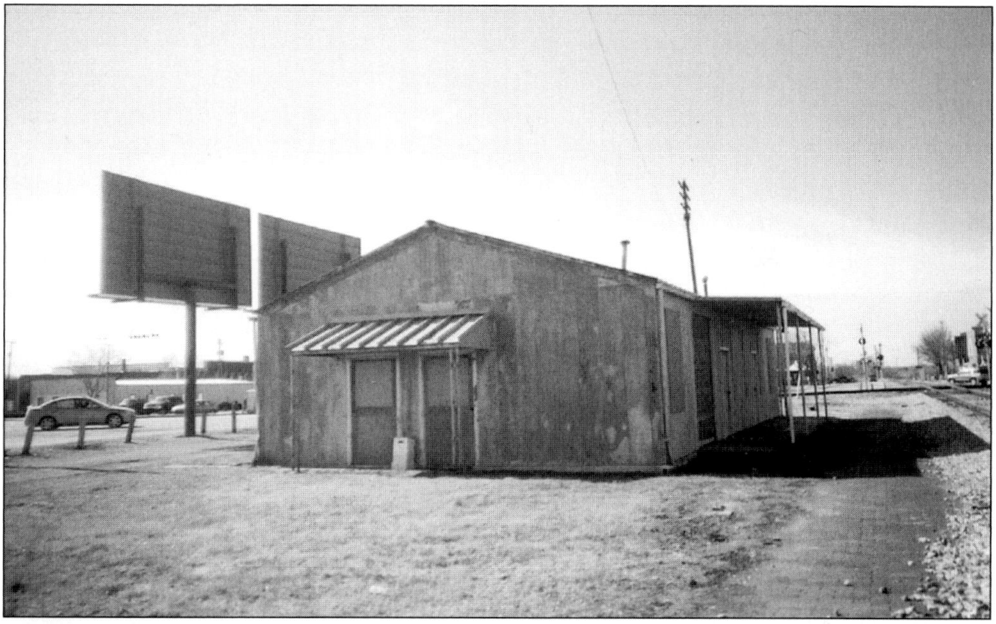

SEYMOUR B&O DEPOT. This photograph shows the Baltimore & Ohio freight house that is located near the junction of the old B&O line and the Milwaukee Line at St. Louis and Jeffersonville Streets. This east-west rail line came to Seymour in 1852, crossing the land of farmer Meedy Shields. The B&O line comes out of Cincinnati and then runs through North Vernon before continuing across the state. This is a very run-down metal structure. The rail is now used by the CSX and Louisville & Indiana Railroad.

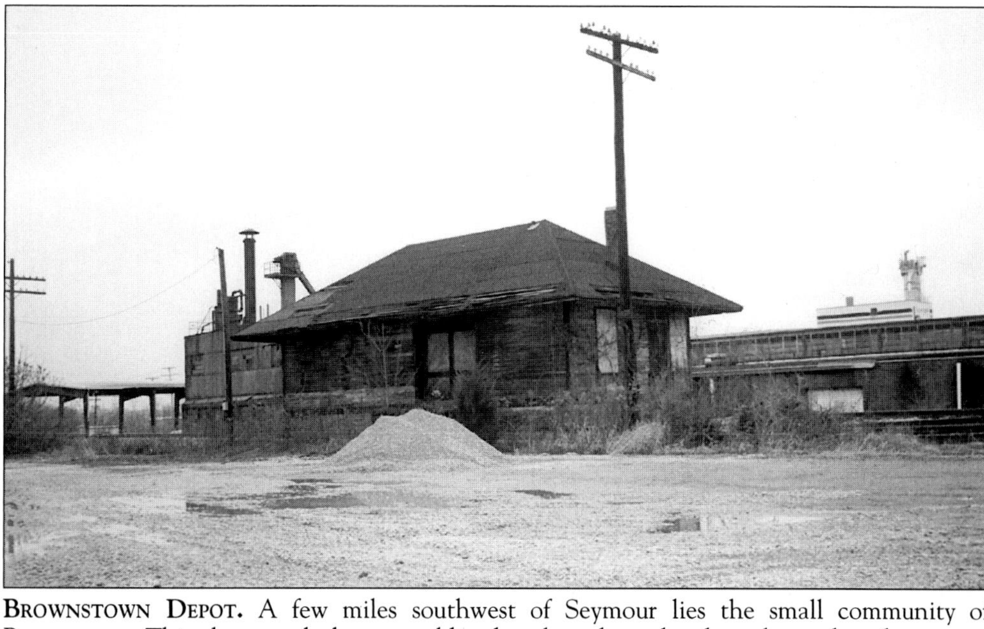

BROWNSTOWN DEPOT. A few miles southwest of Seymour lies the small community of Brownstown. This photograph shows an old and neglected wooden depot located on the current CSX track coming from North Vernon and Seymour. This was a B&O freight depot, built in 1908. It sits on the corner of Depot and Spring Streets. The B&O line then continued west to Mitchell, Shoals, Washington, and Vincennes.

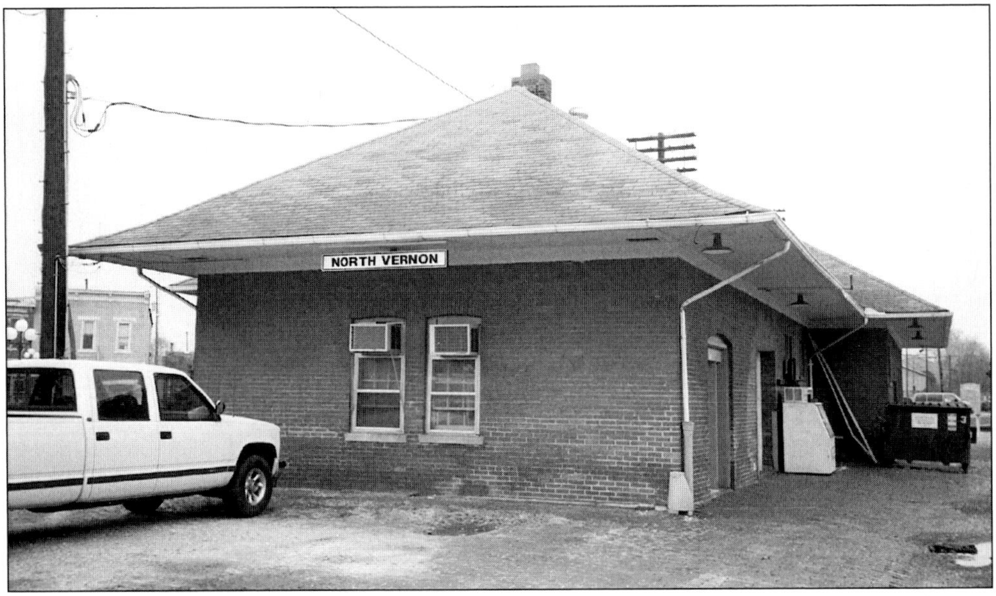

NORTH VERNON B&O DEPOT. North Vernon celebrates "Railroad Days" each June, which gives an idea of how important railroads are in the city's history. This community has a solid rail history, founded in the workings of the B&O Railroad and several others. The brick passenger depot shown here is a B&O depot located at Madison Avenue and Main Street Still in use by CSX, it was built around 1888, after an earlier depot burned. North Vernon once had the third highest railroad traffic in Indiana. The Ohio & Mississippi, the Baltimore & Ohio, the Pennsylvania, and the New York Central Railroads converged here.

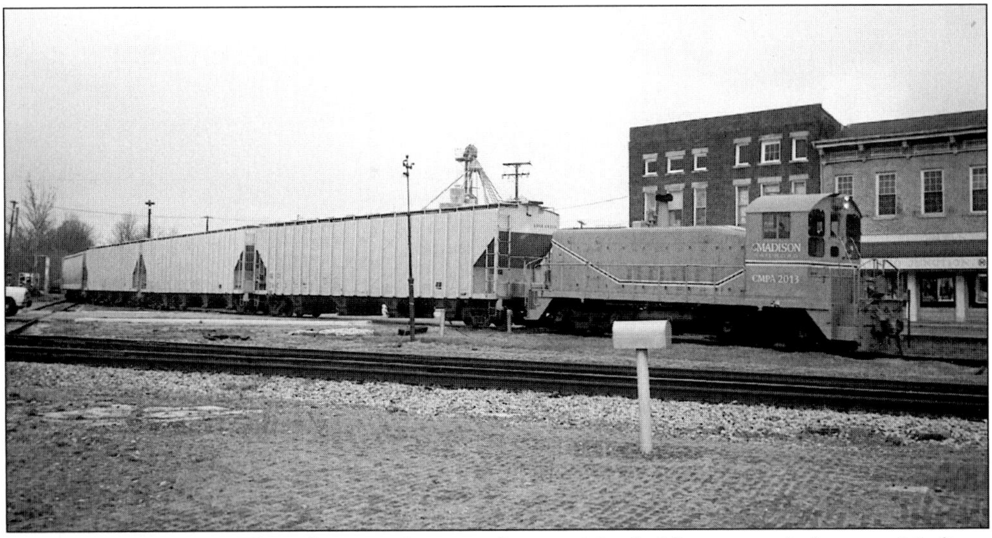

MADISON RAILROAD. This photograph was taken in North Vernon and shows a Madison Railroad train. The Madison Railroad is a Class III railroad that runs between Madison and North Vernon and uses the old Columbus & Indianapolis rail line. This is the same line that began at Madison, went through Columbus, and first reached Indianapolis in 1847. The length of this short line from Madison to North Vernon is nearly 26 miles. The Madison Railroad is owned by the Madison Port Authority and ranks sixth in Indiana Class III railroads in volume of carloads handled.

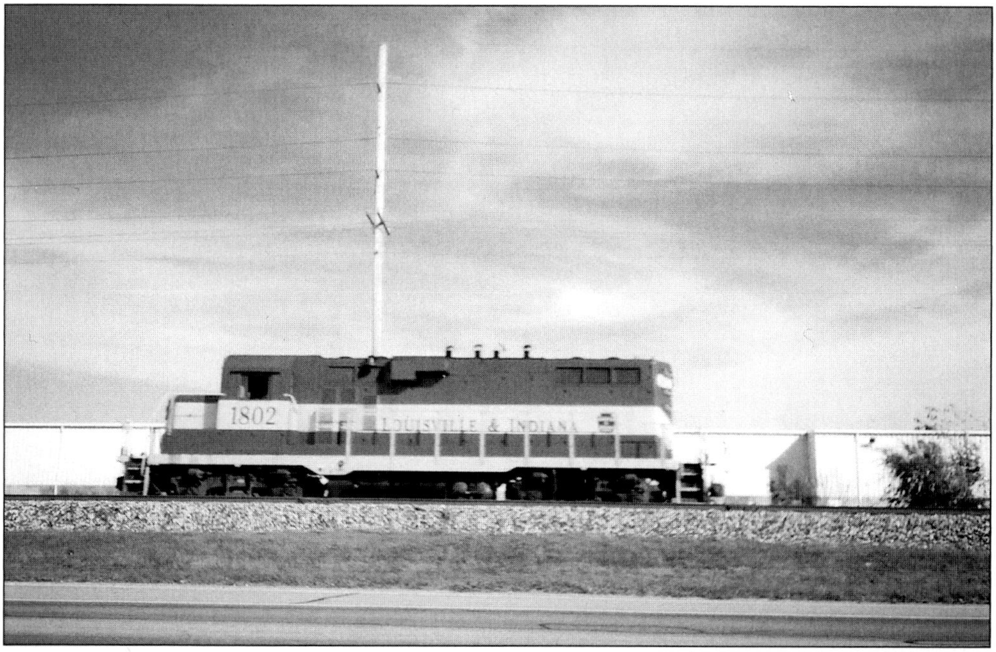

LOUISVILLE & INDIANA. A lone engine heads north near Columbus. This short line uses the old Pennsylvania trackage from Jeffersonville to Indianapolis. The L&I Railroad currently performs business on 113 miles of track, 7 miles of which are jointly owned with other roads. L&I stops at many companies between Louisville and Indianapolis. Chemicals, plastics, auto parts, steel, grain, and scrap metal make up most of the traffic. The L&I Railroad was recently ranked tenth in Indiana Class III railroads in volume of carloads handled.

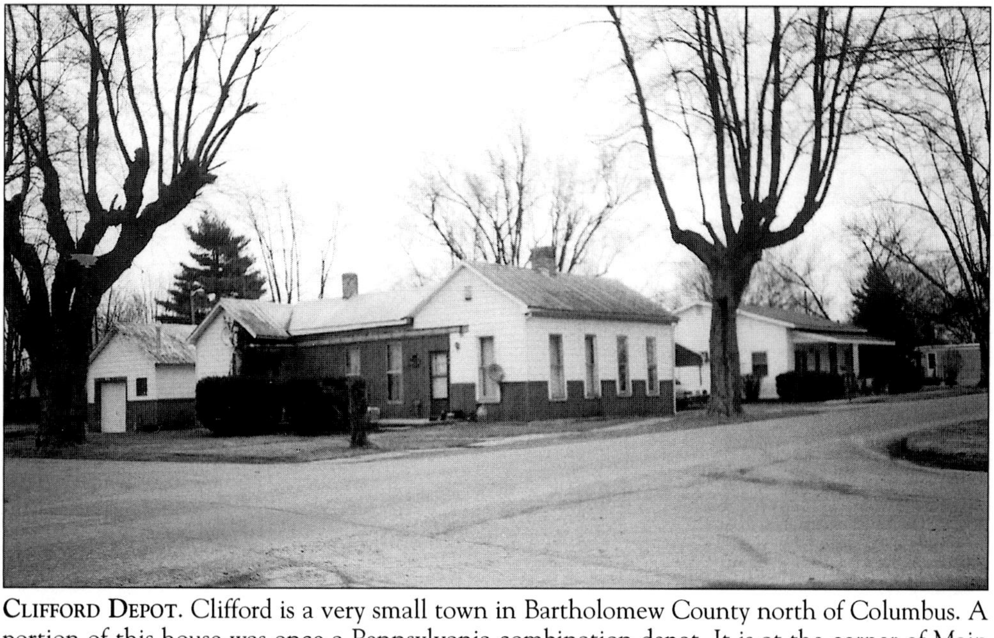

CLIFFORD DEPOT. Clifford is a very small town in Bartholomew County north of Columbus. A portion of this house was once a Pennsylvania combination depot. It is at the corner of Main and Depot Streets. Now a residence, the old wooden depot portion has been altered a great deal. It was built in 1892, and there are currently no tracks or railroad nearby.

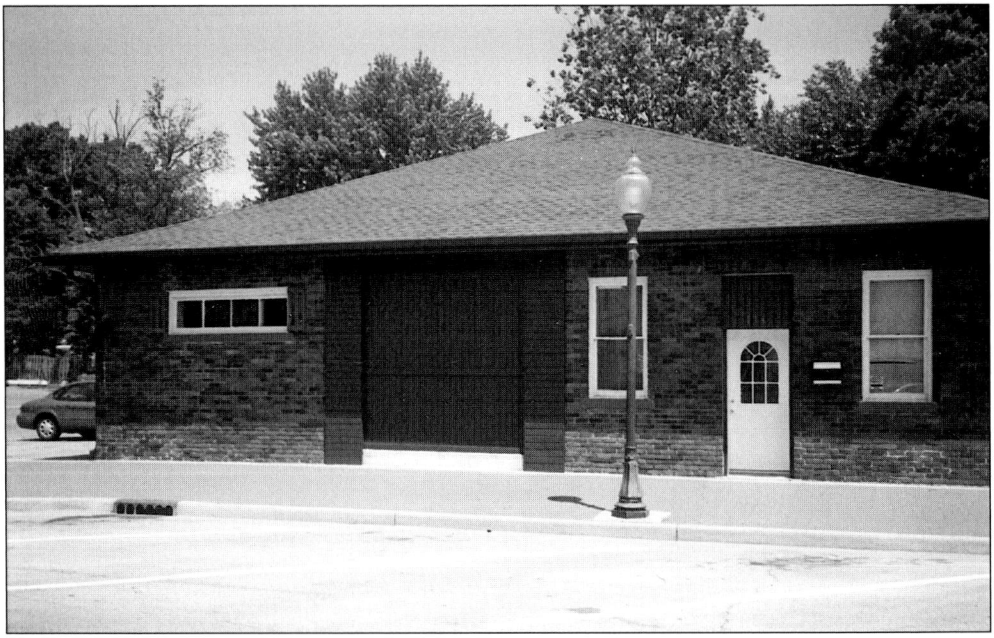

Edinburgh Interurban. This brick building was an Interstate Public Service Company (IPSC) interurban combination depot. It served as a depot and a substation. It is located in Johnson County at 114 Main Street in Edinburgh, about ten miles north of Columbus. In 1991, the station was recognized as part of the Edinburgh Commercial Historic District

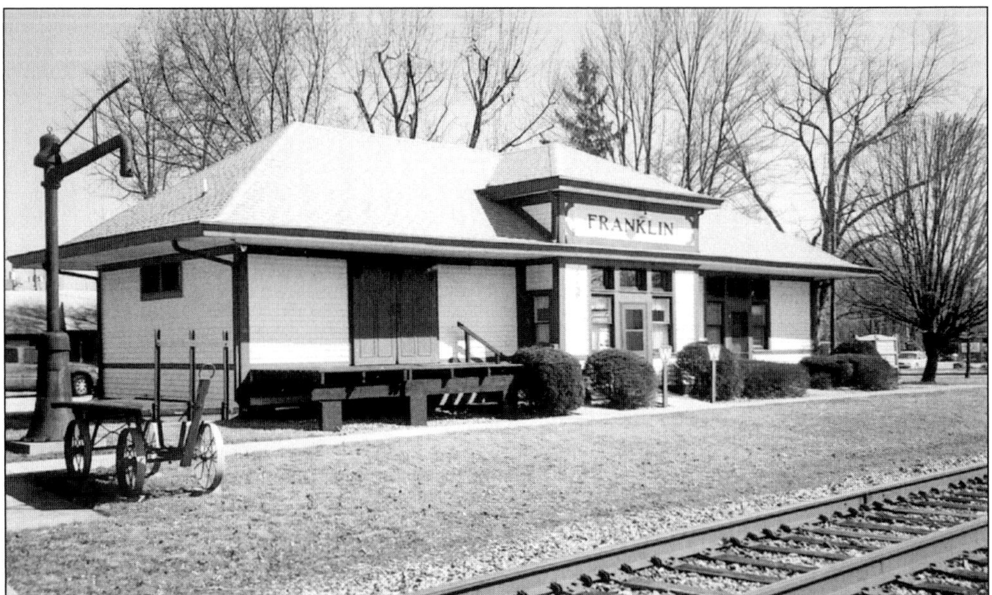

Franklin Depot. The Franklin Chamber of Commerce makes its home in the restored New York Central Railroad Depot of Franklin. It was moved from its Cincinnati Street and Martin Place location in 1978 to its present location on East Jefferson Street. The cost for the location and renovation was about $50,000. This combination depot with clapboard siding was constructed in 1909. A portion of the depot is now preserved as a railroad museum.

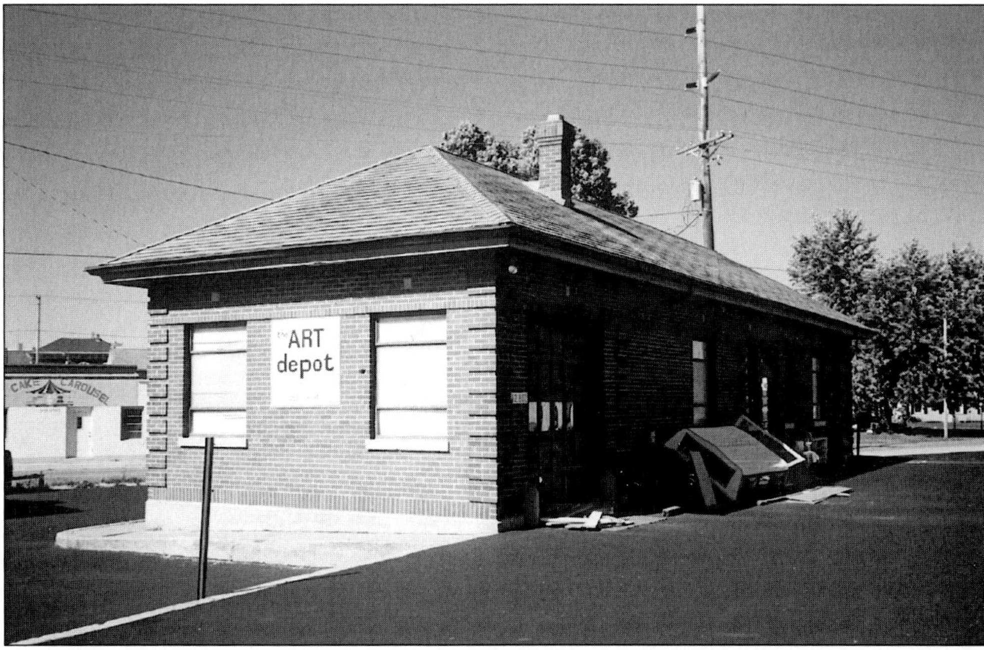

SHELBYVILLE COMBINATION DEPOT. After leaving Franklin, go east to Shelbyville where you will find a combination passenger and freight house on Noble Street This station was a New York Central brick depot and has recently been used as the Art Depot. It was built in 1949. There have been other NYC depots previously near this site.

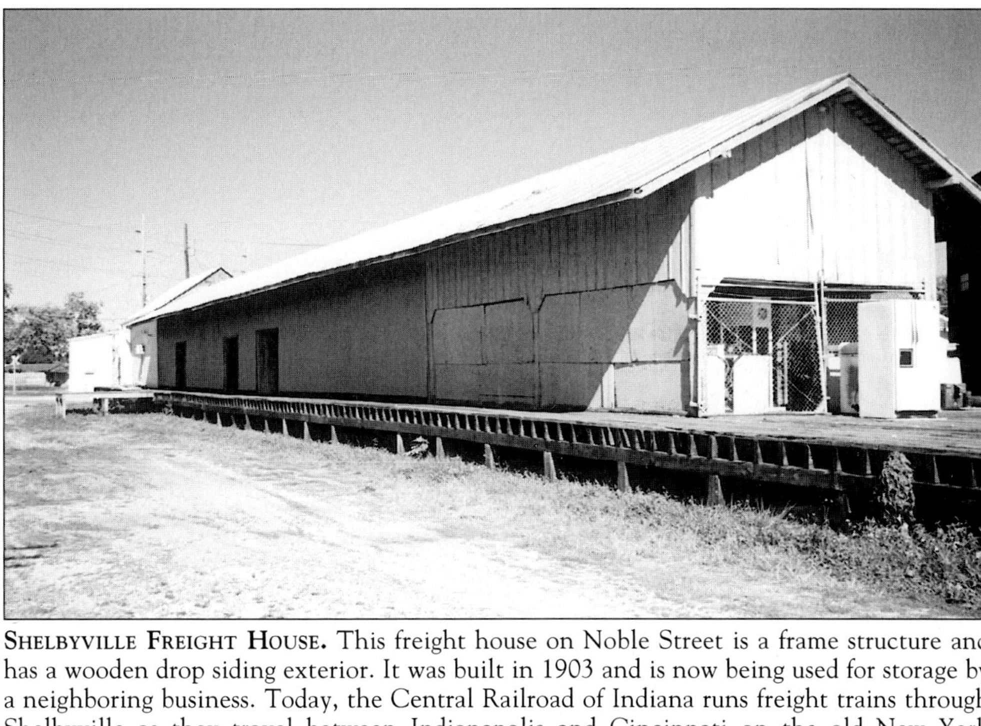

SHELBYVILLE FREIGHT HOUSE. This freight house on Noble Street is a frame structure and has a wooden drop siding exterior. It was built in 1903 and is now being used for storage by a neighboring business. Today, the Central Railroad of Indiana runs freight trains through Shelbyville as they travel between Indianapolis and Cincinnati on the old New York Central line.

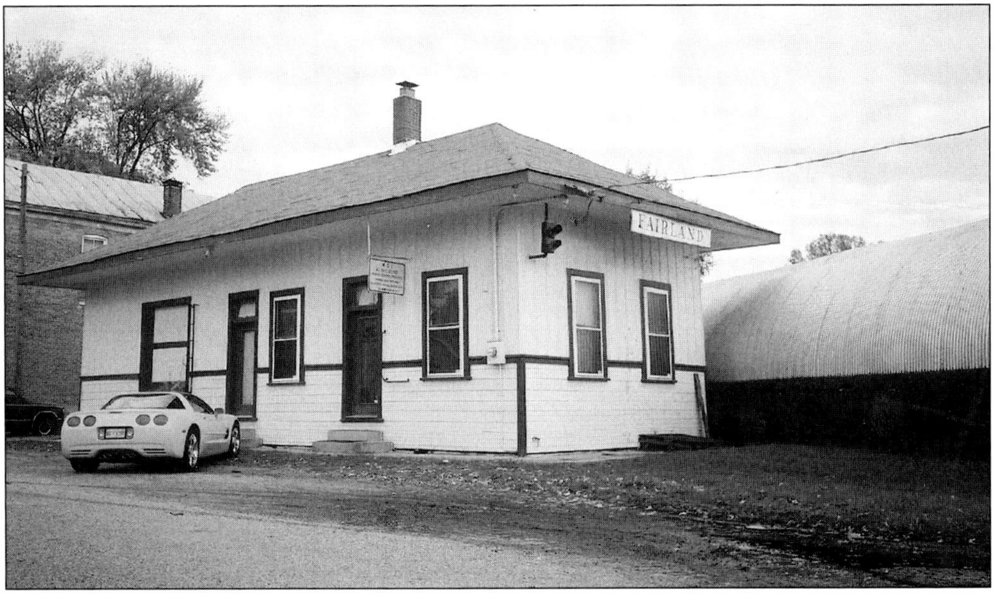

FAIRLAND COMBINATION DEPOT. There is another depot in Shelby County located near the place where Interstate 74 cuts diagonally across Shelby County. This was a CCC&StL depot and currently stands on West Washington Street. It was built of wood in 1909 and was later moved from the original site. The New York Central abandoned the trackage of the Franklin to the Fairland line in the early 1970s.

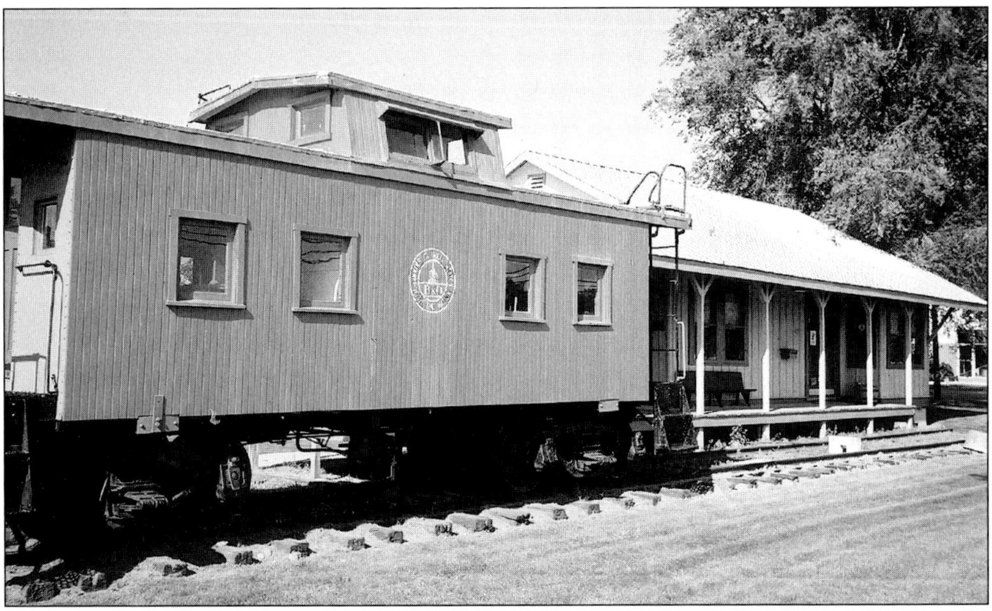

MORRISTOWN CH&D DEPOT. Morristown is a tiny town located just northeast of Shelbyville in Shelby County. There is a Cincinnati, Hamilton & Dayton (CH&D) wooden combination depot on Main Street that is being used as a business. You will find a Baltimore & Ohio caboose sitting at the east end of the depot. The depot was built in 1869, but was moved from its original site and reconstructed in the mid-1970s. It has been listed on the National Register of Historic Places since 1979.

Two

CROSSROADS OF AMERICA THE INDIANAPOLIS AREA

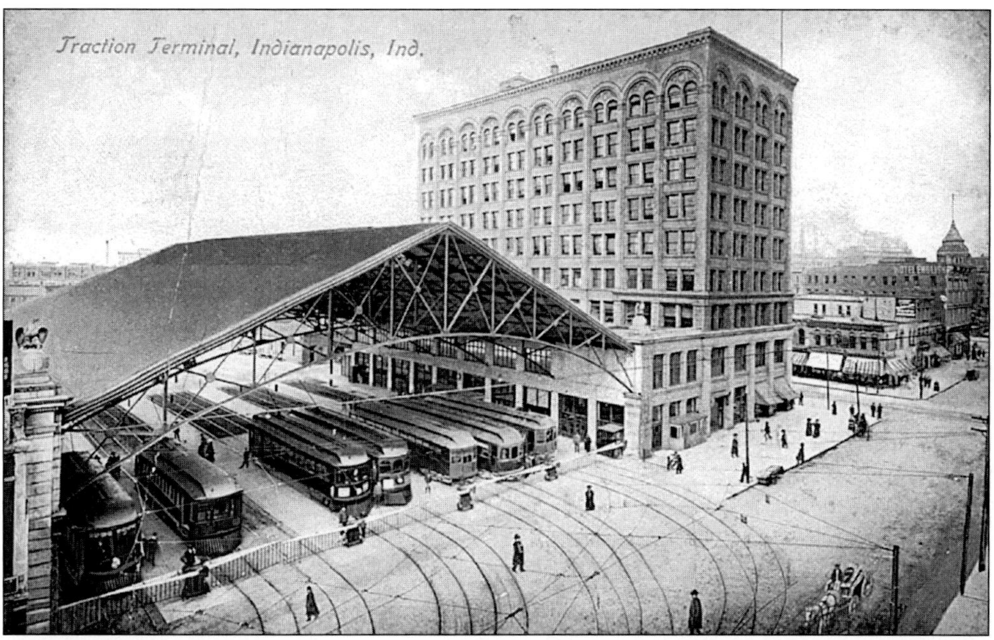

INDIANAPOLIS'S TRACTION INTERURBAN STATION. The Interurban was quite important to Indianapolis as a way to connect the capital city with other less populous neighboring cities. This postcard, postmarked 1907, emphasizes the Traction Terminal garage building. In 1904, the Indianapolis Traction Terminal opened to consolidate the stations of the various interurban lines that had been established. This greatly relieved the traffic congestion from the loading and unloading in the city's downtown. The design of this terminal allowed for several interurban companies to have their own office space, ticket counters, and baggage offices. It had a nine-track train shed. (Postcard by Import Postcard Co.)

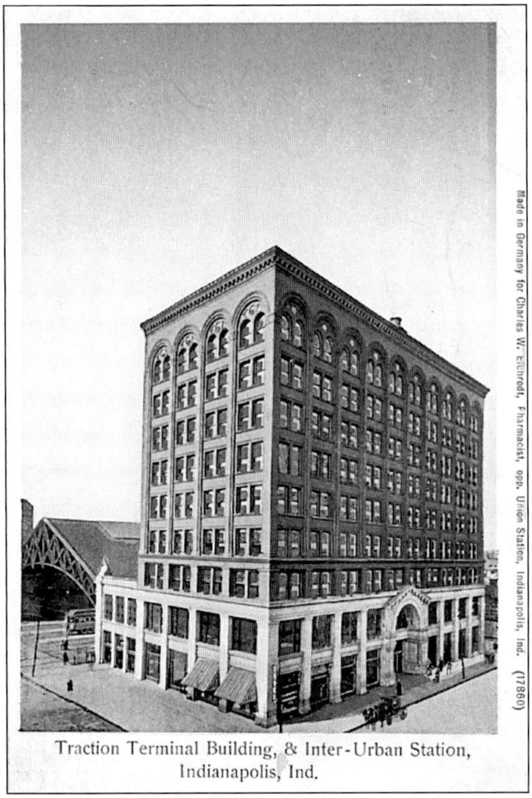

INDIANAPOLIS'S TRACTION TERMINAL BUILDING. This postcard shows the office building used by the Indianapolis Traction Co. The nine-track shed, previously discussed, together with this nine-story building, made up the terminal complex. The card has a 1909 postmark and was sent during the heyday of interurban popularity in Indiana. During the terminal's first week, it handled an average of 10,000 passengers per day. The freight terminal was originally located within the Traction Terminal complex, but as freight traffic increased, more space was needed; in 1918, it was moved to a separate site on Kentucky Avenue. (Postcard by Reichner Bros., Boston.)

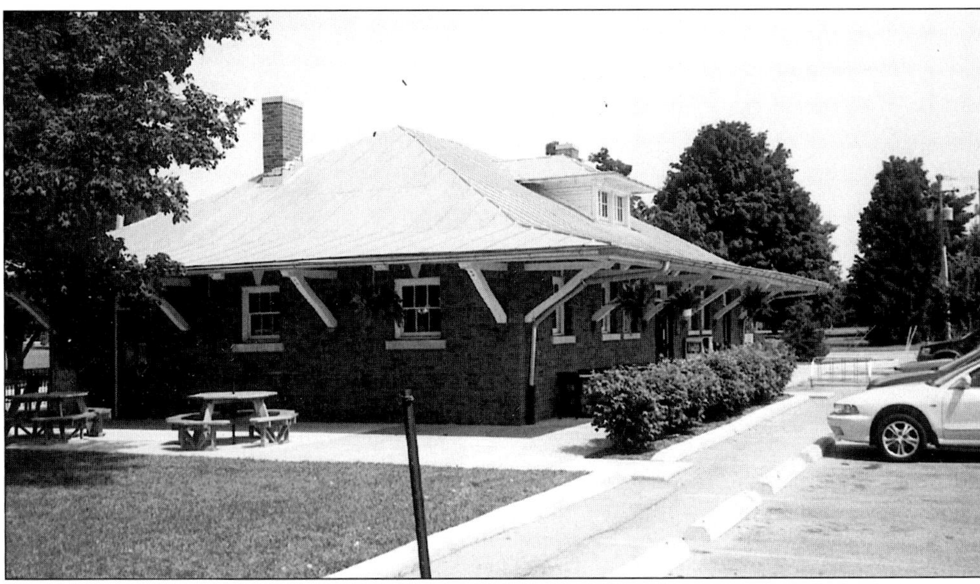

FT. HARRISON INTERURBAN DEPOT. This Union Traction depot was built in 1908 and was on the base property of Ft. Benjamin Harrison. It is located on Aultman Avenue and the Lawton Loop. The depot is currently being used as a gourmet coffee shop. The military fort is now under the control of the Indiana State Park system. This fine brick structure was part of the interurban system, and in 1984, it was added to the National Register of Historic Places.

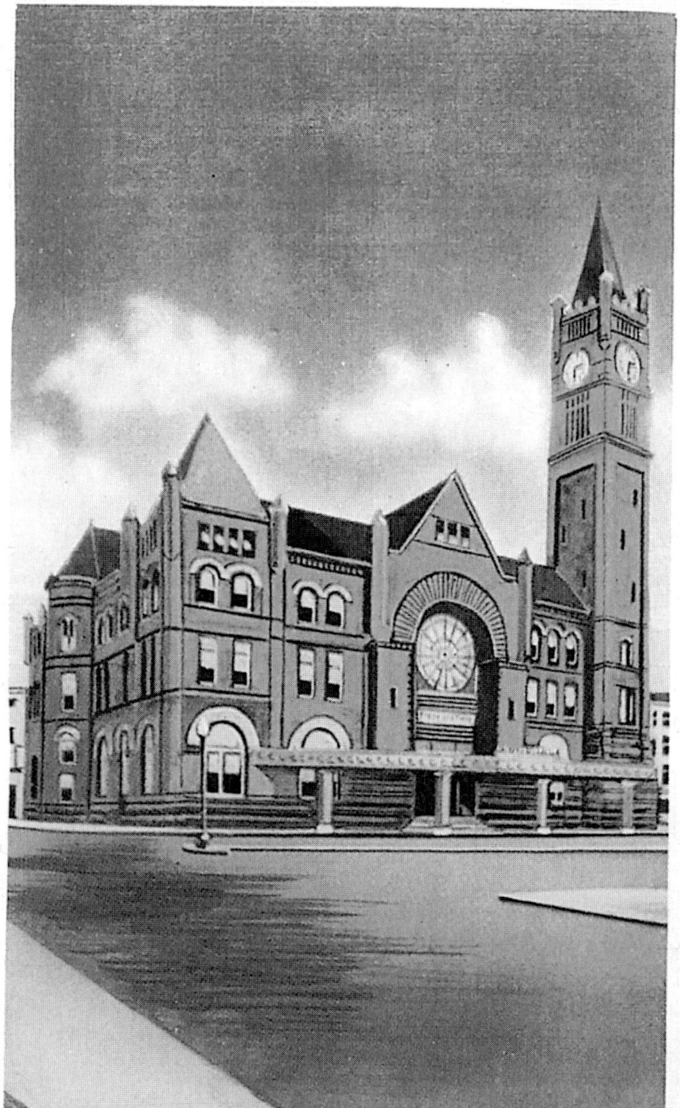

View of Union Station, Indianapolis, Ind. — 5

INDIANAPOLIS UNION STATION. Railroads have always been an important part of the history of Indianapolis. At one time, there were at least seven or eight railroads either entering the city from the east and west or from the north and south. Here is a postcard of Union Station, one of the oldest buildings in the city. This was not the original union station in Indianapolis. The first one, built in 1853, was said to be the first union station in America. It was called Union Depot. By the 1880s, this first structure was becoming quite rundown, which led city leaders and railroad officials to encourage the construction of a new station in 1887. Today, Amtrak has a stop there. The depot was placed on the National Register of Historic Places in 1974. The station is currently part of the Crowne Plaza Hotel at 123 West Louisiana Street and has 26 authentic Pullman train car sleeping rooms named and decorated after famous personalities from the early 1900s. (Postcard by Craft Greeting Card Co.)

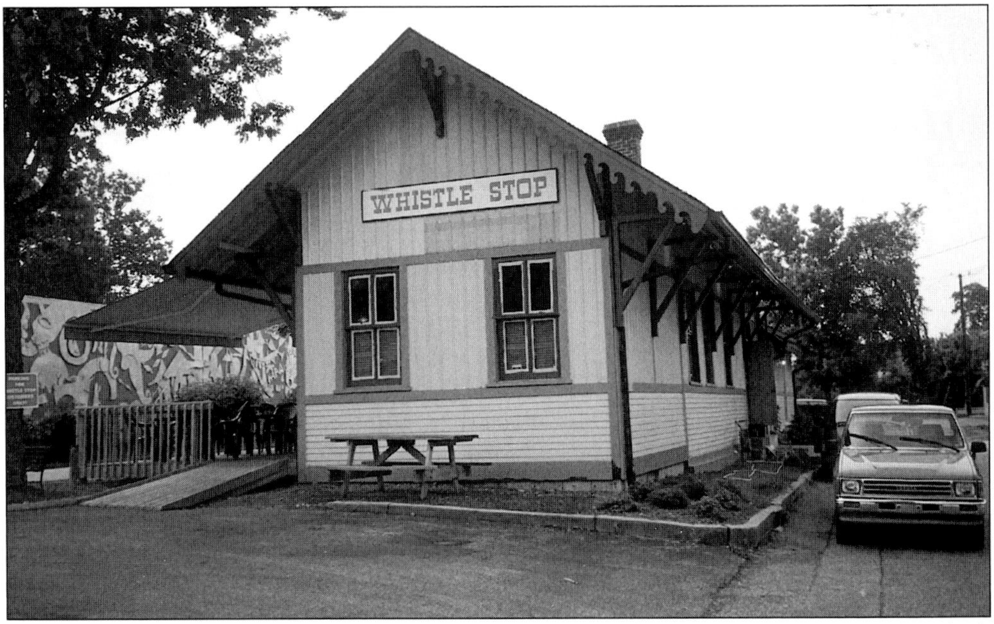

BROAD RIPPLE DEPOT. Within northern Indianapolis is a community called Broad Ripple, which has a wood combination Monon depot that was built in 1898. The Seaboard line abandoned this part of the Monon in 1985. The tracks have been raised and the rail bed turned into a path for walking and running. Made of board and batten, the depot itself is located at Cornell Street and East Sixty-fourth Street. The Broad Ripple area is known for its specialized shopping, and the depot now houses a gourmet food store.

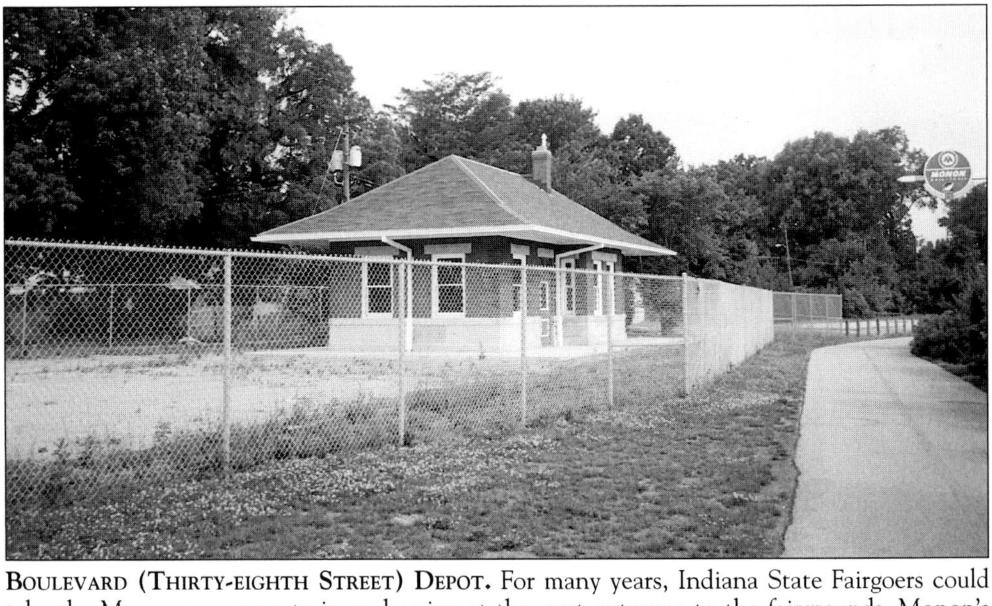

BOULEVARD (THIRTY-EIGHTH STREET) DEPOT. For many years, Indiana State Fairgoers could take the Monon passenger train and arrive at the west entrance to the fairgrounds. Monon's Boulevard combination depot was built in 1922 and is located on Thirty-eighth Street at the main entrance to the Indiana State Fairgrounds. This depot served as a freight house and a passenger station. At the time of this photograph, there was a fence around the perimeter of the property. At right is the "Monon Trail," the salvaged rail bed, used for walking and running.

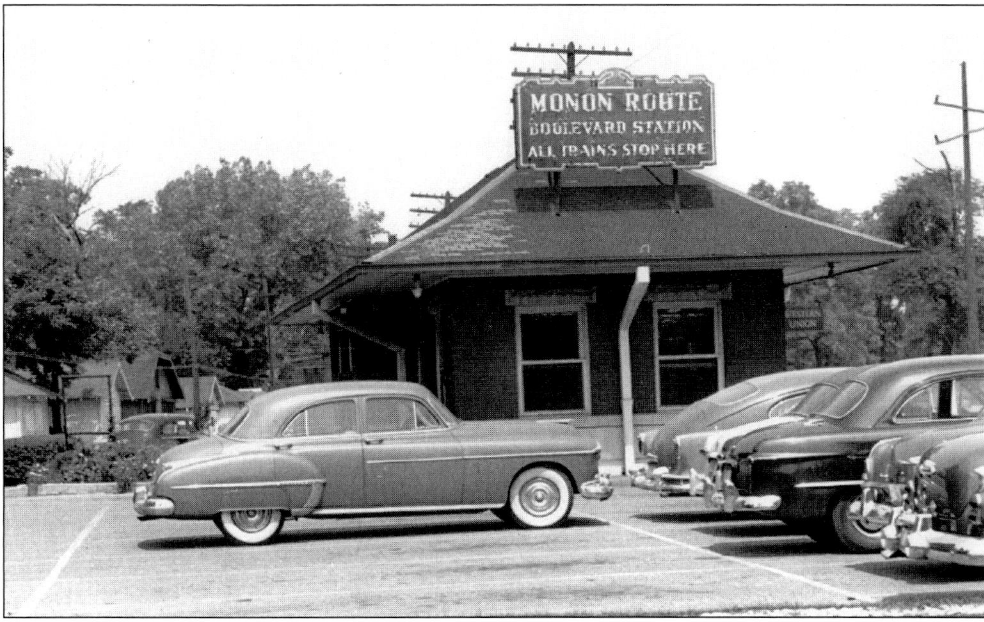

MEET ME AT THE FAIR. This photograph, c. August 1953, shows the Boulevard depot in its heyday. It was taken by rail photographer Ron Stuckey. Notice the sign above the depot. The Indiana State Fairgrounds is located to the east of the depot. Recently the city black-topped over the abandoned rail bed and created an avenue to be used for jogging and walking. It is called the Monon Trail. (Courtesy MRHTS Collection.)

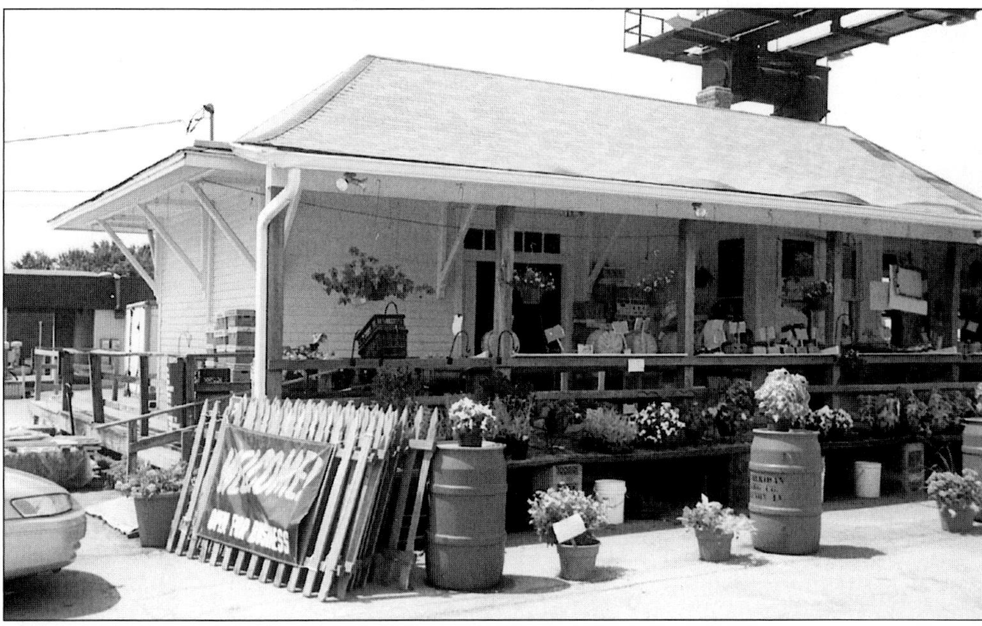

CASTLETON DEPOT. The Lake, Erie & Western Railroad ran through the northern part of Indianapolis and had a depot at Castleton. This LE&W depot was moved across the track and is now a fresh produce business. Built in 1909, it is a wooden combination depot and stands on the south side of Eighty-second Street. It is the only remaining example of this commonly-used LE&W depot style.

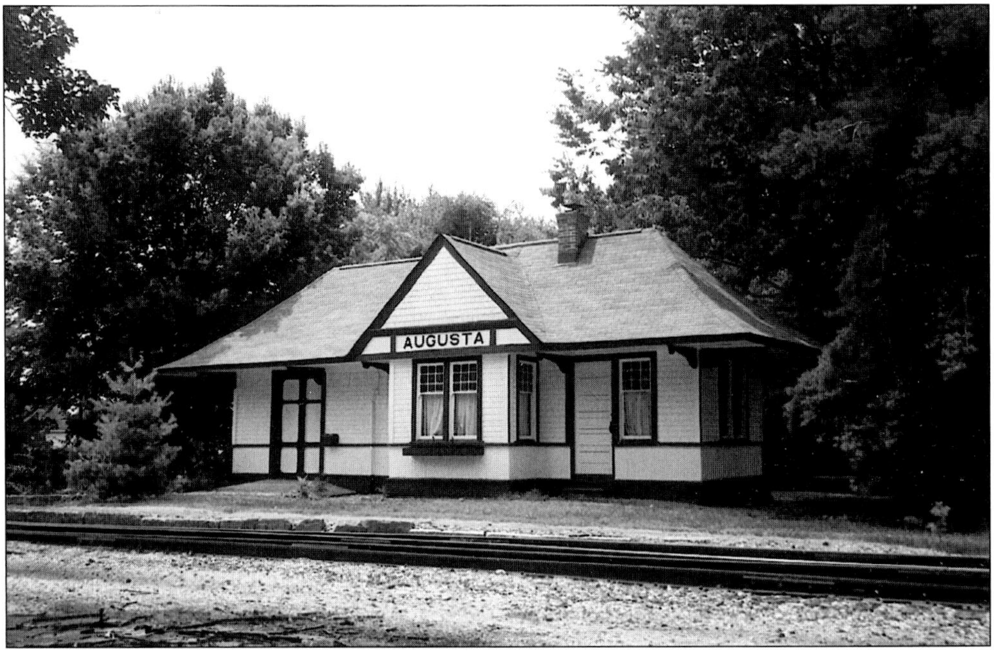

New Augusta Depot. A small area called New Augusta is located on the west side of Indianapolis. This depot is a combination CCC&StL frame building, built is 1896 and since restored. Located off New Augusta Road, the depot is used by the nearby residence to house guests. It was placed on the National Register of Historic Places in 1989.

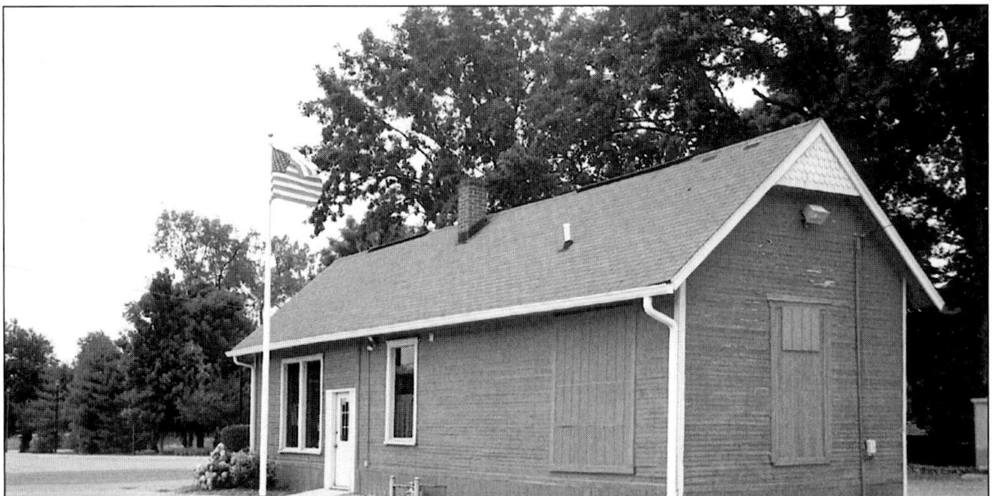

Brownsburg Interurban Depot. The next depot is in Hendricks County. Brownsburg has a Terre Haute, Indianapolis & Eastern (THI&E) combination depot at 205 Green Street. Constructed between 1907 and 1922, the depot is now a business and the rails are long since gone. The THI&E was incorporated in 1907. By 1914, the THI&E had 442 miles of track. It had several branches and eventually connected from Indianapolis to Richmond.

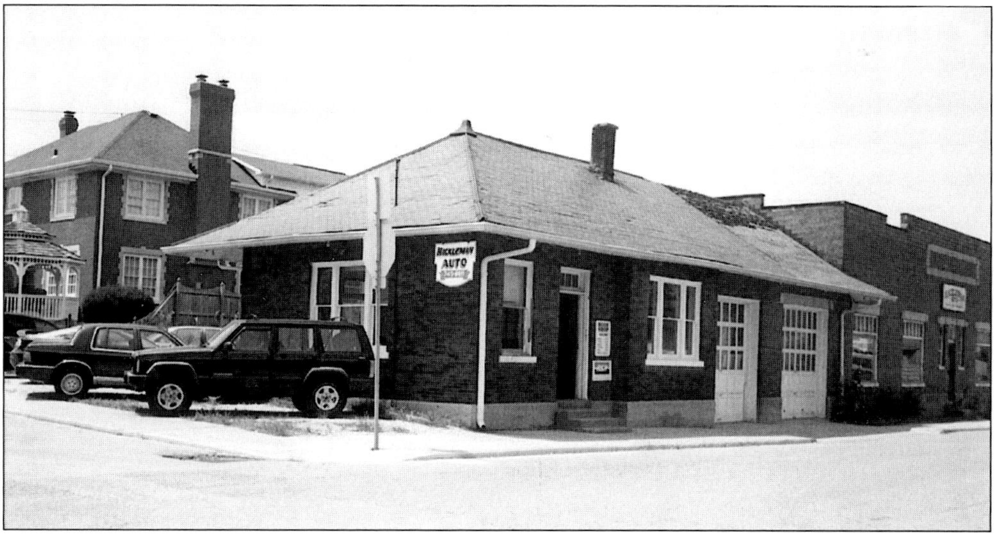

DANVILLE INTERURBAN DEPOT. Southwest of Brownsburg lies the town of Danville. A Terre Haute, Indianapolis & Eastern (THI&E) combination depot stands at the corner of Marion and Indiana. It is now an auto repair garage, and the building has been lengthened through additions. This red brick depot was constructed sometime between 1907 and 1920. The tracks have been paved over.

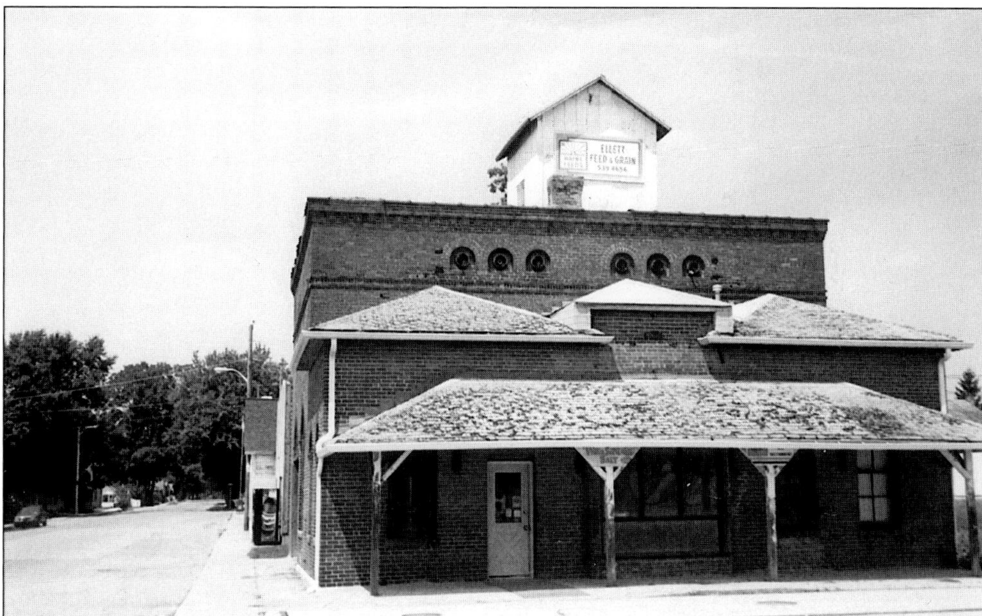

AMO INTERURBAN DEPOT. Amo is an extremely small town situated at the end of County Road #500. Here stands a THI&E combination depot. Built in 1907, the depot is at the corner of Railroad and South Pearl Streets. An *Indianapolis Star* article in July 2001 explained a delay in the renovation of the depot; town officials were excited about getting a $1,750 Indiana Preservation Grant from Historic Landmarks Foundation of Indiana, but were counting on $30,000 from the Build Indiana Fund, which is now in limbo. The depot at Plainfield, also in Hendricks County, is of the same design.

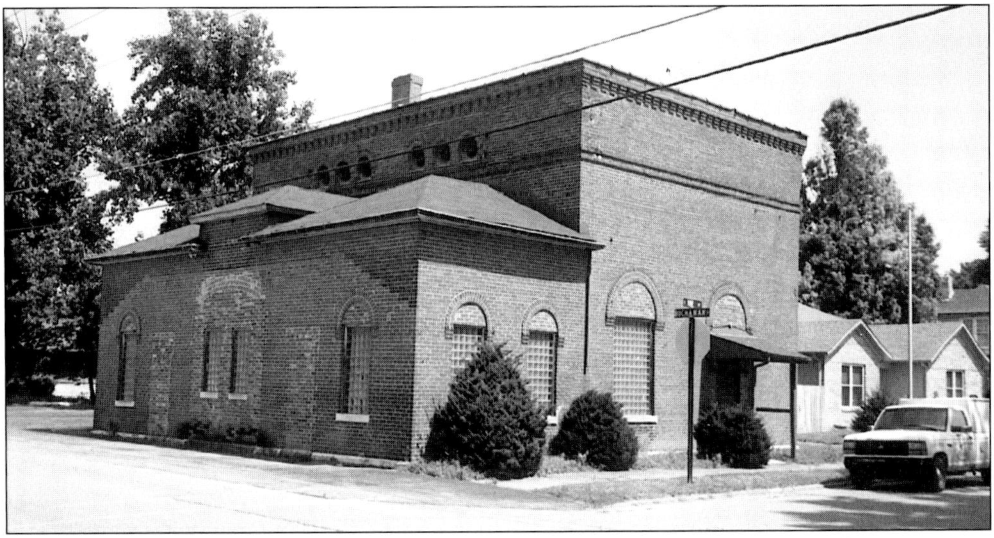

PLAINFIELD INTERURBAN DEPOT. The THI&E depot in Plainfield at 401 South Vine Street is pictured above. Notice that the Amo depot and the Plainfield interurban depots are of the same building design; they were both constructed in 1907. This structure is now being used for municipal purposes and was placed on the National Register of Historic Places in 2002. A recent project to rehabilitate the building resulted in the Western Regional Advisory Committee of the Historic Landmarks Foundation of Indiana awarding Plainfield the 2004 Western Regional Preservation Award.

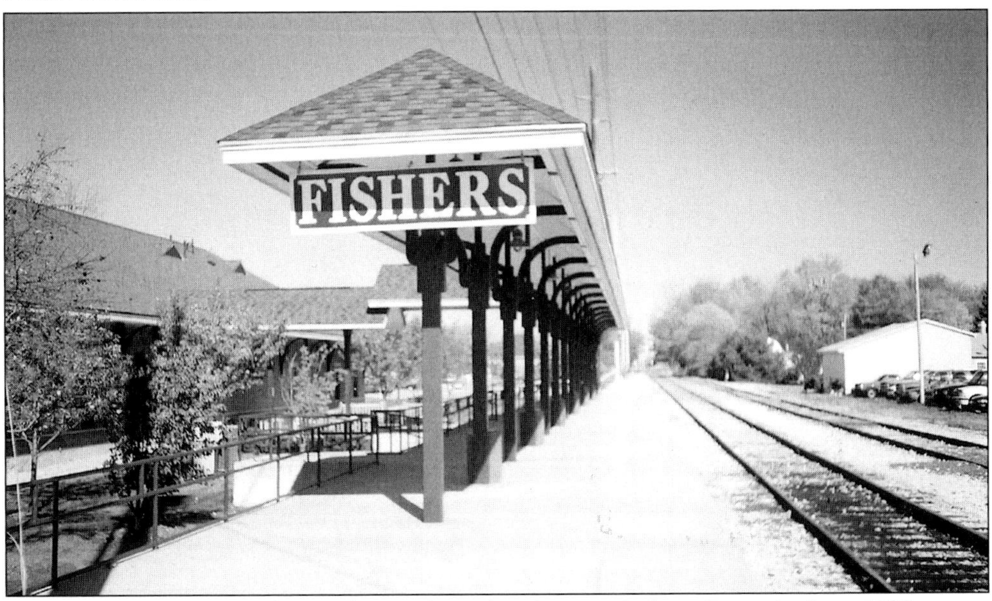

FISHER'S DEPOT. Just north of Indianapolis is this depot at Fishers. It was built in 1999 as part of a huge effort in preservation. The Indiana Transportation Museum's Fair Train runs during the Indiana State Fair in Indianapolis and provides an 11 mile, 30-minute trip between Fishers Station on 116th Street and the Indiana State Fairgrounds. Eight coaches are pulled by diesel engines at the front and rear. It makes about 10 departures daily and runs from around 8:45 a.m. to 10:15 p.m. An exact schedule is usually published in the Indianapolis Star each August The line is also used for hauling freight between Noblesville and Indianapolis.

Three

Eastern Indiana and South

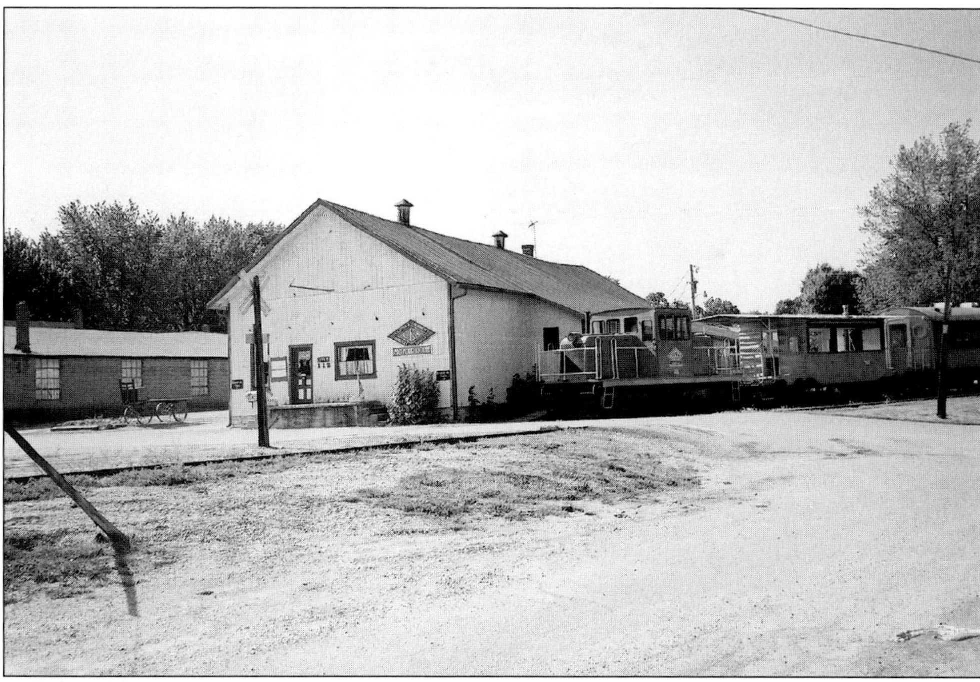

Knightstown Depot. Henry County is located about 30 miles east of Indianapolis. The people in Knightstown have worked hard to retain their railroad heritage. This is the home of the Carthage, Knightstown & Shirley Tourist Railroad (CK&S), which runs tourists between the local towns of Knightstown, Carthage, and Shirley from May to October. The ride covers 10 miles, and passengers enjoy yarns and anecdotes during the journey. The CK&S provides a relaxed 1-hour look at passenger train travel over a 5-mile stretch of the old CCC&StL Railroad. Passengers get a real perspective of what rural Indiana looks like today. The depot is located at 112 West Carey Street.

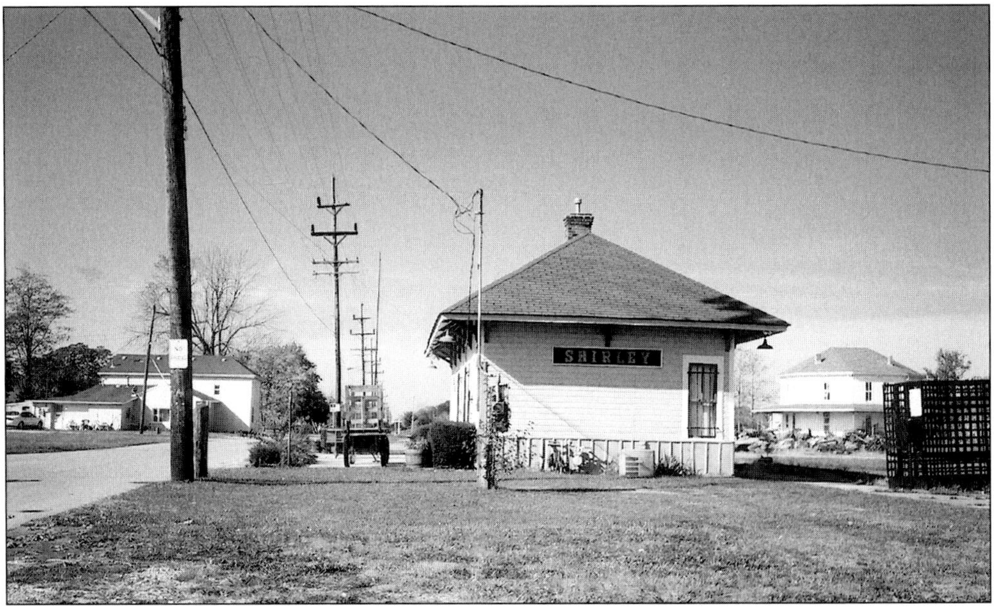

SHIRLEY MUSEUM DEPOT. Shirley is a local town in Hancock County and has a small wooden depot now used as a museum. This depot appears well-cared for and is obviously a source of pride to the community. This Peoria & Eastern (P&E) combination depot was built in 1893 of board and batten siding. It is located on Railroad Street. Shirley is a stop on the CK&S Tourist Railroad.

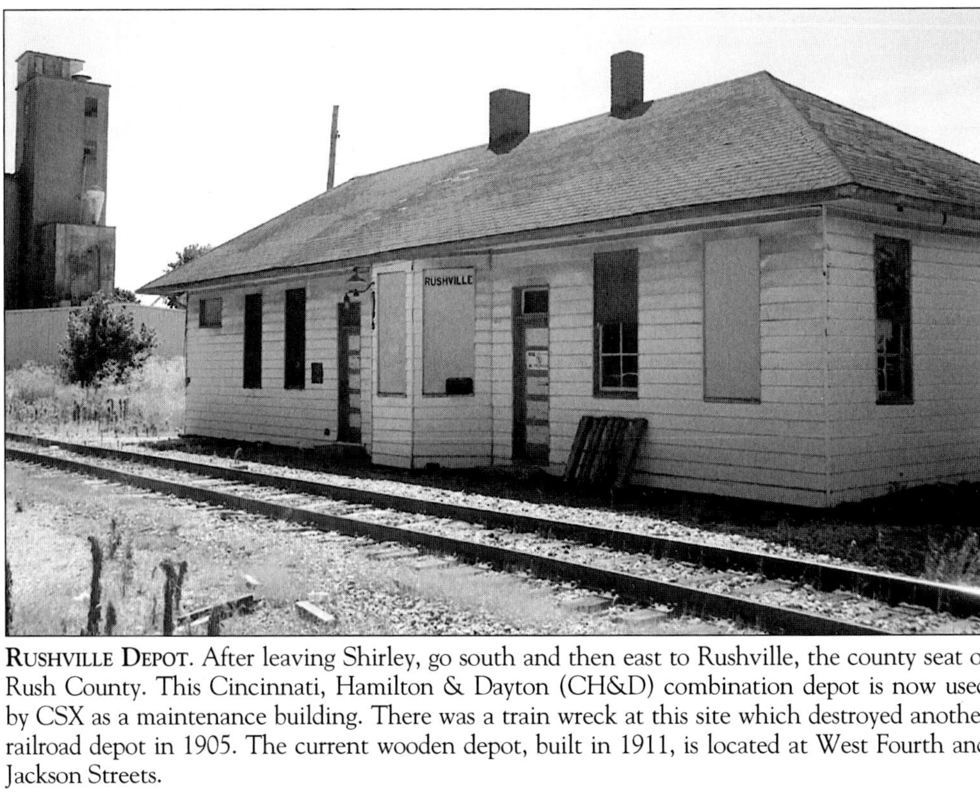

RUSHVILLE DEPOT. After leaving Shirley, go south and then east to Rushville, the county seat of Rush County. This Cincinnati, Hamilton & Dayton (CH&D) combination depot is now used by CSX as a maintenance building. There was a train wreck at this site which destroyed another railroad depot in 1905. The current wooden depot, built in 1911, is located at West Fourth and Jackson Streets.

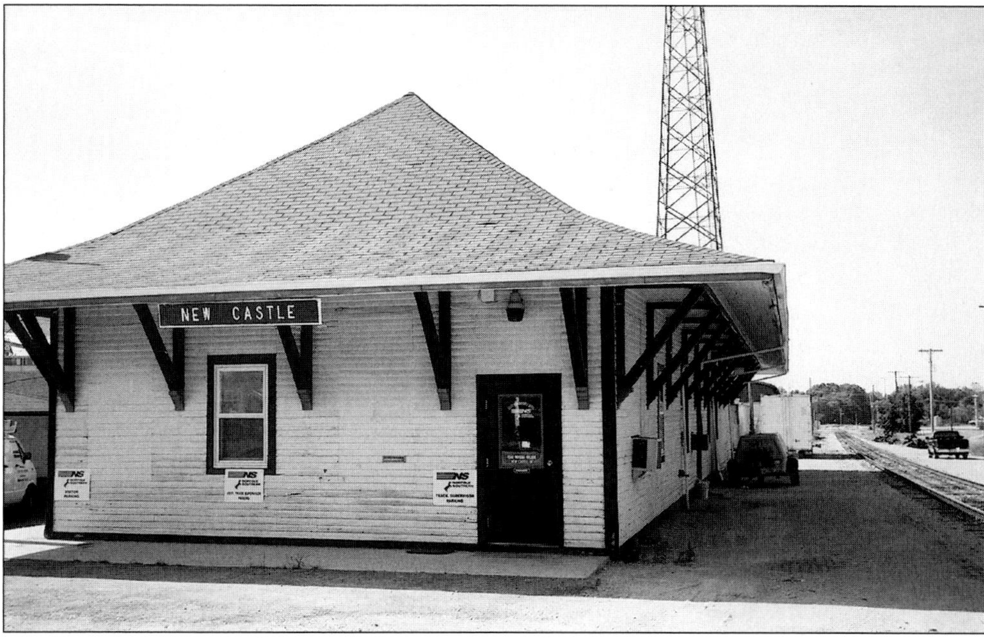

New Castle Depot. Take U.S. 40 east to SR 3, and then go north to New Castle. New Castle has a passenger depot on Indiana Avenue, currently used by the Norfolk Southern Railroad as a railroad office. This framed, wooden structure was built in 1910 by the Lake Erie and Western (LE&W) and PCC&StL.

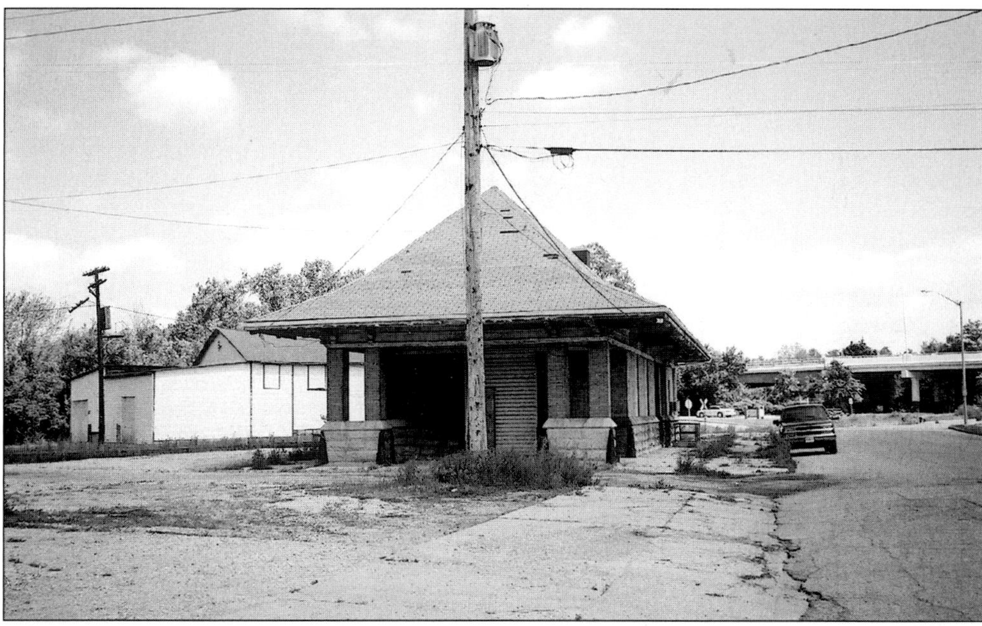

Richmond C&O Depot. On North Third Street at D Street in Richmond is the Chesapeake and Ohio (C&O) passenger depot. It is in poor shape, but not beyond repair. The C&O entered Indiana at Richmond and traveled to Muncie, Marion, Peru, and then on toward Chicago. The tracks are in use by CSX. The lower portion of the depot has rough-faced stone with vertical siding above the windows.

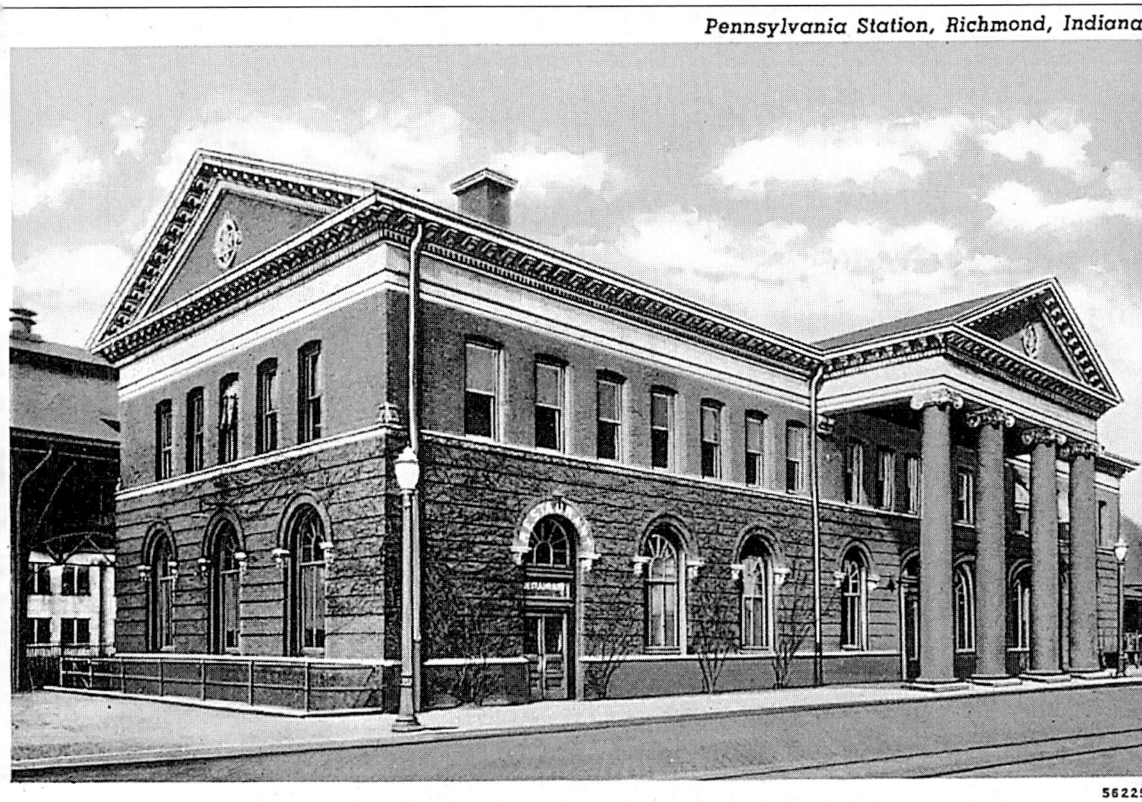

RICHMOND'S PENNSYLVANIA STATION. The Richmond Pennsylvania Railroad Station is a focal point of the Richmond Historical District. It was designed by Daniel Burnham, a famous architect from Chicago. The building was constructed in 1902 in the Neo-Classical style and had a belt course. It was saved through the efforts of Historic Landmarks Foundation of Indiana, Historic Richmond, Neighborhood Preservation Services, and the Urban Enterprise Zone Association. Located on E Street, this large, red-brick structure boasts four magnificent columns. In the depot's prime, the second floor was used for offices and the lower level had a restaurant. This postcard shows its impressive stature. Plans have not been finalized concerning the future use of the station. It was added to the Richmond Railroad Station Historic District in 1987. (Postcard by C. T. American Art Postcard)

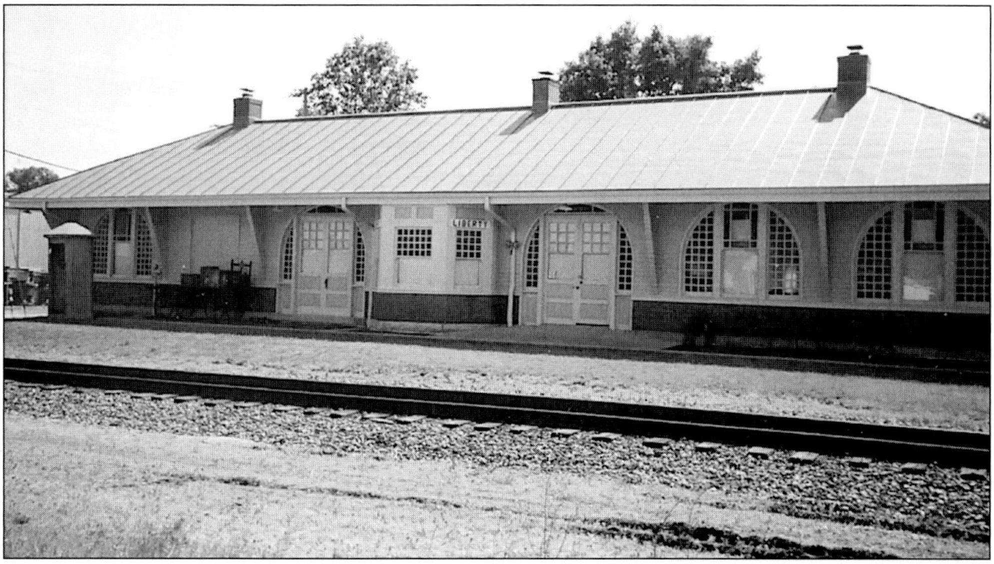

Liberty's CH&D Depot. The town of Liberty is located south on U.S. 27. Liberty has a CH&D passenger depot on High Street that has been restored and is now a museum. This wooden depot was built in 1902 by the Cincinnati, Hamilton & Dayton (CH&D) Railway. The nearby tracks are used by thc CSX Railroad. Notice the brick lower walls, the bevel siding, and the arched Romanesque windows. Liberty is near the Whitewater Memorial State Park, which is home to the 200-acre Whitewater Lake.

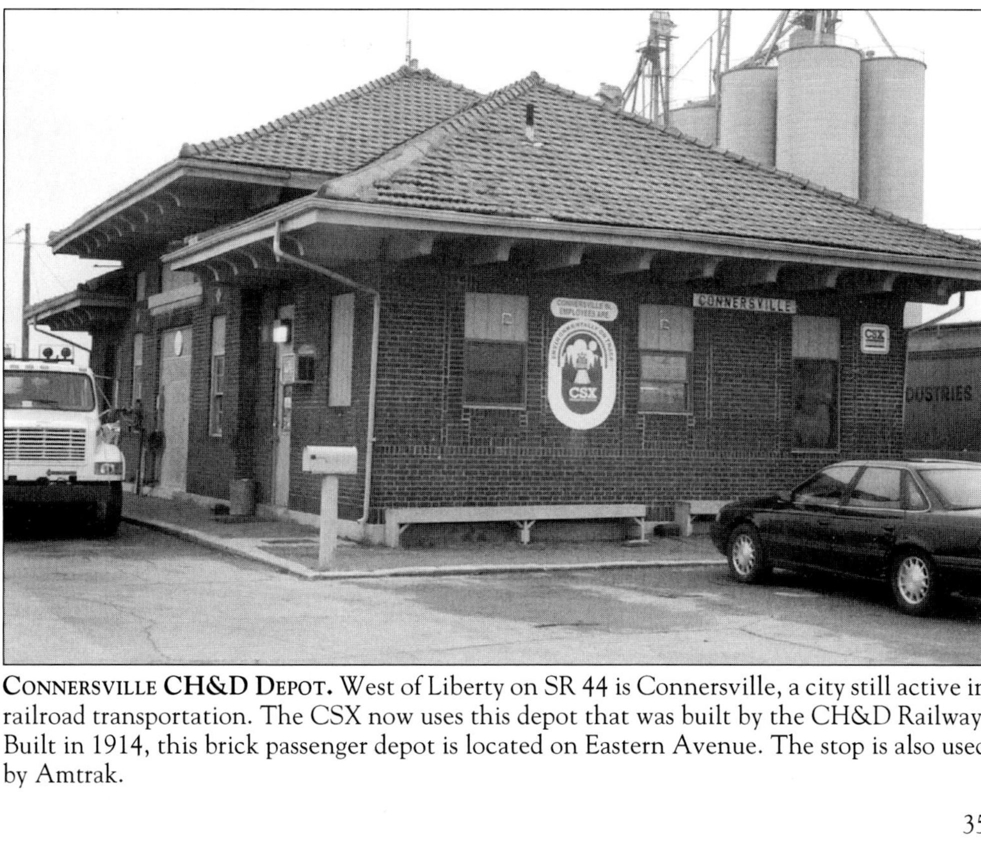

Connersville CH&D Depot. West of Liberty on SR 44 is Connersville, a city still active in railroad transportation. The CSX now uses this depot that was built by the CH&D Railway. Built in 1914, this brick passenger depot is located on Eastern Avenue. The stop is also used by Amtrak.

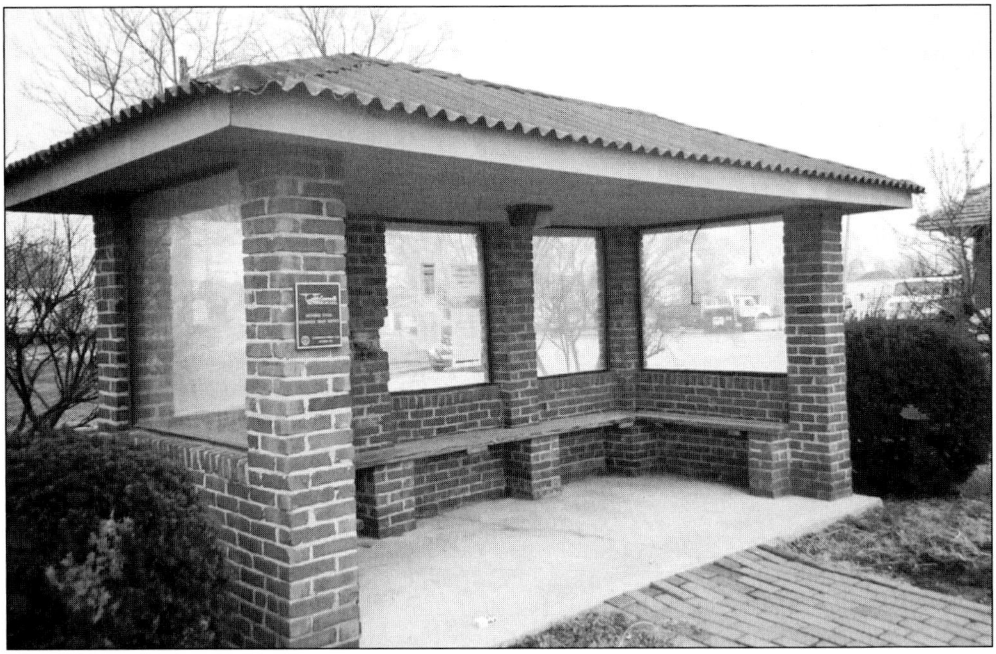

AMTRAK SHELTER. The Amtrak still passes through here as it proceeds to Indianapolis; the Cardinal heads toward Crawfordsville, Lafayette, Dyer, and Chicago. This is the waiting shelter for the Amtrak passenger train, which makes its Connersville stop quite early in the mornings. This shelter has been restored in recent times.

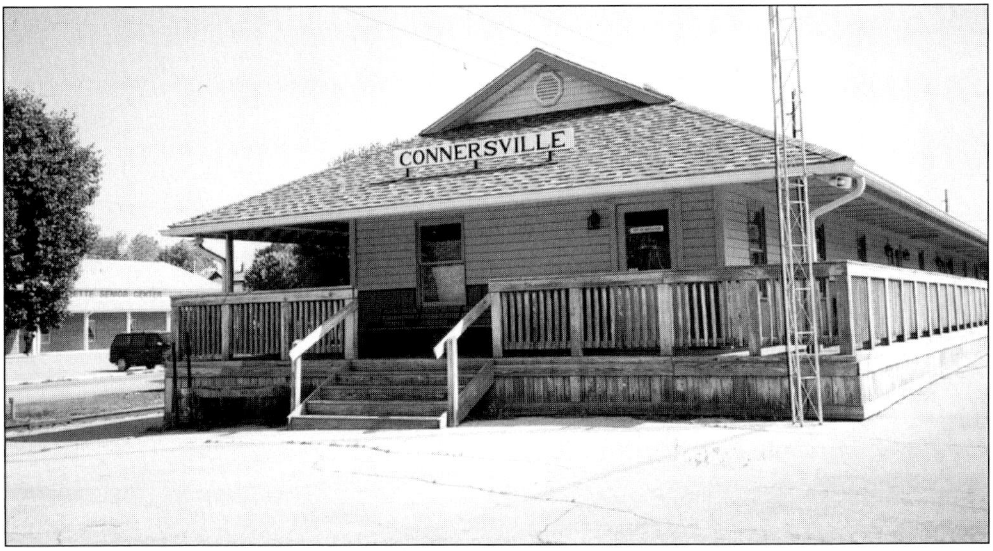

WHITEWATER VALLEY TOURIST RAILROAD. Connersville is also the home of the Whitewater Valley Tourist Railroad. This depot was built expressly for the WVRR. The railroad runs 19-mile excursion routes between Connersville and Metamora, offering a two-hour lay over in Metamora, good for shopping, eating, and sightseeing. The present Whitewater Valley Railroad was formed as a not-for-profit corporation in 1972, and began weekend passenger operations in 1974. Further information regarding the WVRR can be found in chapter nine.

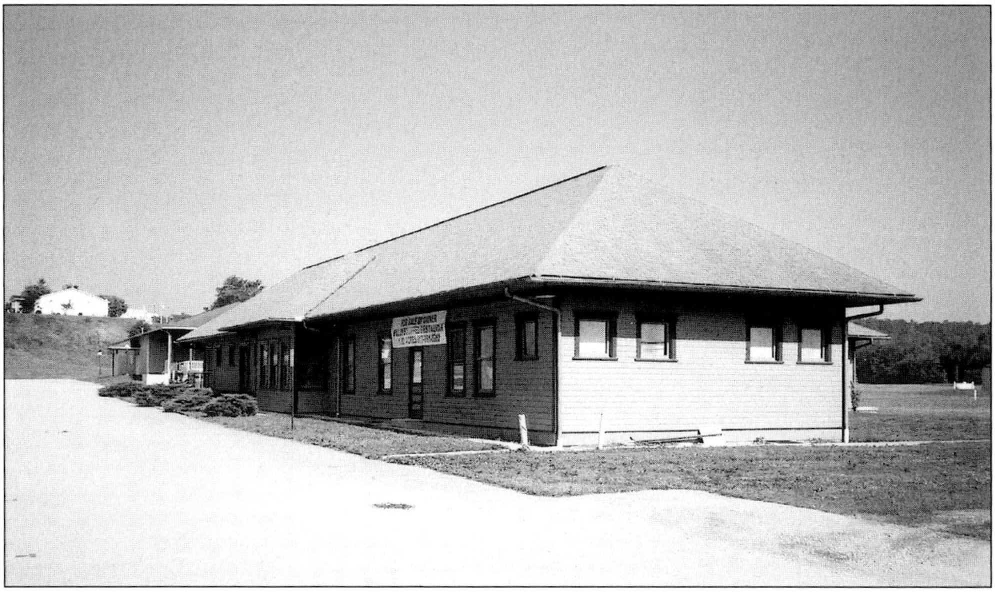

Brookville (Metamora). Take SR 121 south from Connersville to US 52, and go east to Metamora. The depot now standing at Metamora is the same building moved from Brookville. It has been altered and is somewhat difficult it identify. A CCC&StL combination depot, it was built of wood and is now a restaurant on U.S. 52.

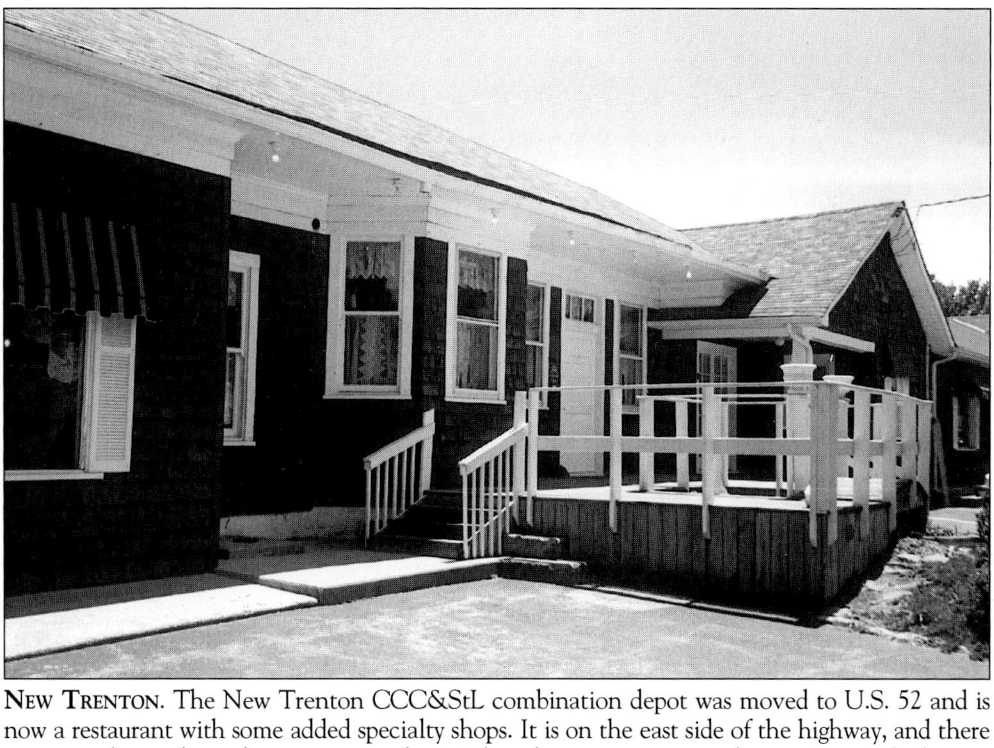

New Trenton. The New Trenton CCC&StL combination depot was moved to U.S. 52 and is now a restaurant with some added specialty shops. It is on the east side of the highway, and there are no tracks nearby to designate it as a depot. Though an attractive wooden structure, it looks very little like a railroad depot.

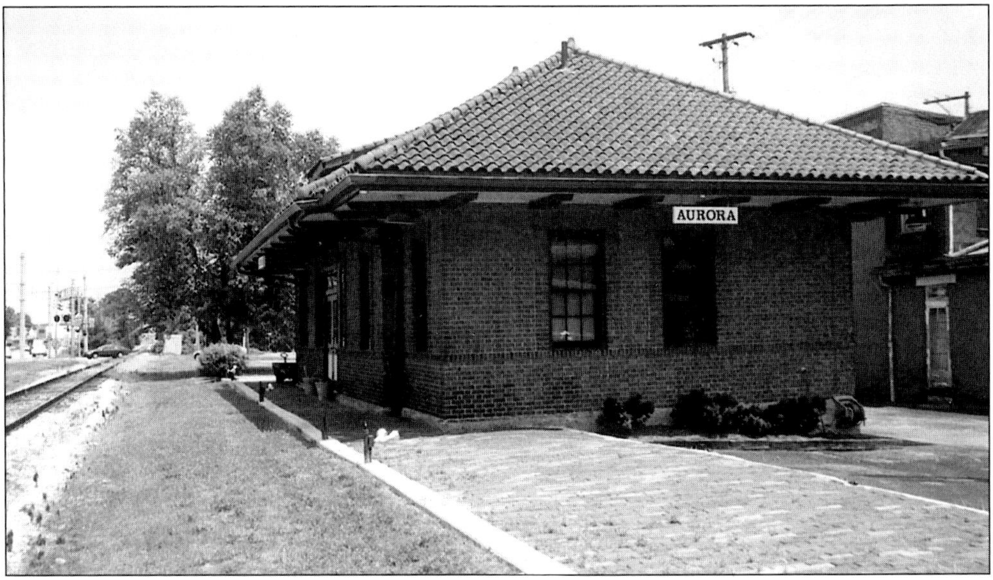

Aurora's B&O Depot. In the southeast corner of the state is Dearborn County, which is located near Cincinnati, Ohio. There are two depots worth visiting: one in Aurora and the other in Lawrenceburg. The B&O brick passenger depot in Aurora was built in 1915 and is on Second Street. It is currently a business office. This depot was included as part of the Downtown Aurora Historic District in 1994. CSX uses the tracks. A restored 1850s Victorian home, Hillforest Mansion, sits above, overlooking the Ohio River in Aurora.

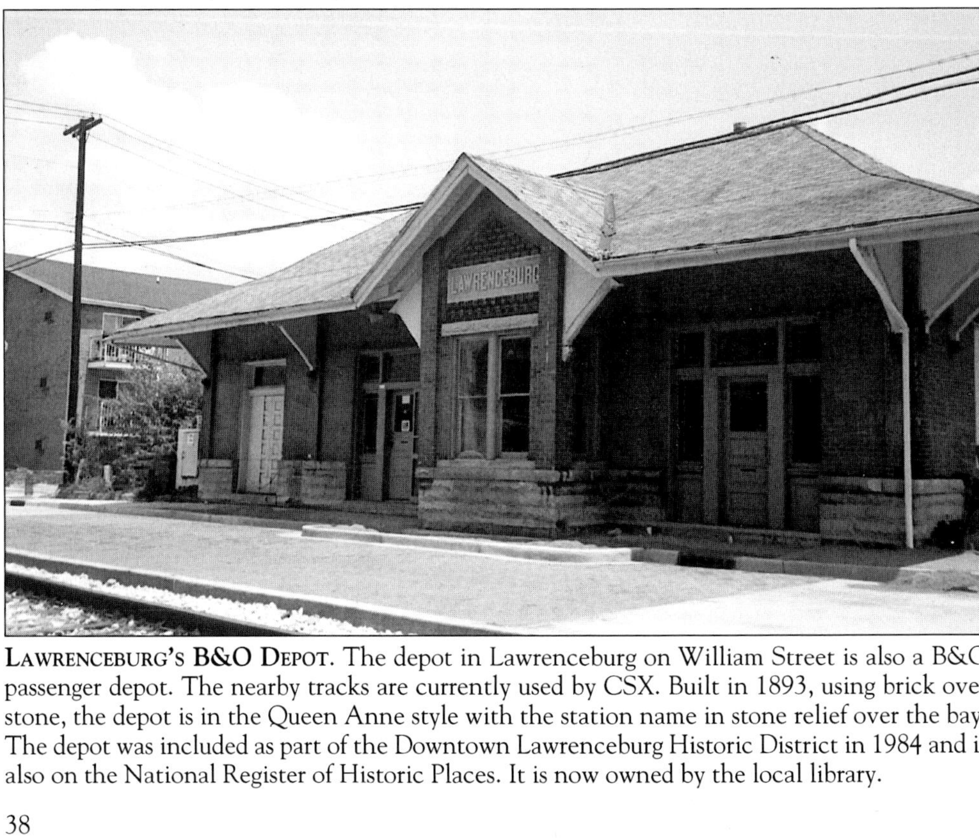

Lawrenceburg's B&O Depot. The depot in Lawrenceburg on William Street is also a B&O passenger depot. The nearby tracks are currently used by CSX. Built in 1893, using brick over stone, the depot is in the Queen Anne style with the station name in stone relief over the bay. The depot was included as part of the Downtown Lawrenceburg Historic District in 1984 and is also on the National Register of Historic Places. It is now owned by the local library.

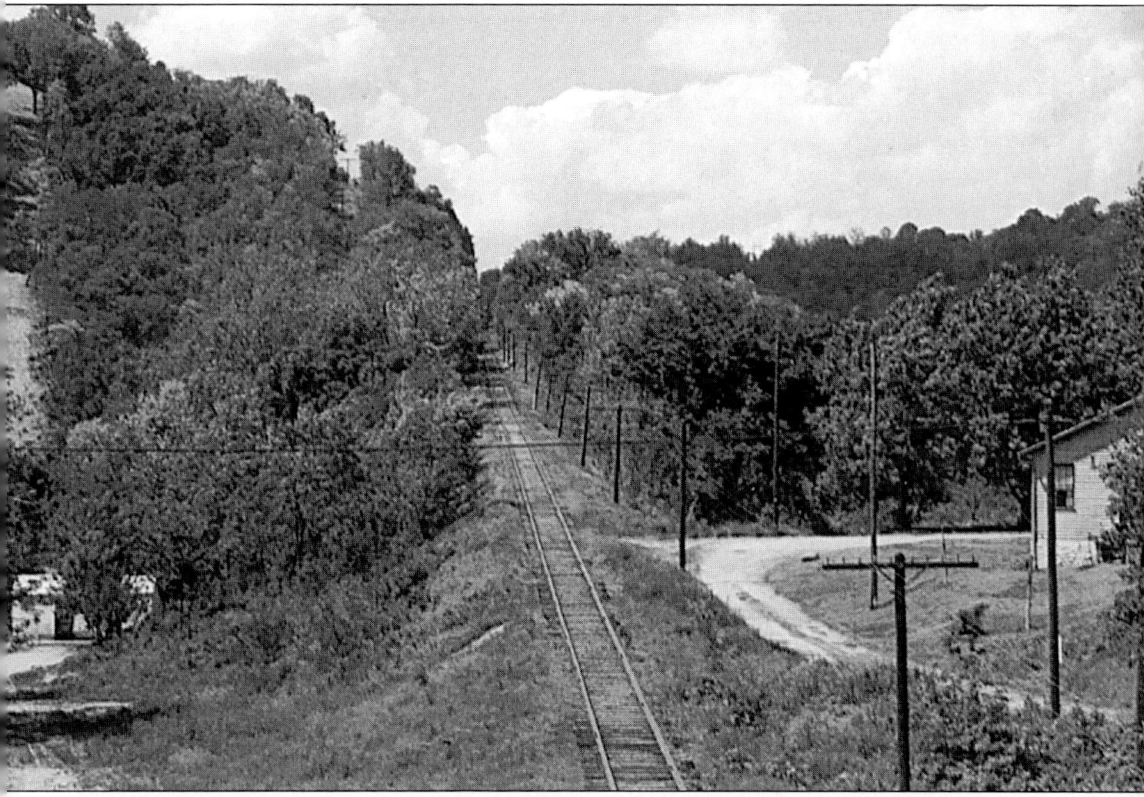

Madison's Incline. In 1832, the Indiana legislature chartered eight railroad companies. By 1835, the Madison to Indianapolis charter had begun, and construction started in September 1836, after surveys and contracts were completed. The rugged terrain and steep incline from the Ohio River to the land above Madison was a real challenge for the Irish workers. The incline, having an average grade of 5.89 percent, was not completed until 1841. It was not until 1844 that rail was completed to Columbus, only about halfway to Indianapolis. The last rail was finally laid in Indianapolis in October 1847. This postcard shows the incline cut, now abandoned and overgrown with trees. The grade is still one of the steepest in the country. While in use, it was too steep for regular locomotives to climb, and the results were even more dangerous when cars descended the hill and gravity had its way. (Postcard by Dexter Press Inc.)

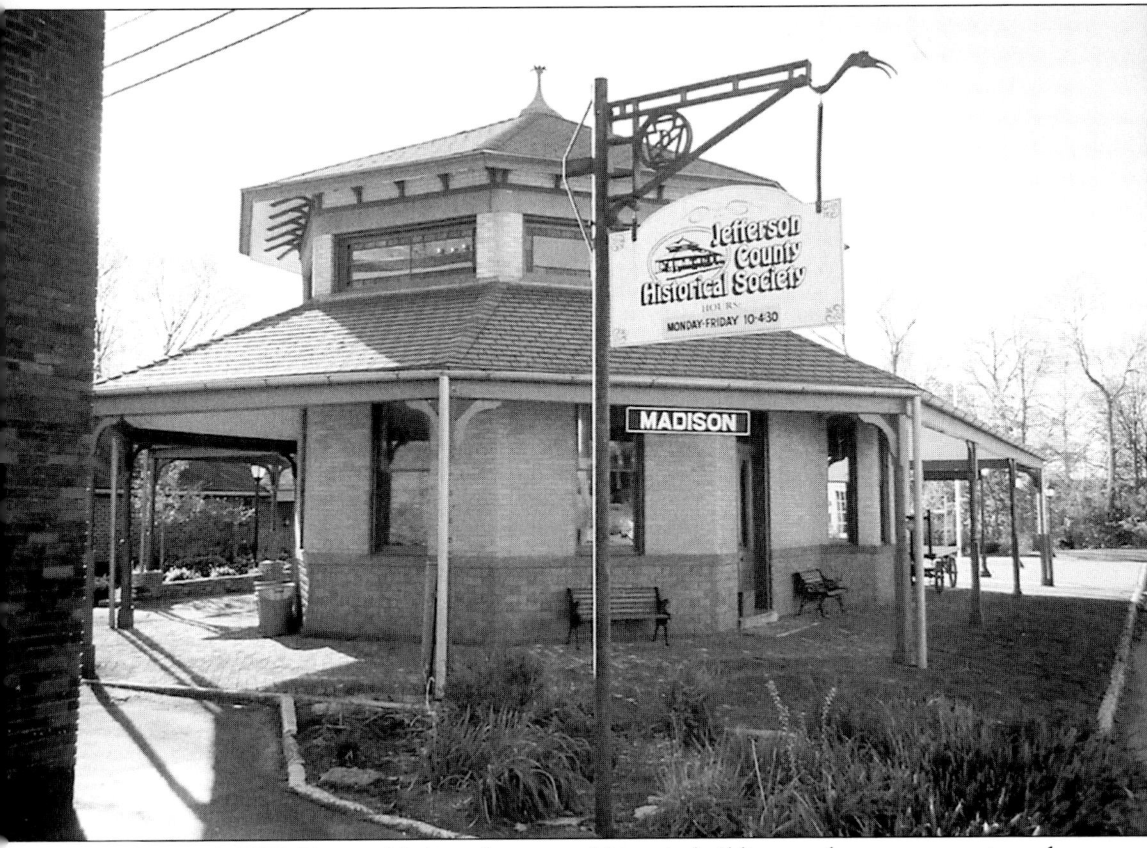

MADISON'S PRR DEPOT. Madison has several historic buildings and numerous antique shops. On Mill Street at First Street, you will find the Pennsylvania Railroad brick passenger station. Built in 1894 at a cost of $5,600, it was actually the fourth passenger depot in Madison. This building served as a passenger depot until 1931 and was used as a community center during the Depression. It is part of the Madison Historic District, which was placed on the National Register of Historic Places in 1973.

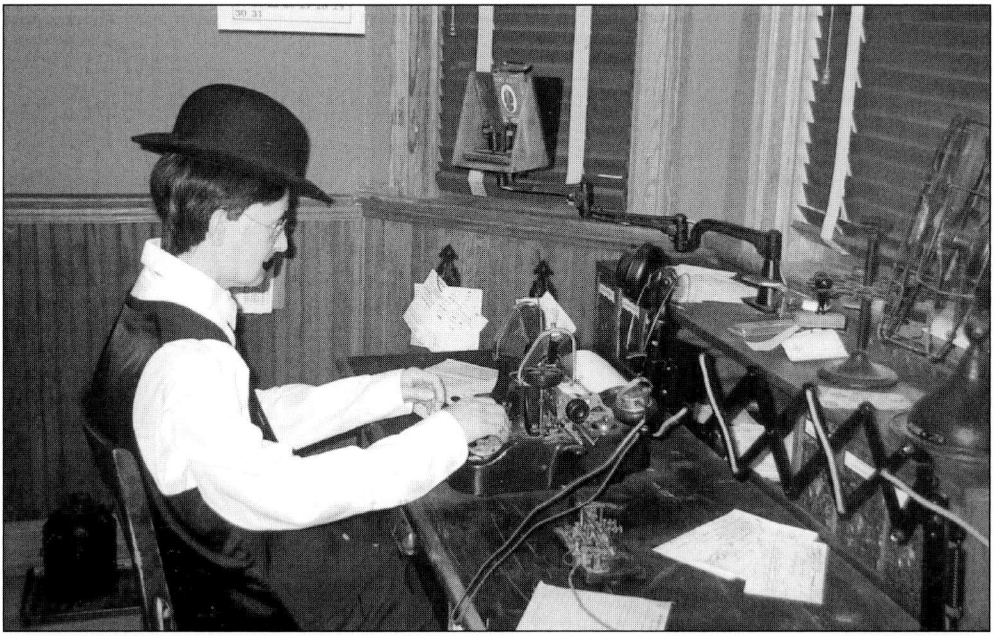

MADISON AGENT AT WORK. This scene was created by the Madison Historic Society to express the various daily tasks of the passenger agent. It can be seen in the clerk's office at the PRR depot at Madison. Note the scissors-like phone, railroad stamp holder, old-time typewriter, and forms—all tools for the agent's daily tasks.

MUDSILL TRACKS. Within the Madison depot are various informative railroad displays, including this exhibit of the components of a mudsill railroad track. A wood plate is used to distribute the weight of the rails and ties over the ground. At the base is a large timber with a smaller notched-out timber crossing above it. Another notched out timber supports the steel track that was nailed into place. The size of the mudsill is determined by the nature of the soil supporting it.

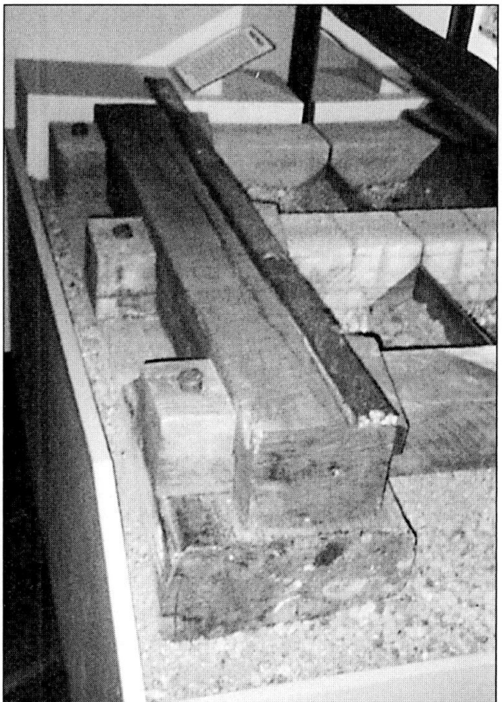

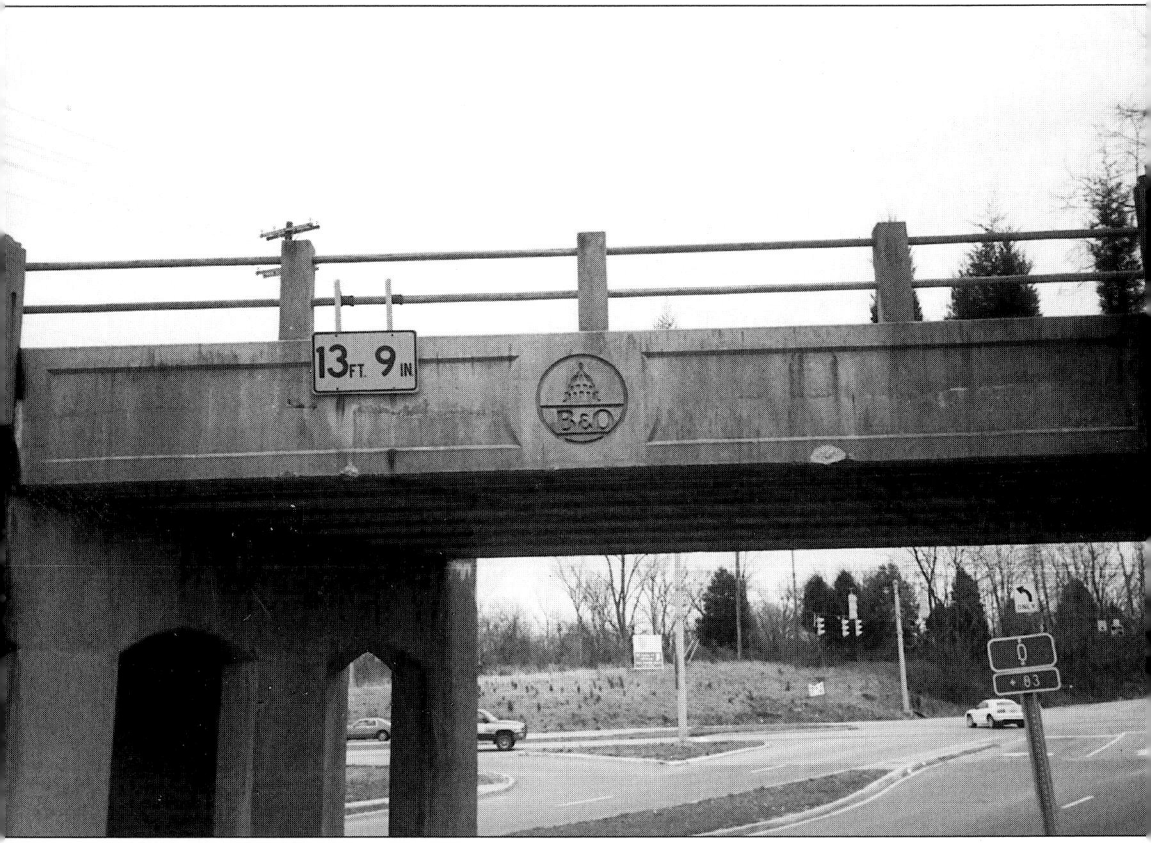

Charlestown Viaduct. In April 2001, the Louisville Courier-Journal printed an article stating that the railroad viaduct in Charlestown was to be torn down. The viaduct carried workers to the Indiana Army Ammunition Plant for many years, up to and including World War II. For many Charlestown residents, the demise of the viaduct was probably good news. It was a visual barrier near a busy intersection and had created water drainage problems for the town. The article was a reminder that yet another part of our railroad heritage was to soon disappear. I made sure I had a camera the next time I was in Charlestown. The viaduct, built in the 1940s, is now gone, but the image remains. The depot on Depot Street (no longer on maps) is also gone.

Four

New Albany's Railroad History

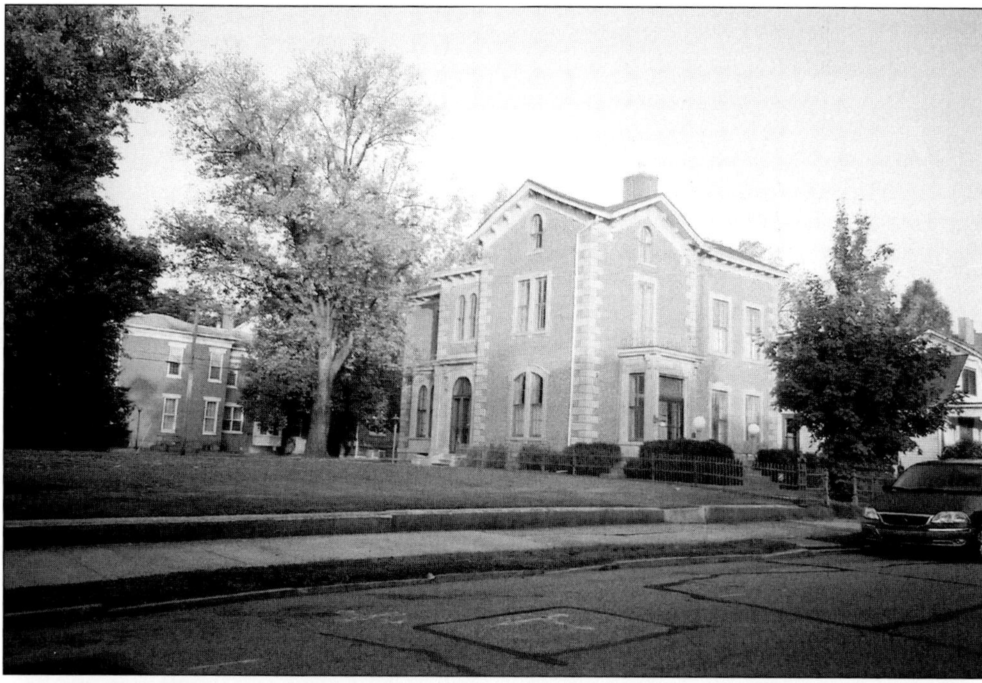

James Brooks Home. James Brooks was born in Orrington, Maine, in 1810. His family moved to Cincinnati when he was a youngster, and in the 1820s, Brooks moved downstream to New Albany. In 1830, the Louisville and Portland Canal was built on the Kentucky side of the Ohio River. Because of this new trade revenue, Louisville began growing at a rate above that of New Albany. Brooks felt that a railroad would help offset this revenue loss for New Albany. In January 1847, the Indiana legislature passed an act so that the road from New Albany to Salem might be privatized and completed as a railroad. So in spring 1847, the New Albany and Salem Railroad was chartered in Providence (now Borden), with James Brooks and six others. After organization, Brooks became the first president. This photograph shows the New Albany home of Brooks on East Ninth Street. He was president of the railroad until 1859.

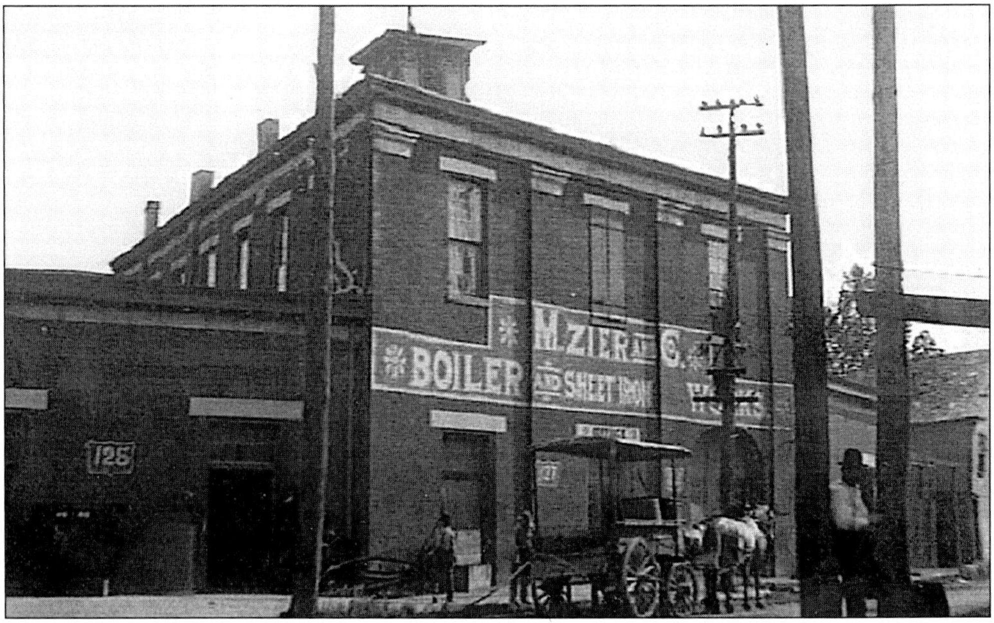

NEW ALBANY & SALEM DEPOT. The New Albany & Salem Railroad (NA&S), which later became the Monon, used at least five different buildings in New Albany over the years to meet its needs for freight houses and passenger depots. The NA&S's earliest structure was the combination passenger depot and freight house located at 125 East Oak Street, built for $18,000. The exact date of its construction is not always agreed upon, and some speculate it may have been as early at 1851. It was used by the Monon until 1891. This photograph, taken after 1895, shows that M. Zier and Company moved into the old depot after the NA&S built a freight house on Sycamore Street and a passenger depot on Vincennes Street. (Courtesy New Albany Floyd County Public Library—Emma Carleton Collection.)

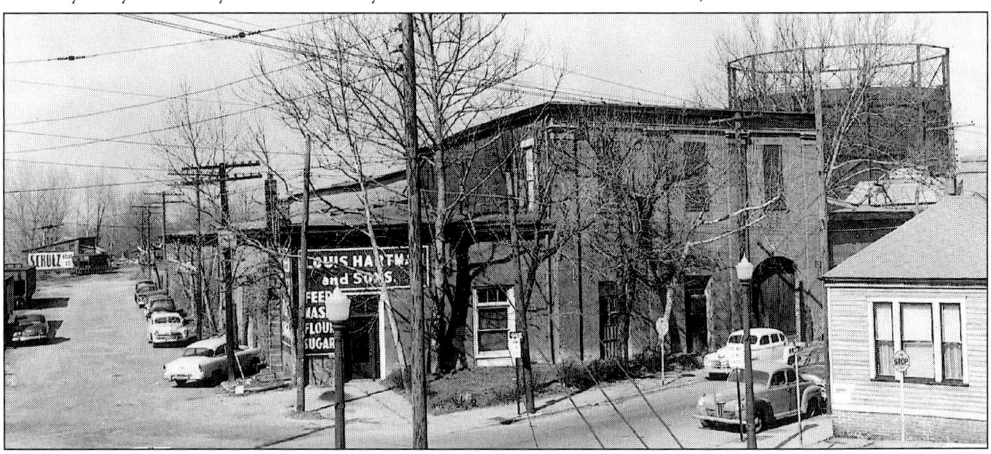

NA&S DEPOT. This photograph was likely taken in the late 1940s or early 1950s. John Hartman and Sons Company occupied the building at that time. The two-story brick depot was 300 feet long and 110 feet wide after an addition was built in the 1890s. It had huge beams measuring three-feet square, the size of whole tree trunks. It was heavily damaged by fire in March 1995, and had to be torn down by order of the New Albany Fire Chief. It was demolished on August 9, 1995, but stood longer than any other Monon depot in town. (Courtesy New Albany Floyd County Public Library—Reisz/Coleman Collection.)

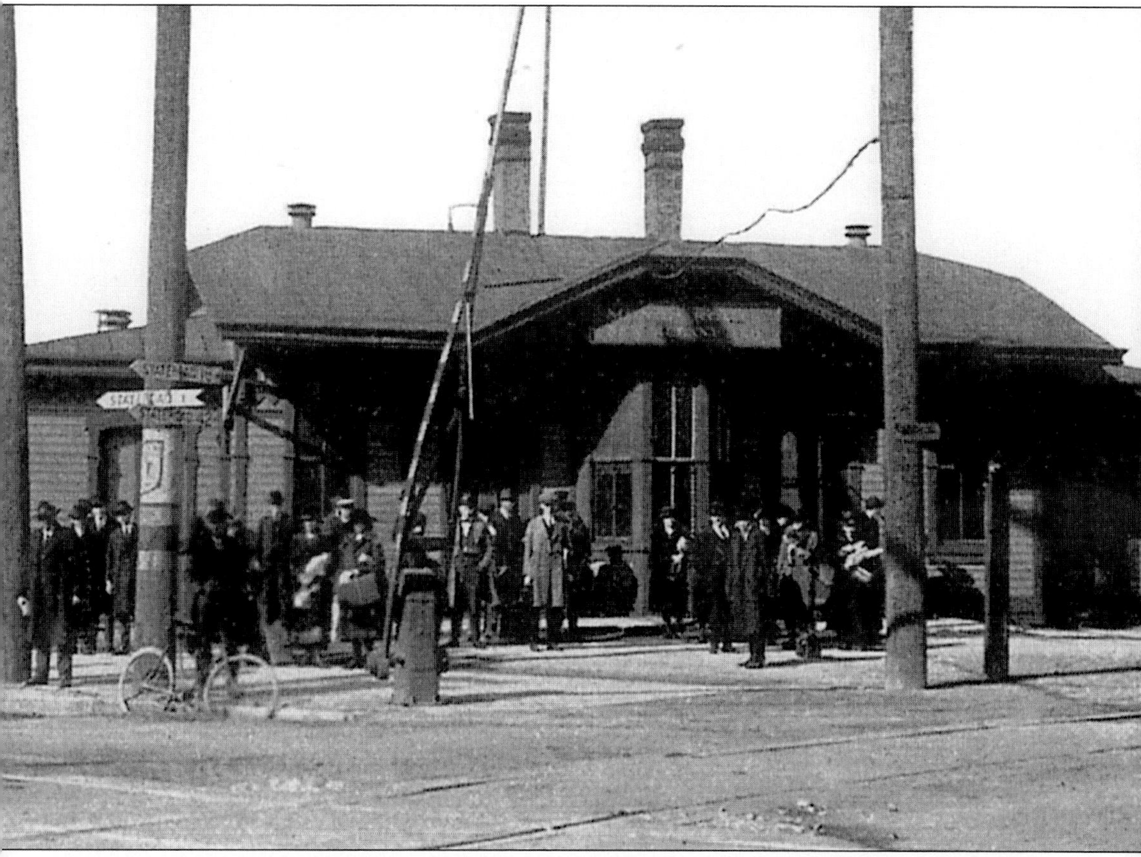

LOUISVILLE, NEW ALBANY & CHICAGO PASSENGER DEPOT. The *New Albany Ledger* of March 15, 1884, mentions that "the painting of the elegant new passenger station of the LNA&C Railway at Vincennes and Main Streets is nearly completed." This photograph was taken from the book *Picturesque New Albany* (1923). A map from the *Ledger* of September 20, 1887, shows this LNA&C passenger depot at the corner of Main Street and Vincennes Street. It stood from 1884 to about 1937 and was the second passenger depot of the Monon Railroad in New Albany. By 1939, fire insurance maps showed a filling station on this property.

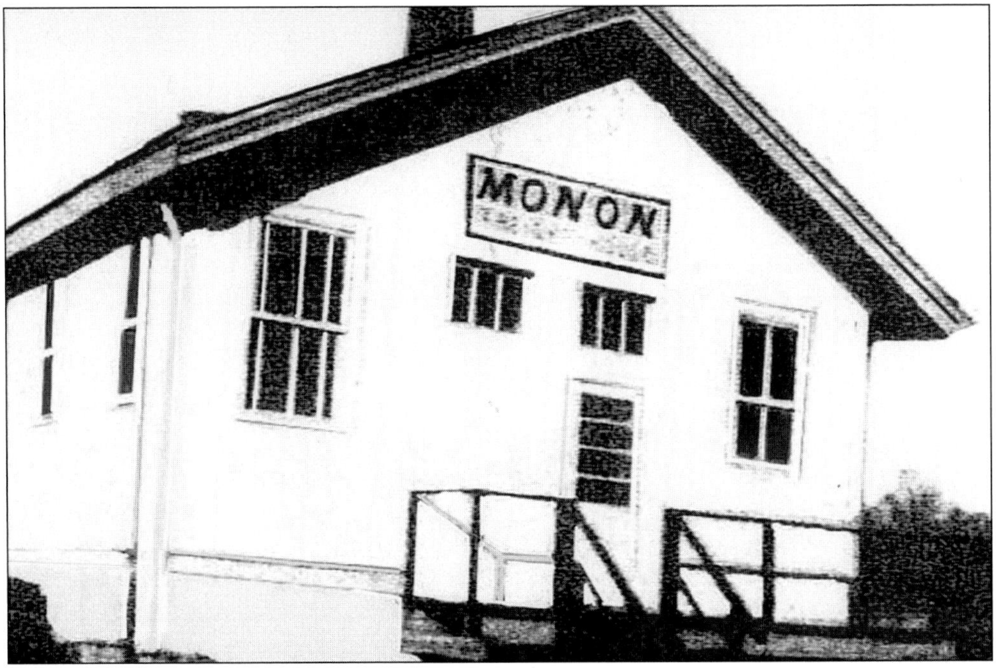

CI&L (MONON) FREIGHT HOUSE. This photograph shows the second Chicago, Indianapolis & Louisville freight house. It appeared in the *New Albany Tribune* on November 21, 1962, as the Monon Railroad announced their plans to build a new and larger freight house in New Albany. Constructed around 1896, this wooden depot was used until about 1963. It was built on Culbertson Avenue (previously Sycamore Street) and sat parallel to the CI&L tracks at the intersection of Culbertson Avenue and Bank Street.

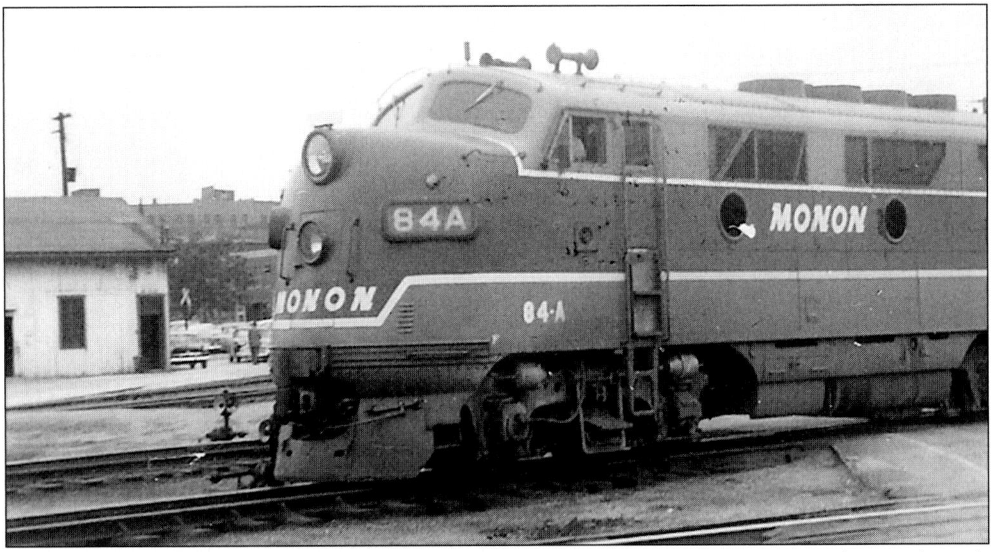

CI&L FREIGHT HOUSE. This photograph shows the same freight house from another angle with a Monon F-3 diesel locomotive to the right. This F-3, #84A diesel was purchased by Monon in May 1947, to be used with passenger units. It had 1500 horsepower and was part of Monon's effort to move from steam locomotives to diesels. (Courtesy New Albany Floyd County Public Library Archive.)

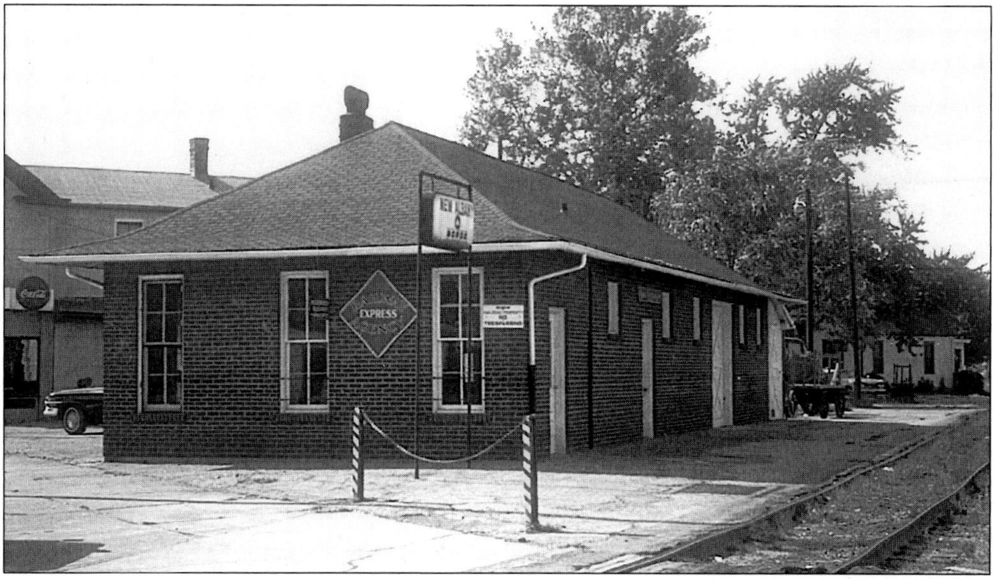

CI&L DEPOT. This third CI&L (Monon) passenger depot was built in 1937. A 1939 insurance map shows the depot at 1623 Market Street. Monon used this red brick depot as a ticket office until 1967; it stood vacant from 1967–1971. The image above shows the Monon tracks looking north of Market Street. (Courtesy Bob McCord.)

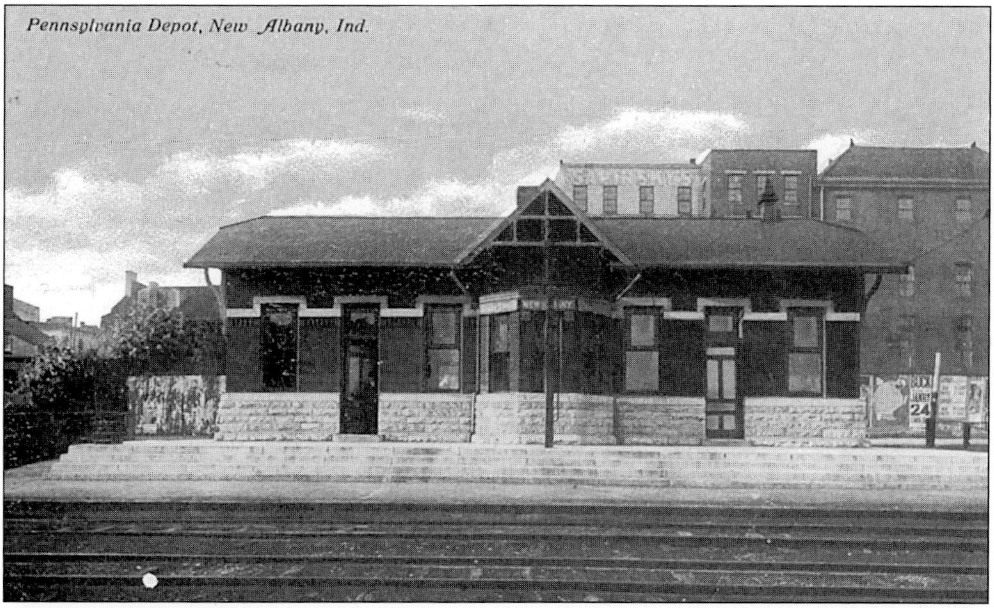

JM&I PASSENGER DEPOT. In 1866, the merger of the Indianapolis & Madison Railroad with the Jeffersonville Railroad brought to New Albany the Jeffersonville, Madison & Indianapolis Railroad (JM&I). The JM&I had been mentioned in the *New Albany Ledger* as early as May 1866; the line was owned and operated by the Pennsylvania Railroad (PRR). This postcard shows the JM&I passenger depot, which was located between Pearl and State Streets, south of Main Street and north of the tracks. An article in the *Ledger* of April 1883, said, "Work was to commence for a new brick depot, 200 feet x 37 feet." The JM&I at one time had a total of 224 miles of track. (Postcard by F. M. Kirby and Co.)

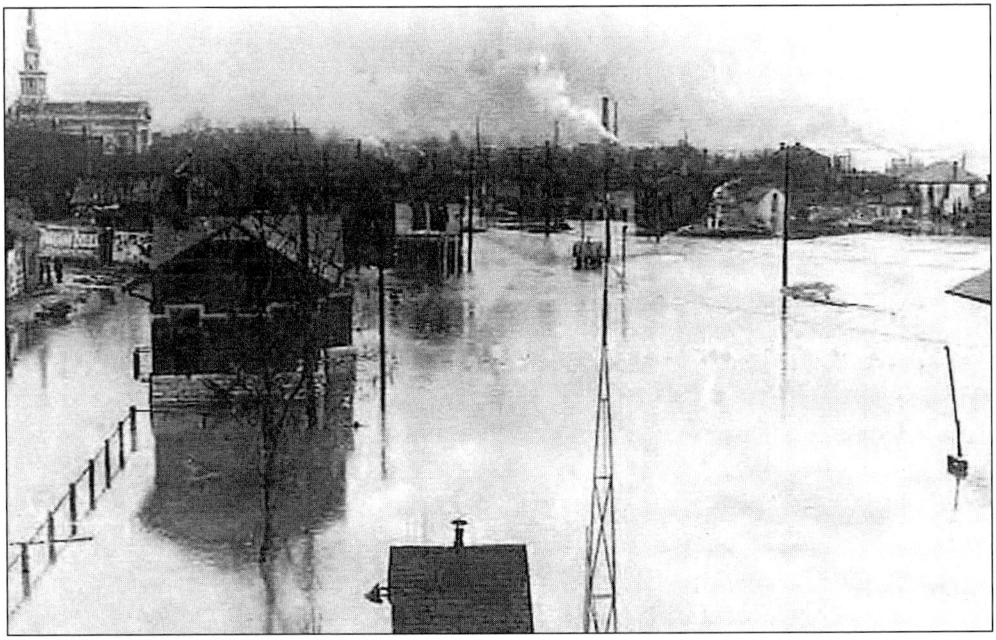

The 1907 Flood. This photograph shows the JM&I passenger station as it looked during the flood of 1907. The tracks ran between the passenger depot and the freight house, the roof of which you can see to the far right. The rail lines and structures took a real beating through the years with floods in 1907, 1913, and 1937. (Courtesy New Albany Floyd County Public Library Archives.)

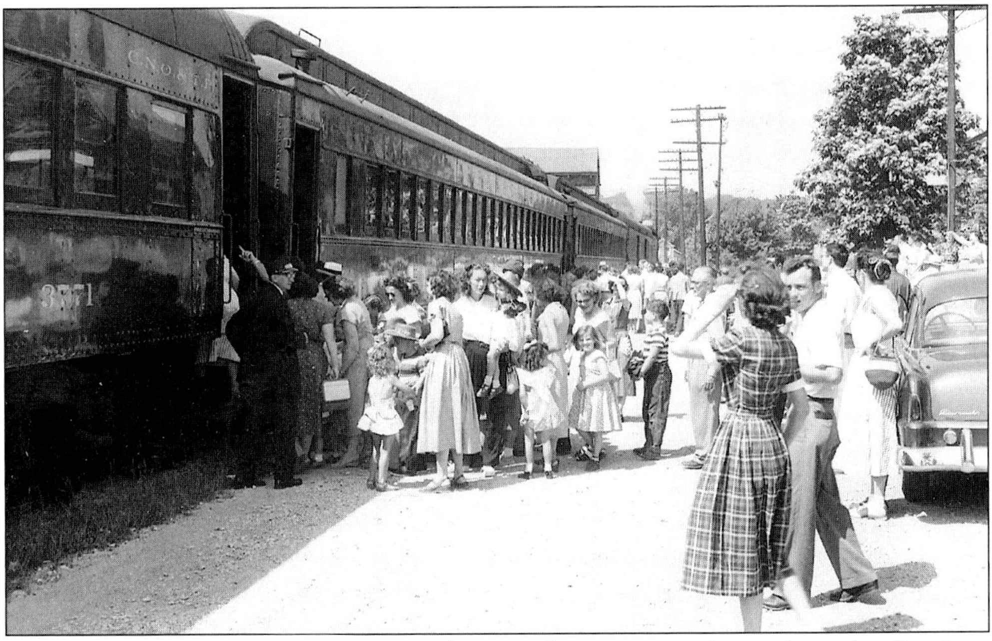

Last Southern Passenger Service. This crowd prepares to depart from the Southern Passenger Depot, which was the depot first used by the JM&I. This date in 1953 marked the last excursion of the Southern passenger service for New Albany. Earlier photographs show that the Louisville & St. Louis Air line also used this passenger station. (New Albany Floyd County Public Library Archives.)

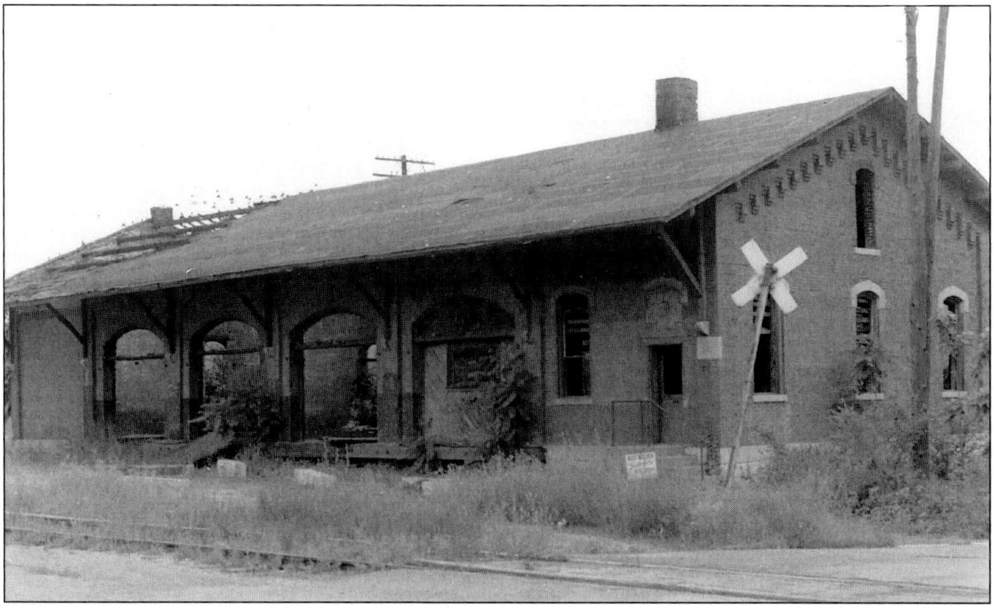

JM&I Freight House. New Albany boasts a varied and full rail history, but has very little to show for it today in the way of rail structures. The only building remaining is the freight house that belonged to the Jeffersonville, Madison & Indianapolis Railroad. It was a furniture store warehouse for many years, but now stands vacant. This early photograph shows the freight house before its conversion. The roof was in very poor shape at the time. Note the high-water mark (small stone block) to the left of the railroad warning cross-buck. (Courtesy Ron Stuckey.)

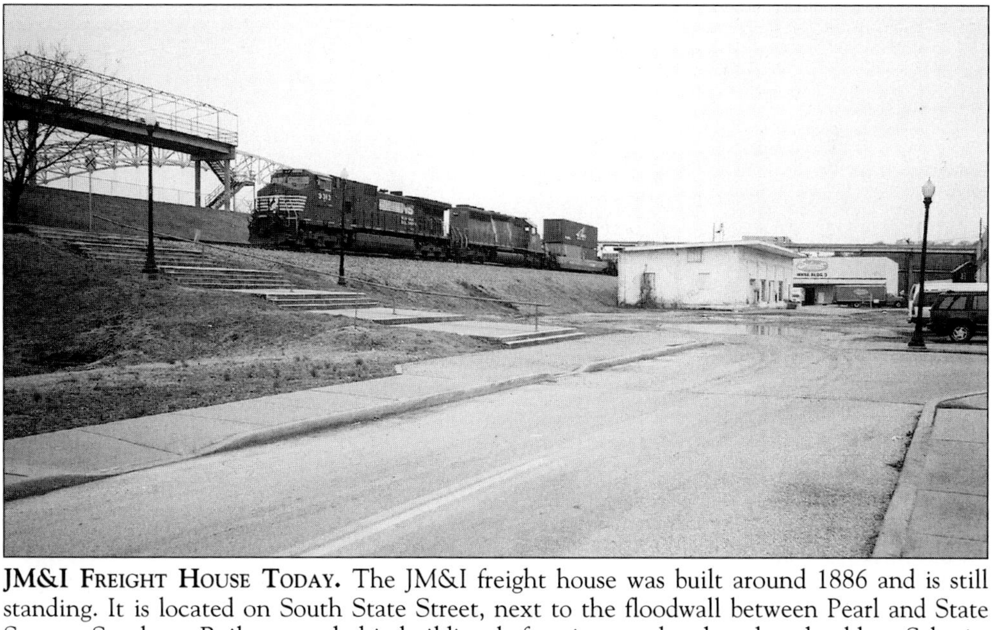

JM&I Freight House Today. The JM&I freight house was built around 1886 and is still standing. It is located on South State Street, next to the floodwall between Pearl and State Streets. Southern Railway used this building before it was abandoned and sold to Schmitt Furniture for storage. The roofline was greatly altered several years ago. A Norfolk Southern freight heading east is pictured here on the tracks, which were relocated onto the floodwall when the levee was constructed.

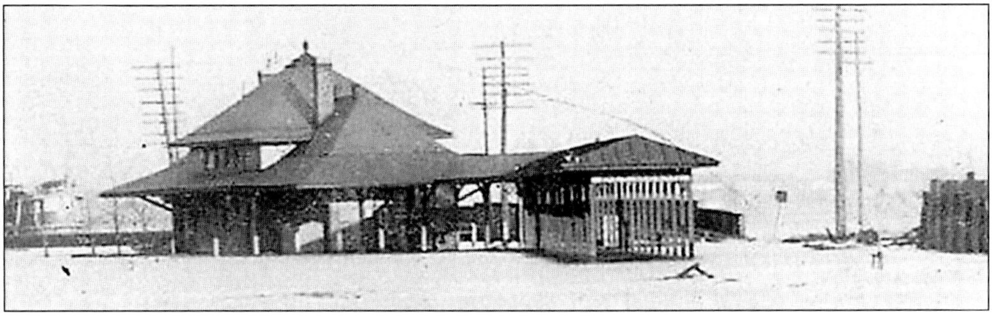

SOUTHERN PASSENGER DEPOT. This photograph shows the Louisville, Evansville & St. Louis Air line passenger station, which was located at West First and Lower Water Streets. The depot would receive additional heavy damage in future floods. To the right of the depot, a small portion of Fenger's Coal Yard can be seen right on the river. The depot was built in 1899. In some photographs, it is named as the Southern Railway passenger station, but it was not until 1900 that the Louisville, Evansville & St. Louis Air line merged into the Southern Railway. (Courtesy New Albany Floyd County Public Library Archives.)

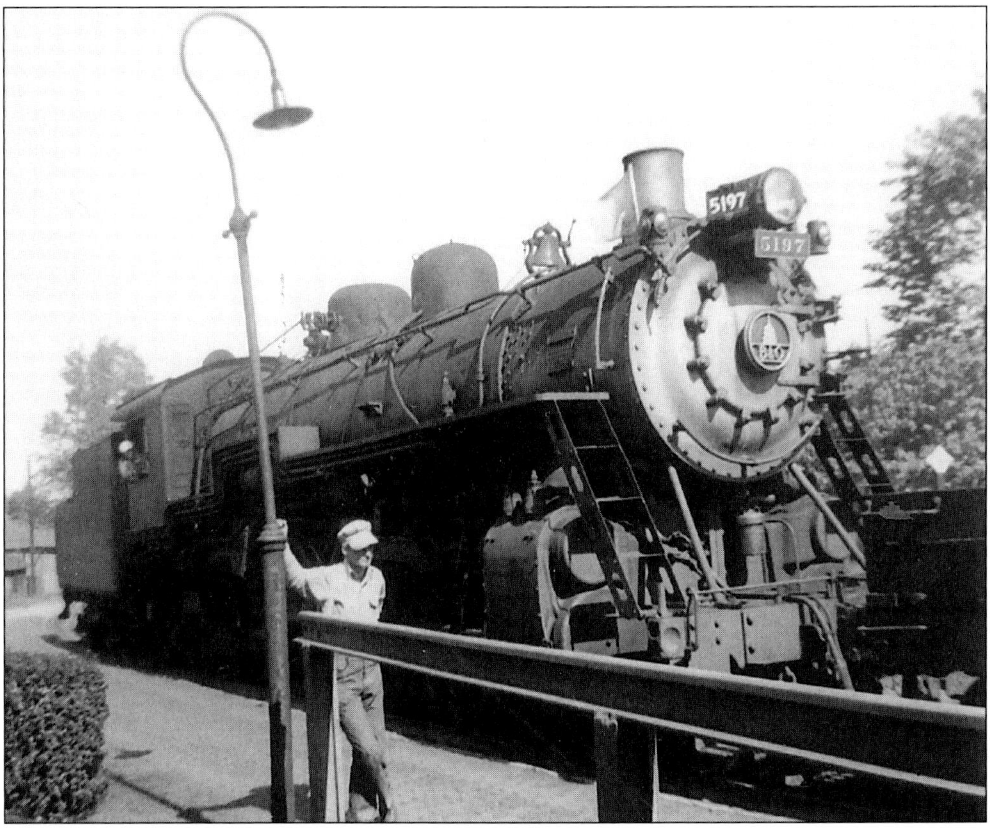

STEAM LOCOMOTIVE. This photograph shows the famous Baltimore & Ohio logo, which depicts the United States capitol building, on the front of the steam locomotive. The exterior lamp would have been beneficial when taking on water and coal or dealing with mechanical problems. Steam locomotive No. 5197 is pictured here with the tender. The Ohio & Mississippi (O&M) began entering New Albany on the K&IT Bridge in 1870. The O&M merged into the B&O in 1893.

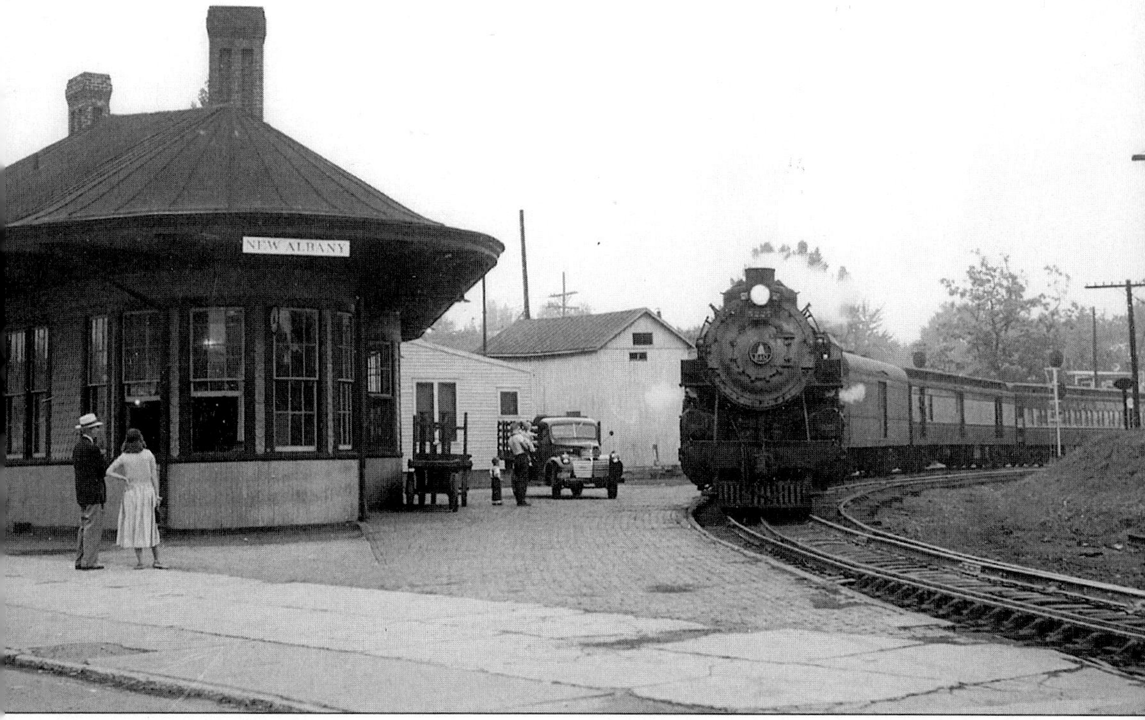

New Albany's B&O Depot. The Baltimore & Ohio (B&O) depot was located on the corner of Vincennes and Stone Streets and was completed January 7, 1888, by the Ohio & Mississippi Railroad. This photograph was probably taken in the late 1930s or early 1940s, based on the truck in the center. The B&O steam locomotive leads a passenger train heading west into the station. This depot was one of the more scenic depots of New Albany.

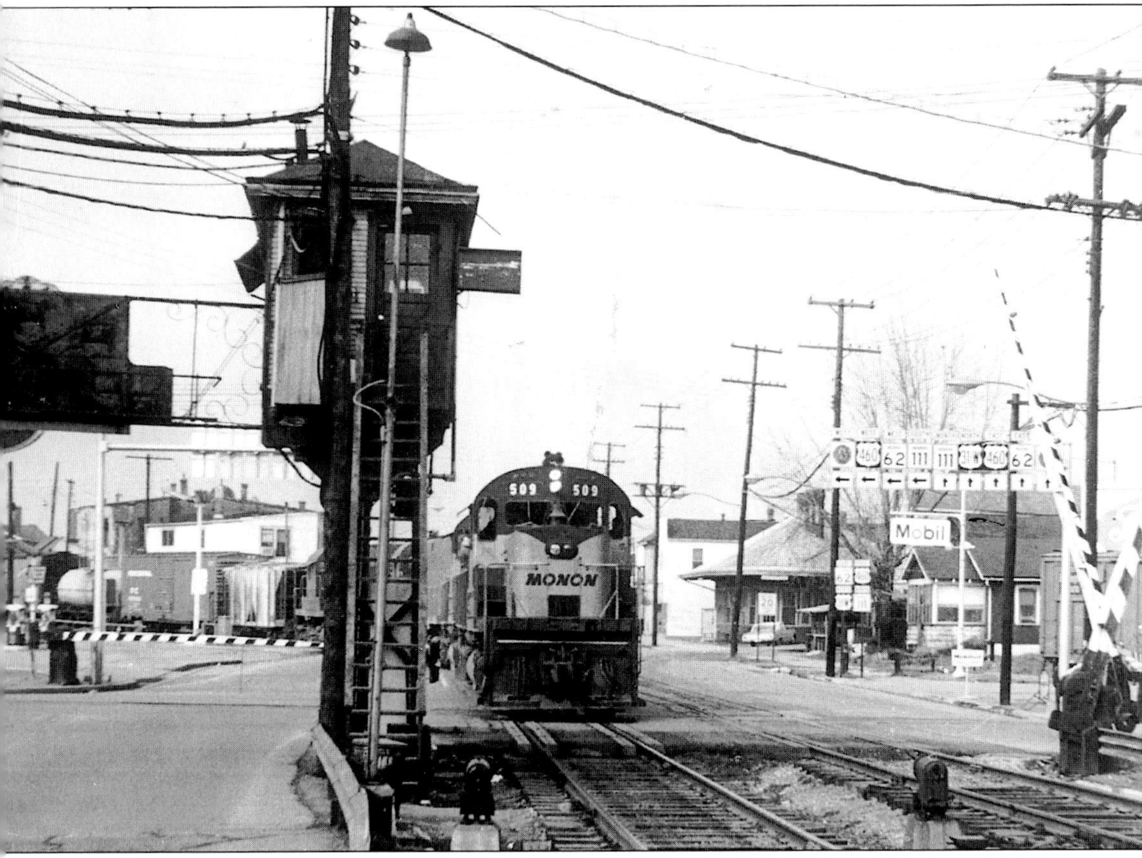

NEW ALBANY'S B&O DEPOT. This photograph was taken looking north on Vincennes Street. A Monon diesel, #509, heads south toward the Kentucky & Indiana Terminal Bridge. The B&O depot can be seen to the right of the engine and to the left of the Mobil Oil sign. A local attorney, Steven Beardsley, tried diligently to save this depot, but a fire destroyed it on the evening of April 6, 1981. A freight house was built just east of the passenger depot. (Courtesy John Fuller.)

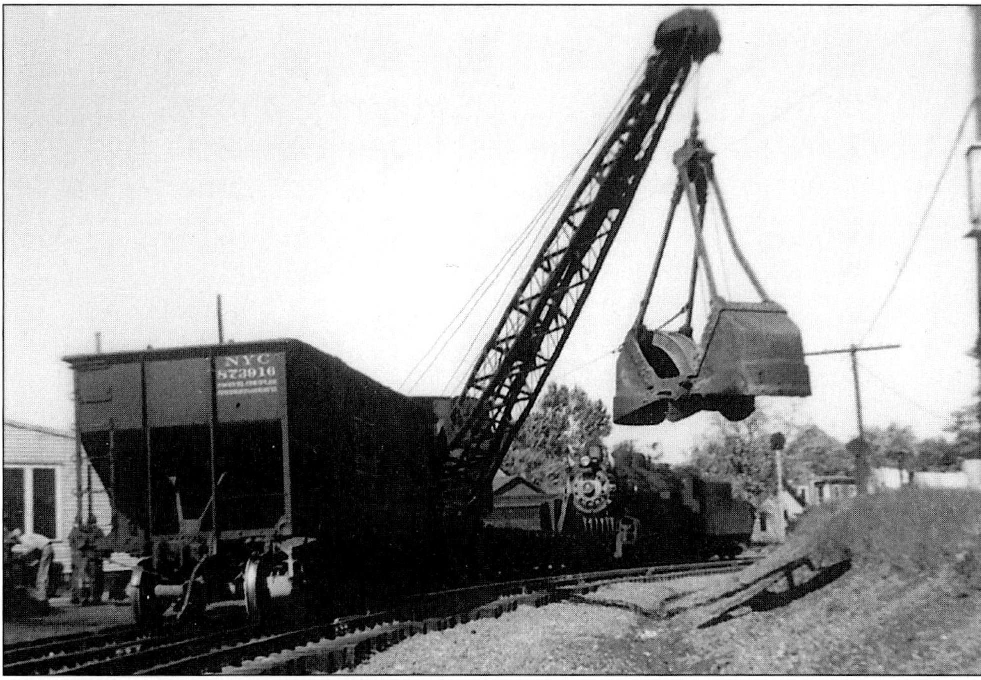

STEAM SHOVEL. Two natural resources that were vital to the steam locomotive were water and coal. The shovel here is unloading a coal shipment from a New York Central hopper No. 873916. A steam locomotive can be seen in the background. The photograph was taken east of the New Albany B&O passenger depot. This B&O line proceeded east through New Albany into Jeffersonville.

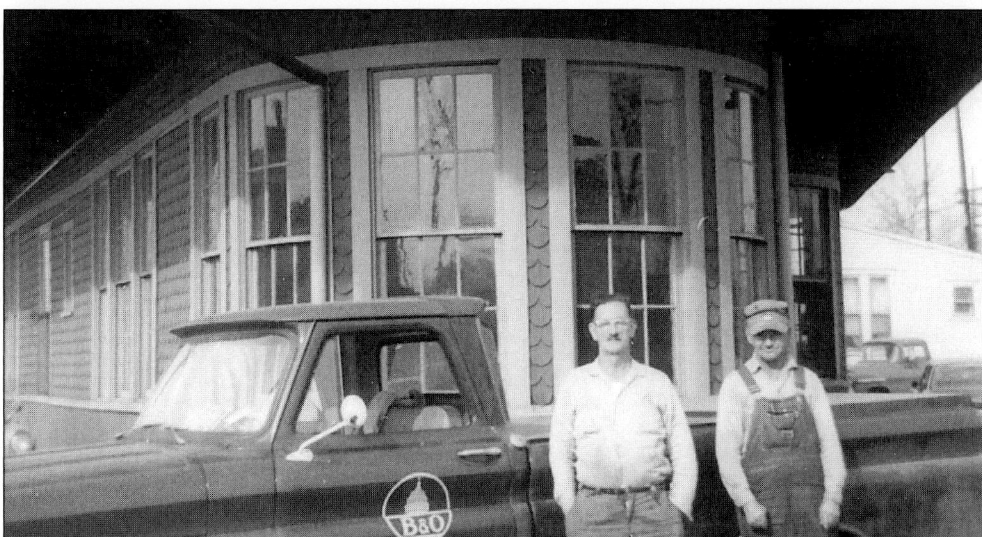

B&O EMPLOYEES. Taken in the early 1950s, this photograph shows the B&O depot with a B&O pickup truck in the foreground. Can you remember when pickup trucks had white painted rearview mirrors as seen here? These vehicles were quite important to the railroad, and could be used for small parcel deliveries, track maintenance, and many other tasks. The B&O once had a freight house east of the depot.

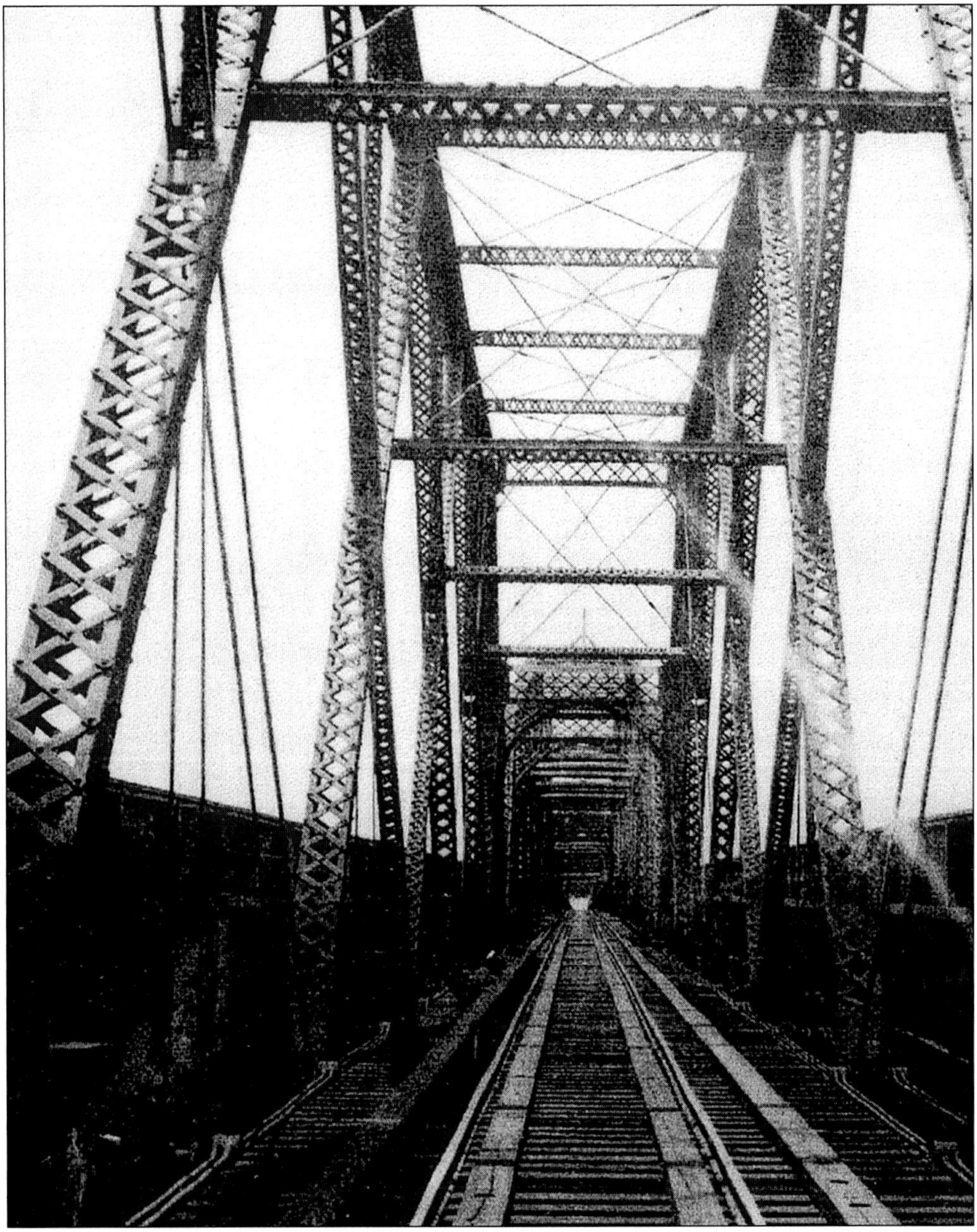

Kentucky and Indiana Railroad Bridge. This photograph, taken from *Art Works of New Albany*, shows the first K&I bridge, begun in 1881 and completed in 1885. It connected the Portland area of Louisville with New Albany's Vincennes Street and had been financed mainly by W. S. Culbertson and W. T. Grant. The first train crossed on October 16, 1886, and the bridge's name was changed to the Kentucky & Indiana Bridge & Railroad Co. in 1900 after it was purchased by the Southern, B&O, and Monon Railroads. The purchase price was a bargain, $700,000, following a bankruptcy. This image shows the single trackage of the K&I Bridge. The structure also had lanes on each side for pedestrians and horse-drawn wagons, as specified by both Indiana and Kentucky legislatures. By 1910, it was obsolete, with as many as 75 train and 96 streetcar crossings per day.

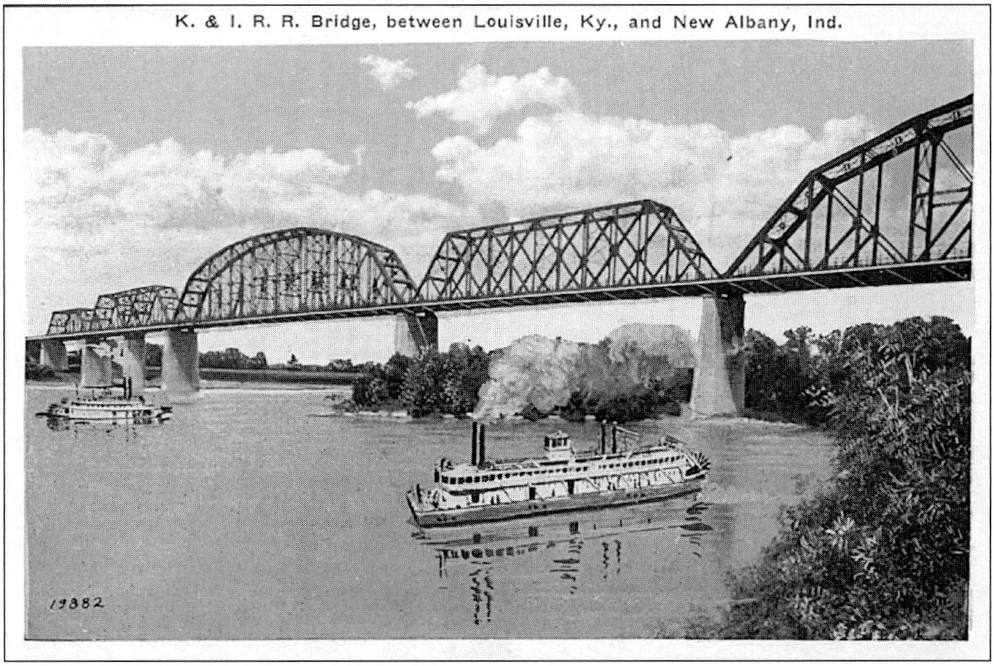

A Second Kentucky and Indiana Railroad Bridge. This postcard shows the second K&IT Bridge, erected between 1910 and 1912. In 1910, the B&O, Monon, and Southern railroads agreed to change the name of the bridge to the Kentucky and Indiana Terminal Railroad Company. The K&I was one of the largest and heaviest plain truss bridges in the world at the time it was completed, in 1912. The new span had two tracks and retained the need for wagon ways and turnouts. (Postcard by the Kyle Company.)

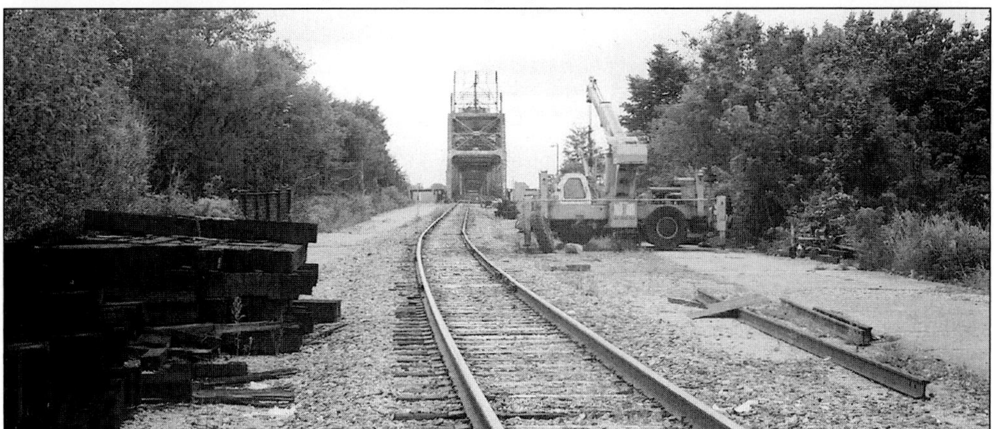

K&I Railroad Bridge Today. This photograph shows the K&I Bridge as it is today. About 15 years ago, the Southern Railway was allowed to alter their entrance into New Albany from the K&I Bridge. Instead of looping to the east and circling under the bridge, they were permitted to turn directly west and onto their tracks. The tracks on the right are used by the Norfolk Southern today, and the tracks on the left are used by CSX. There used to be a toll booth at the far left of the tracks. Cars were no longer able to use the bridge after 1979. The complete span, including approaches, measured nearly 6,000 feet in length and 225 feet in height from its highest point to the normal river surface.

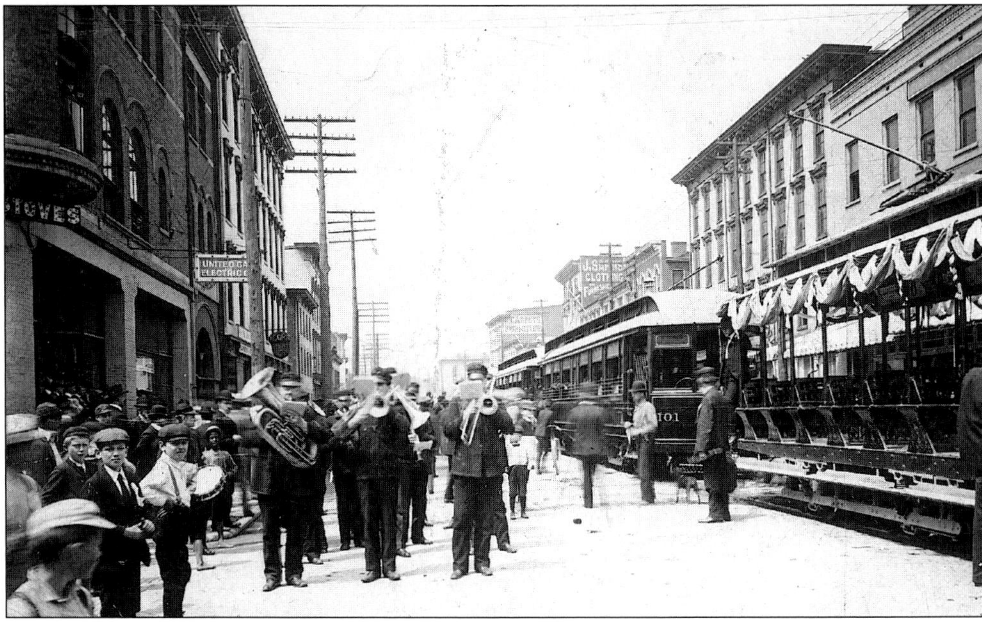

INTERURBAN CELEBRATION. The band is playing, and there's reason to celebrate—a new interurban. One of the building storefronts on Pearl Street was to be the depot for the interurban. Another of the interurban depots in New Albany was located at 138 East Spring Street (Courtesy New Albany Floyd County Public Library Archives.)

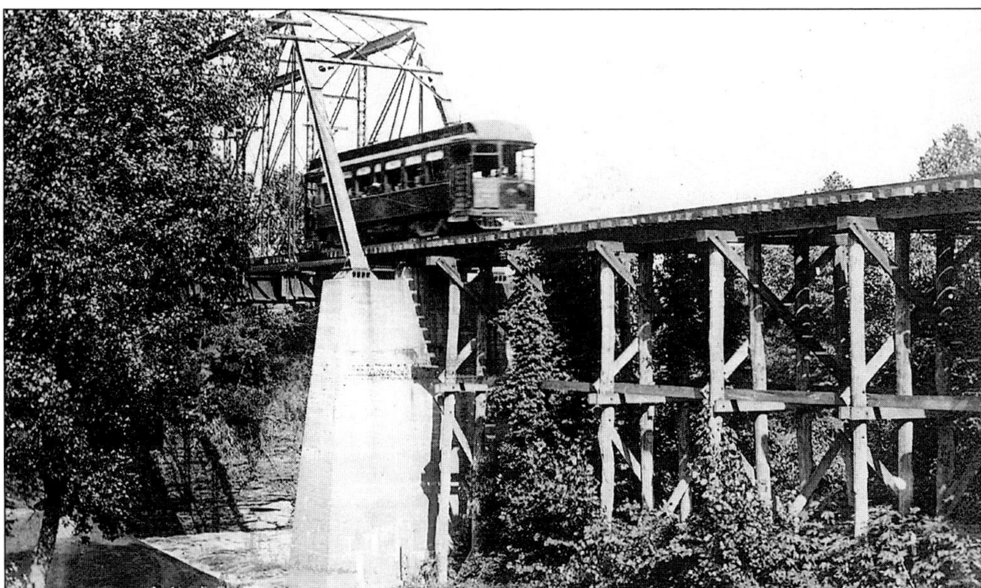

NEW ALBANY BRIDGE OVER SILVER CREEK. Here, the interurban heads across the Silver Creek River Bridge. This line went through Clarksville, Emery Crossing, and on to Jeffersonville. In 1932, streetcar service in Jeffersonville and New Albany was replaced by buses. From 1891, when streetcar service first came to New Albany, through the ultimate switchover to bus service, the owners of the streetcar service changed names no less than five times. (Courtesy New Albany Floyd County Public Library Archives.)

INTERURBAN ADVERTISEMENT. Glenwood Park was a bustling place in the days of the Louisville & Southern Indiana Traction Company (L&SIT). This advertisement promotes boating, fishing, dancing, tennis, and an assortment of activities at the park. A very important part of the advertisement was mention of a streetcar connection to neighboring Louisville. When the L&SIT was formed in 1903, it had already acquired the New Albany Street Railroad Co. It was in direct competition with the Daisy line of Louisville. In 1905, the L&SIT bought out the Daisy line. (New Albany Floyd County Public Library—Hedden Family Collection.)

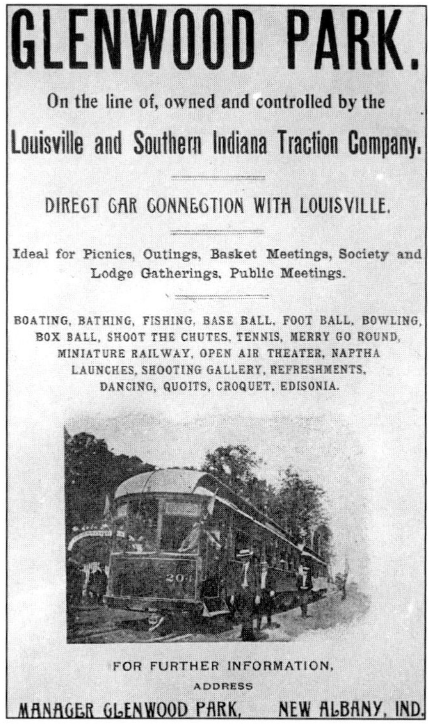

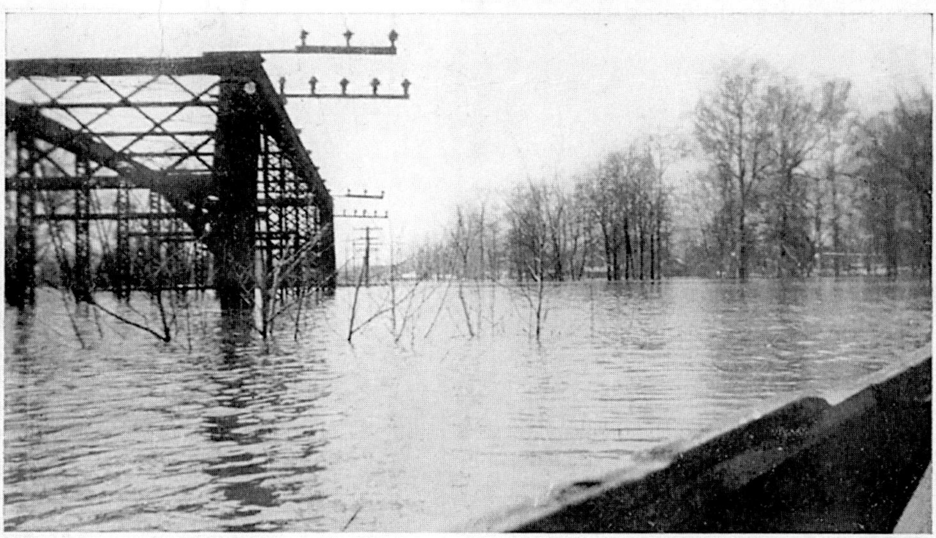

408 Old Interurban Bridge over Silver Creek in New Albany.

INTERURBAN BRIDGE. This old postcard shows the results of the 1907 flood on the interurban bridge that crossed Silver Creek east of uptown New Albany. A 1959 article in the *New Albany Valley News* stated that the interurbans, called Big Reds, "roared into New Albany, going right down Spring Street after crossing the web-structured bridge over Silver Creek. The tracks were on an island of grass that extended from Beharrel Street to Silver Street." The heyday of the interurban in Indiana ended by 1932 as the private automobile became a great threat. (Postcard by Julian R. Fisher, Louisville, Kentucky.)

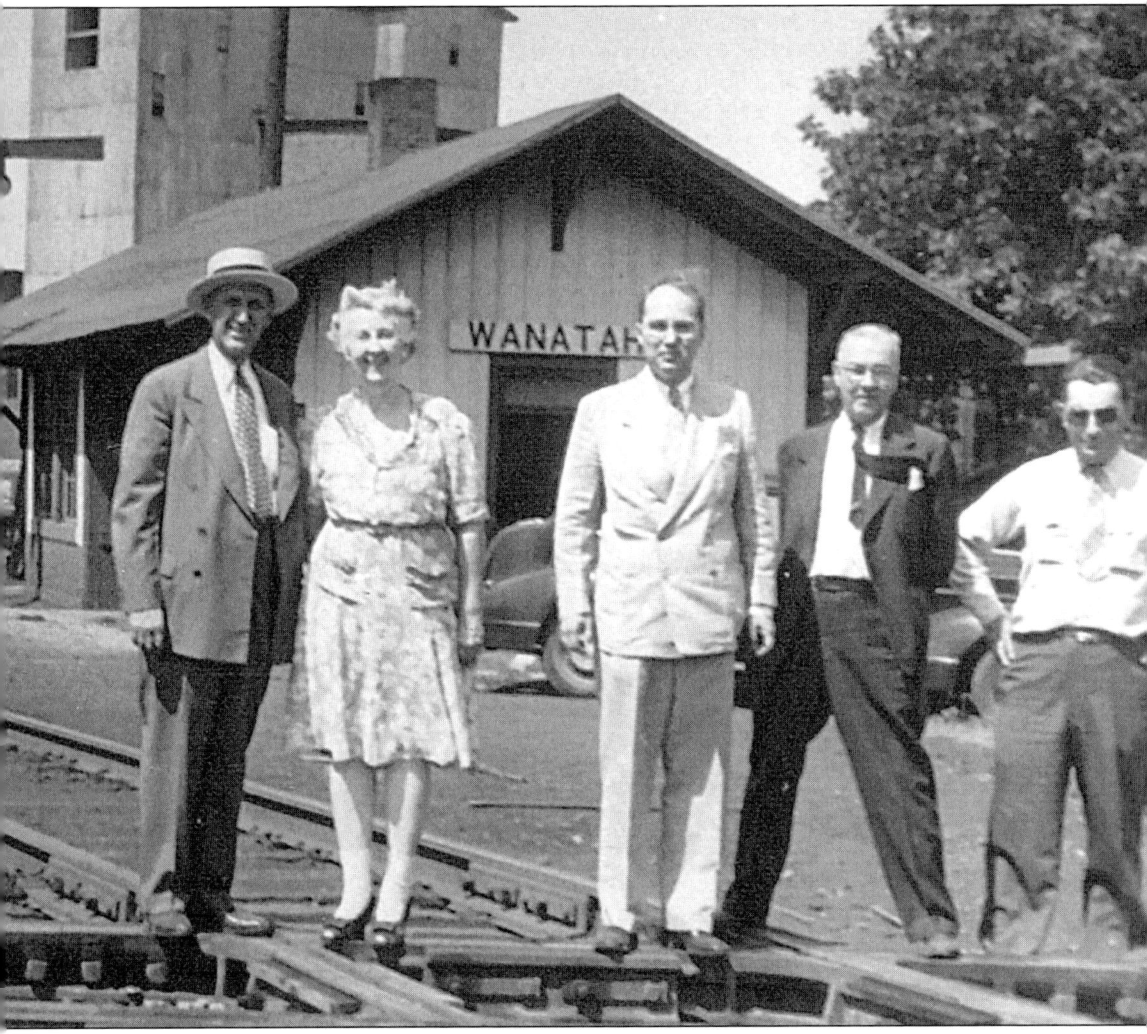

RAILROAD CHIEF. Pictured at center is Monon President John West Barriger, between some local dignitaries at the Wanatah depot in northern Indiana. Barriger became president of the CI&L in 1945, bringing several innovations to the company. He eliminated the old steam locomotives and replaced them with "first-generation" diesel engines. He also replaced problem bridges and tracks. After World War II, he had the Monon shops convert 28 U.S. Army hospital cars into coaches, grille coaches, dining-parlor cars, dining-bar lounges, and mail-baggage cars. He also had a new logo designed for the Monon Route—a circle containing the letter M with an Indian arrowhead pointing upward. He resigned at the end of 1952. (Courtesy MRHTS Collection.)

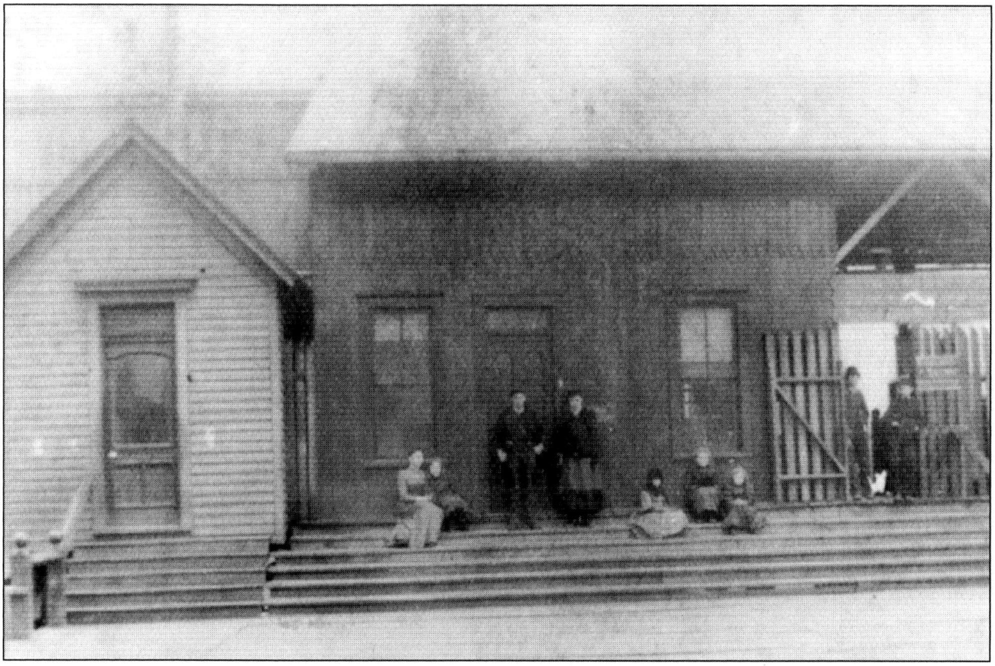

Silver Hills Street Car. This photograph was taken about 1894 and shows the interurban station at West Eighth Street. The small building to the left was the men's waiting room, while the other building was the women's waiting room. It was common in those days for the men to have a separate waiting area from the women. (Courtesy New Albany Floyd County Public Library Archives.)

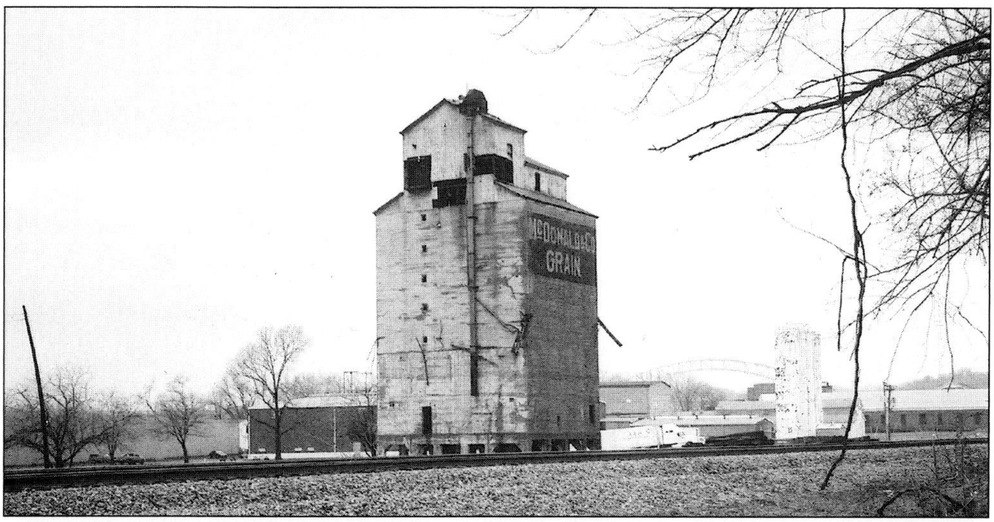

Grain Elevator. South of the Norfolk Southern tracks in New Albany stands this grain elevator. The photograph looks southwest with the tracks in front of the structure. The Norfolk Southern has high visibility in New Albany as the tracks run right along the north side of the floodwall. The Ohio River is south of the floodwall, and to the right of the building you can see the Sherman-Minton auto bridge which crosses the Ohio River. The grain elevator advertises the McDonald Grain Company.

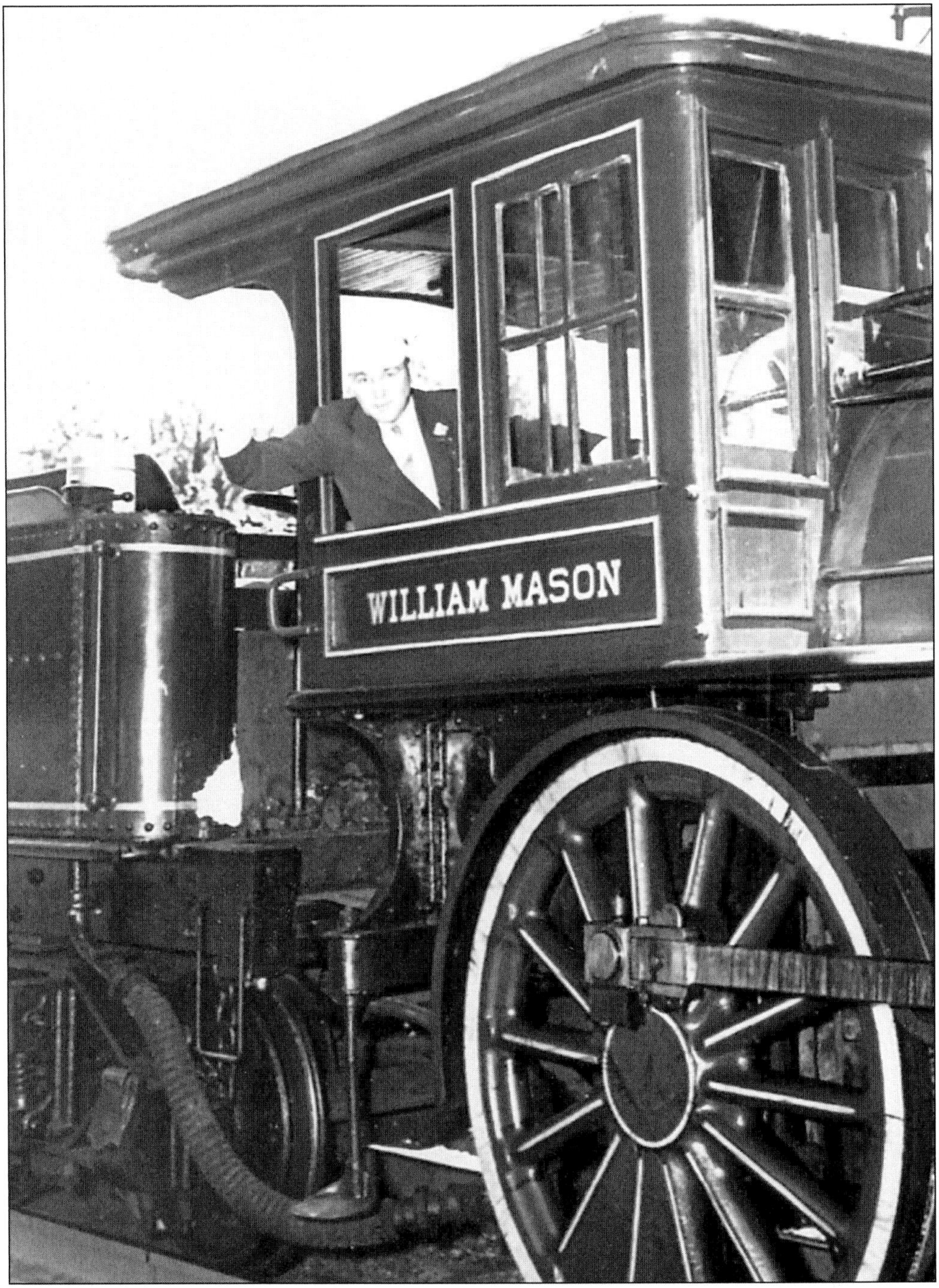

The William Mason. New Albany, as the birthplace of the Monon, fully celebrated the Monon Centennial in 1947. Pictured above is president of the Monon Railroad, John Barriger, sitting in the cab of the William Mason steam locomotive. The William Mason, #25, was borrowed from the Baltimore & Ohio Railroad for this time of reflection and celebration. It traveled from Hammond to New Albany during the four-day festivities. The William Mason was constructed in 1856 and rebuilt in 1926. (Courtesy MRHTS Collection.)

Five

Tracing the Monon Route

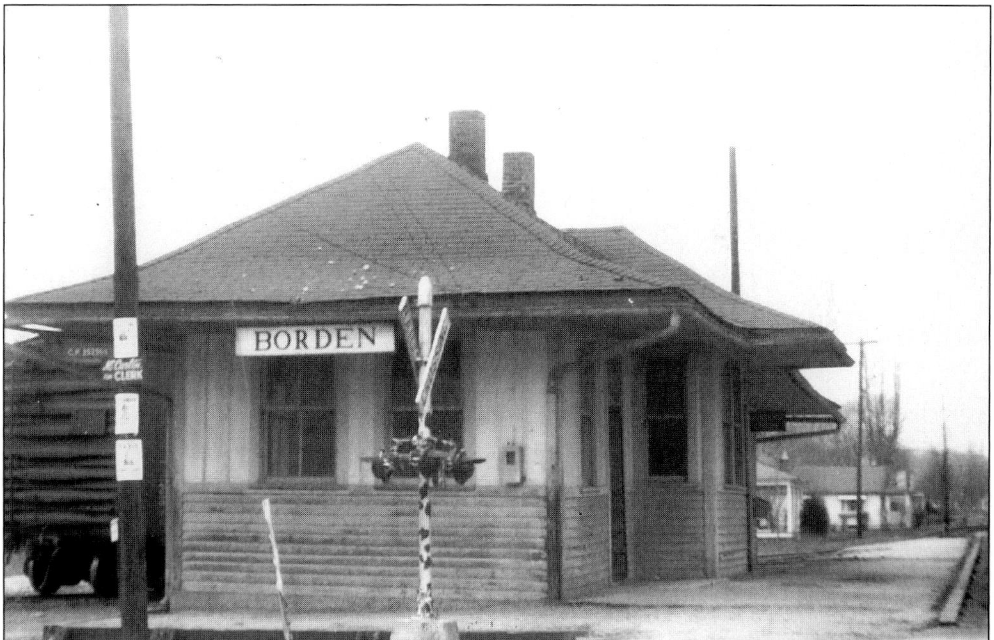

Borden Monon Depot. Under the leadership of James Brooks, the New Albany & Salem Railroad started at Providence (now called Borden) in 1847. It was here that Brooks met with six associates and organized the railroad. This chapter will identify Monon depots that have been demolished, some that are still standing, and the depots of other railroads located in towns shared with the Monon. Borden is about twenty miles northwest of New Albany. The berry and produce business of the Borden community was quite dependent on the Monon to transport crops to market. The Borden Monon depot has been torn down since this photograph was taken. (Courtesy Harry C. Jackson Collection.)

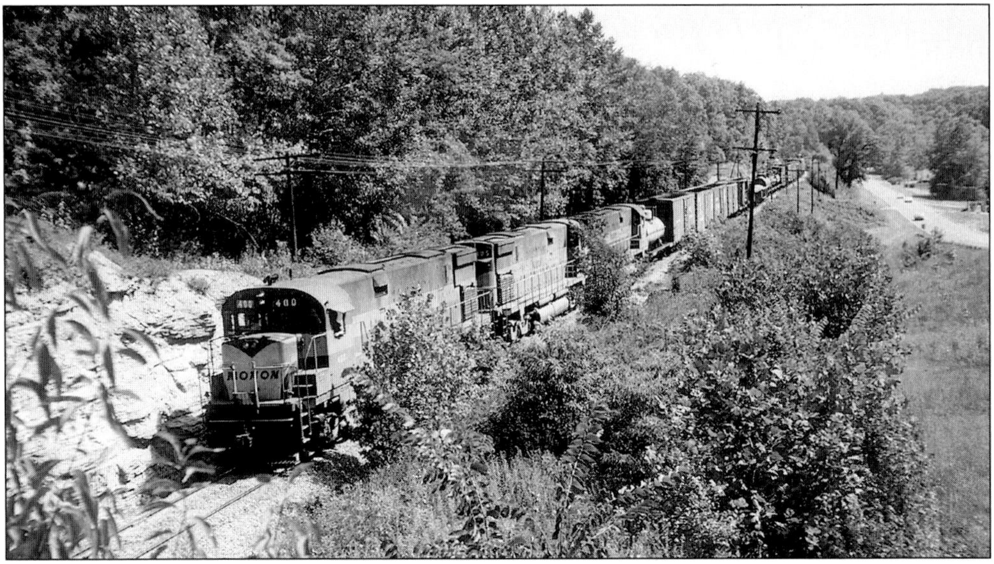

Monon Diesel Pulling the Knob. This September 1964 photograph shows Monon diesel #400, a C-628 heavy road switcher, leading a train north of Borden. "The Knob," as the hill is called, was often a challenge to the Monon. Here, three engines help to make the steep grade. The engine was manufactured by Alco (American Locomotive Company). This particular engine was used for several years after the Monon merged with the L&N. It was retired from Conrail in 1978. (Courtesy MRHTS Collection.)

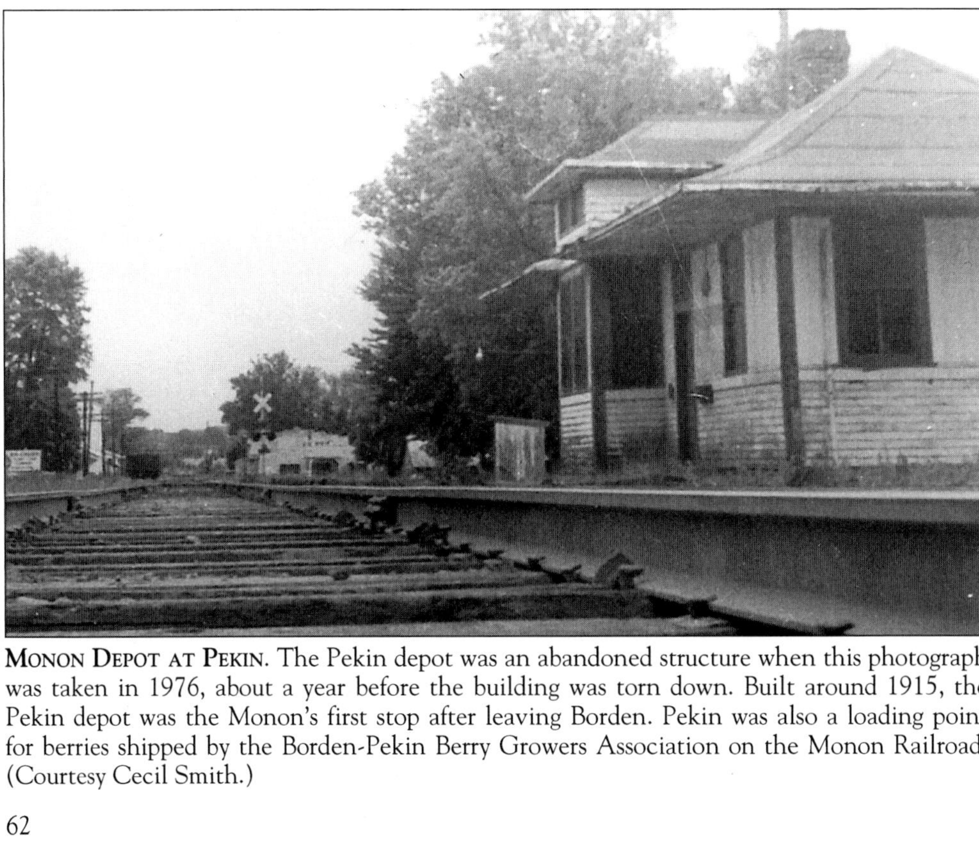

Monon Depot at Pekin. The Pekin depot was an abandoned structure when this photograph was taken in 1976, about a year before the building was torn down. Built around 1915, the Pekin depot was the Monon's first stop after leaving Borden. Pekin was also a loading point for berries shipped by the Borden-Pekin Berry Growers Association on the Monon Railroad. (Courtesy Cecil Smith.)

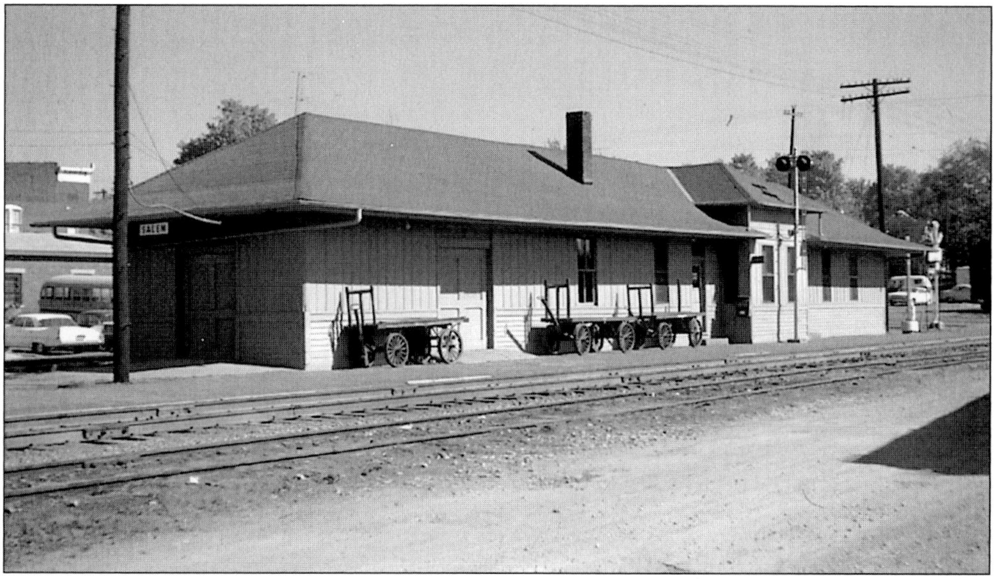

MONON DEPOT AT SALEM. In 1951, Brooks admitted that he had always intended to build the line from New Albany to Lake Michigan, but chose the name New Albany & Salem to better calm investors. This photograph shows the last depot that the Monon Railroad built in Salem around 1909. It was used by the Louisville & Nashville until its closing in 1973. This photograph was taken by Tom Smart on October 17, 1964, a number of years before the depot was razed in 1982. (Courtesy MRHTS Collection.)

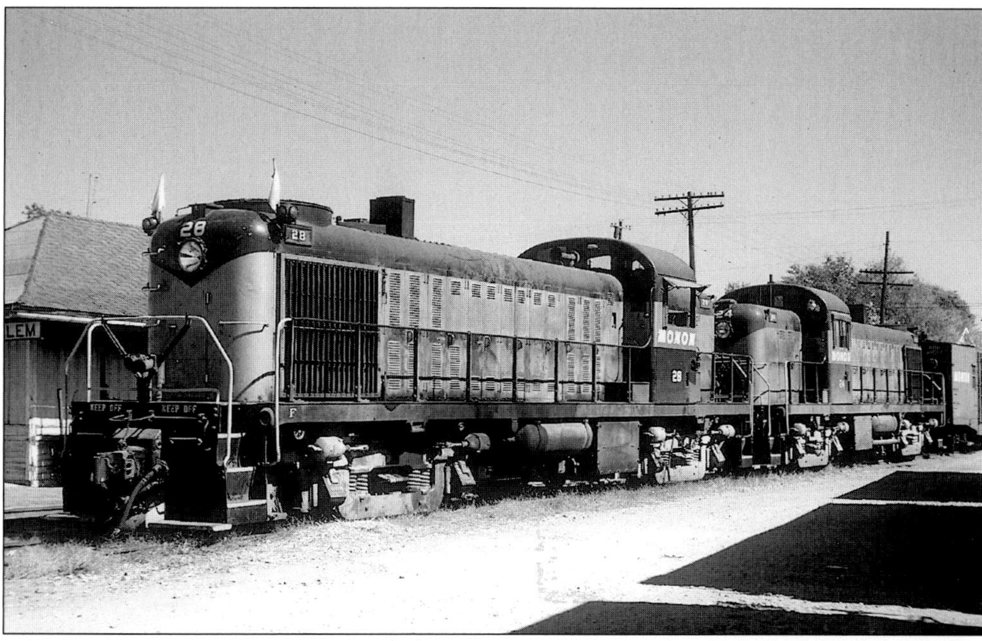

RS-2S AT THE SALEM DEPOT. Pictured above are two RS-2 diesels stopped in front of the Salem Monon station. Alco manufactured the RS-2 diesel locomotive, a road switcher with 1500 horsepower. Monon purchased nine of these engines in 1947, during the time when they were converting to an all diesel fleet. This photograph was taken October 5, 1963, by Tom Smart. (Courtesy MRHTS Collection.)

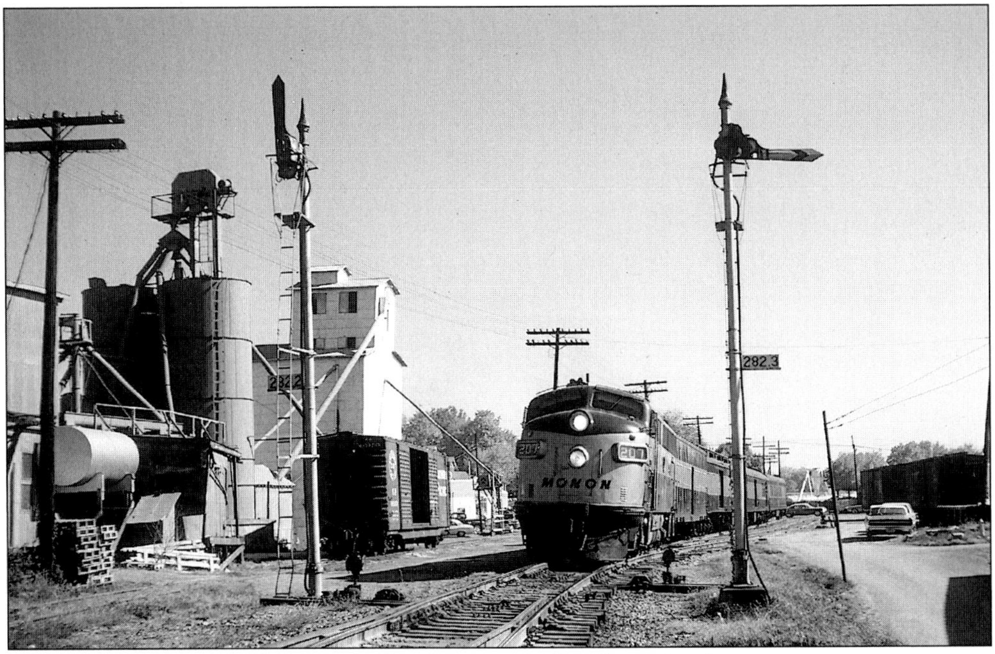

F-3's at Salem. This photograph shows an F3-A diesel #207 pulling a passenger train into Salem. The F-3 locomotive was a 1500 horsepower streamlined cab unit. The old Monon rail line still runs through Salem today and is used by CSX and the Canadian Pacific. Tom Smart took this photograph on October 17, 1964. (Courtesy MRHTS Collection.)

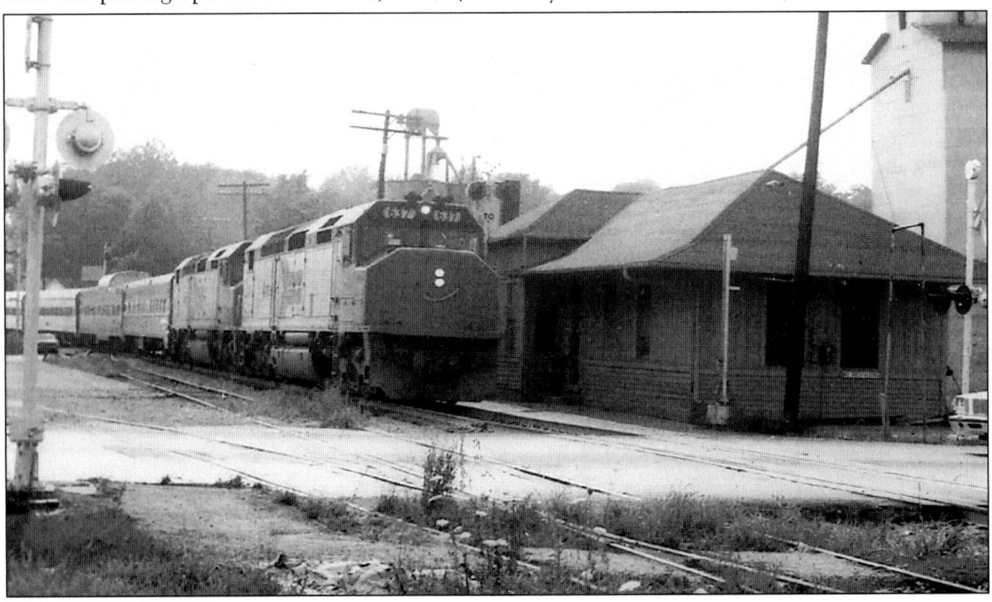

Amtrak Passenger at Salem. A southbound Amtrak passenger train passes through Salem in 1977. In the late 1960s and early 1970s, when passenger service was at an all time decline, the federal government became involved in saving passenger train service. Amtrak was created in 1970, struggling financially since its birth. Because of this, many regions in America have lost passenger service. Today, Indiana still has Amtrak train service largely because Chicago, a major Amtrak destination, is so near its northwest border. (Courtesy Cecil Smith.)

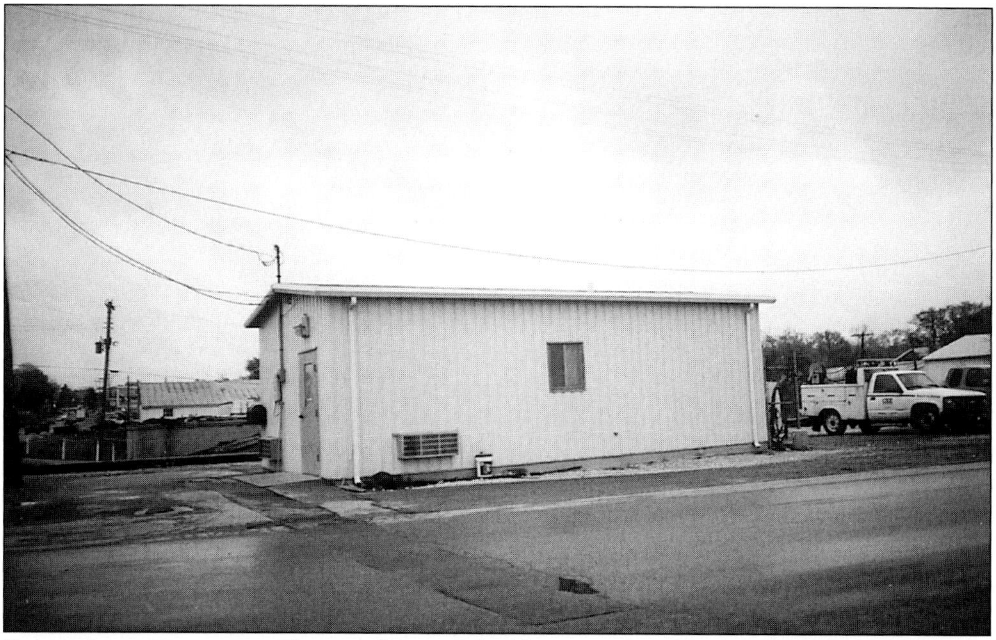

SALEM SHOP BUILDING. This small metal building stands near the location of the now-demolished depot. This structure was built by the Louisville & Nashville Railroad at 401 South Main Street. Currently, the CSX uses this shop building as a place for workers to meet, store equipment, and file paperwork.

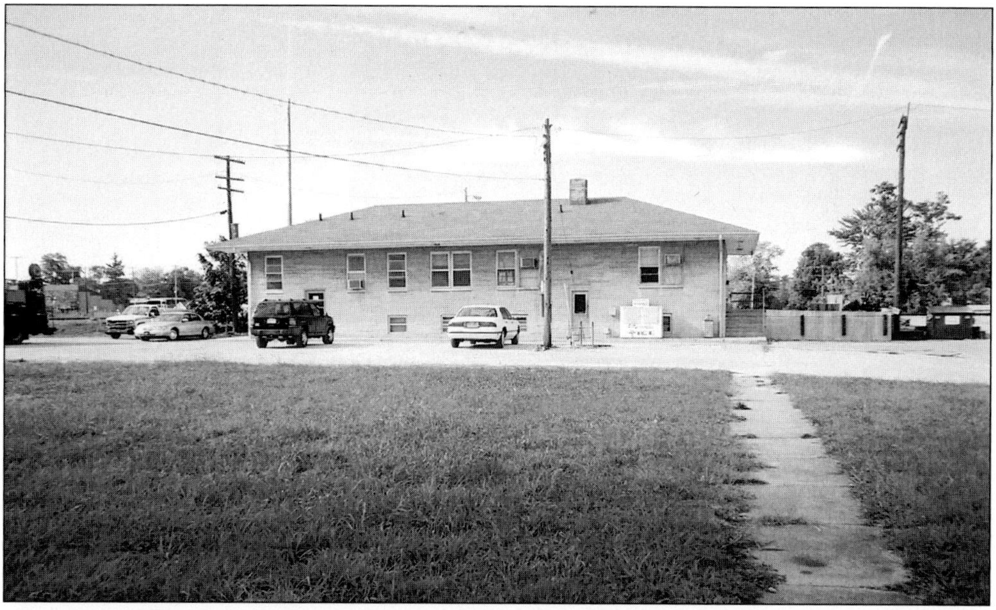

MITCHELL B&O STATION. Mitchell has a strong railroad history, with the Monon arriving in 1851 and the Ohio & Mississippi arriving soon after, in 1857. The O&M later became the Baltimore & Ohio. Mitchell no longer has the Monon depot, but is does have this stone B&O depot on Mississippi Street, now used by CSX. The Monon and B&O at one time interchanged almost 5000 carloads per year. By some estimates, Mitchell has between 15 and 20 CSX trains going through the town each day.

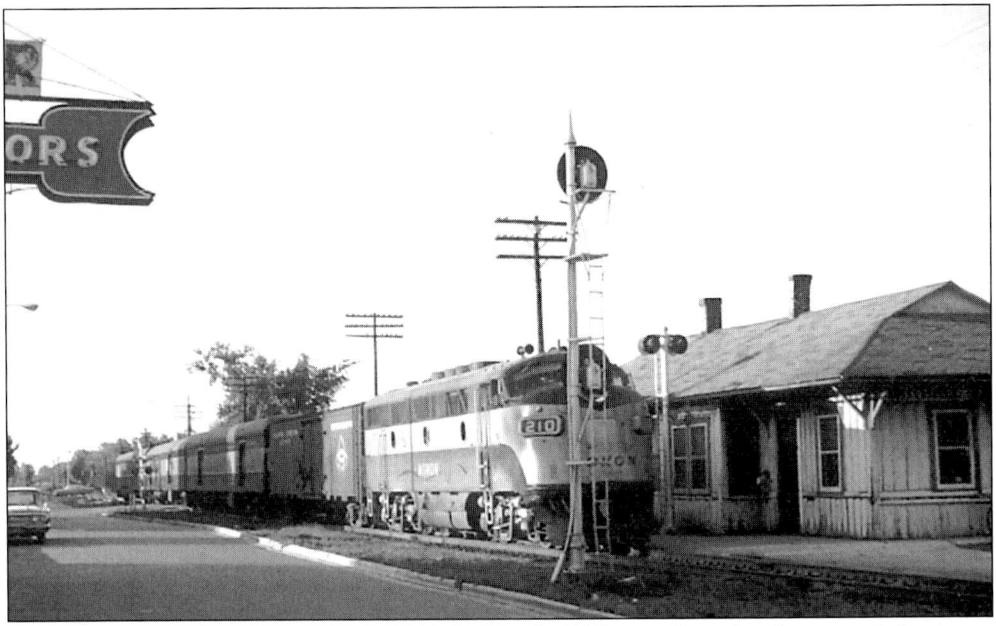

MITCHELL MONON DEPOT. Built in 1892, the Mitchell Monon depot has been razed. It was an important part of the Monon line and, with the B&O depot, kept the little town of Mitchell quite busy. This photograph, taken by Charles Huffer on October 17, 1964, shows an F-3 diesel (#210) passenger train stopped at the station. (Courtesy MRHTS Collection.)

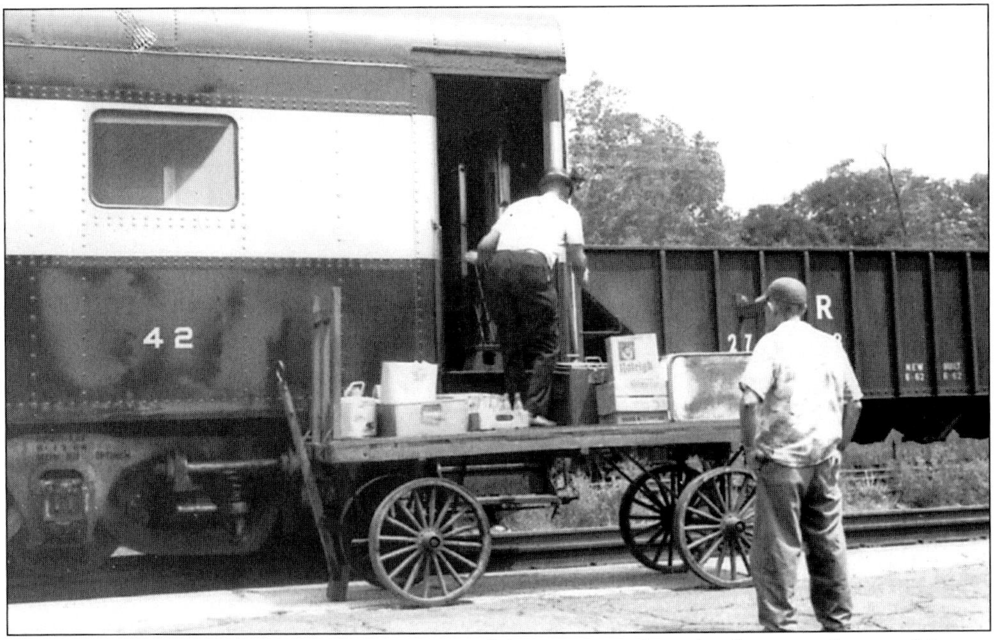

COACH #42 AT MITCHELL STATION. Pictured here are workers loading supplies on Monon passenger car #42 at the Mitchell Monon depot. At each stop, the passenger trains had to handle packages, luggage, drinks, food, and mail. Note the hopper car to the right on the other track. The use of passenger cars had diminished greatly by the 1950s and early 1960s. This photograph was taken on July 15, 1964. (Courtesy MRHTS Collection.)

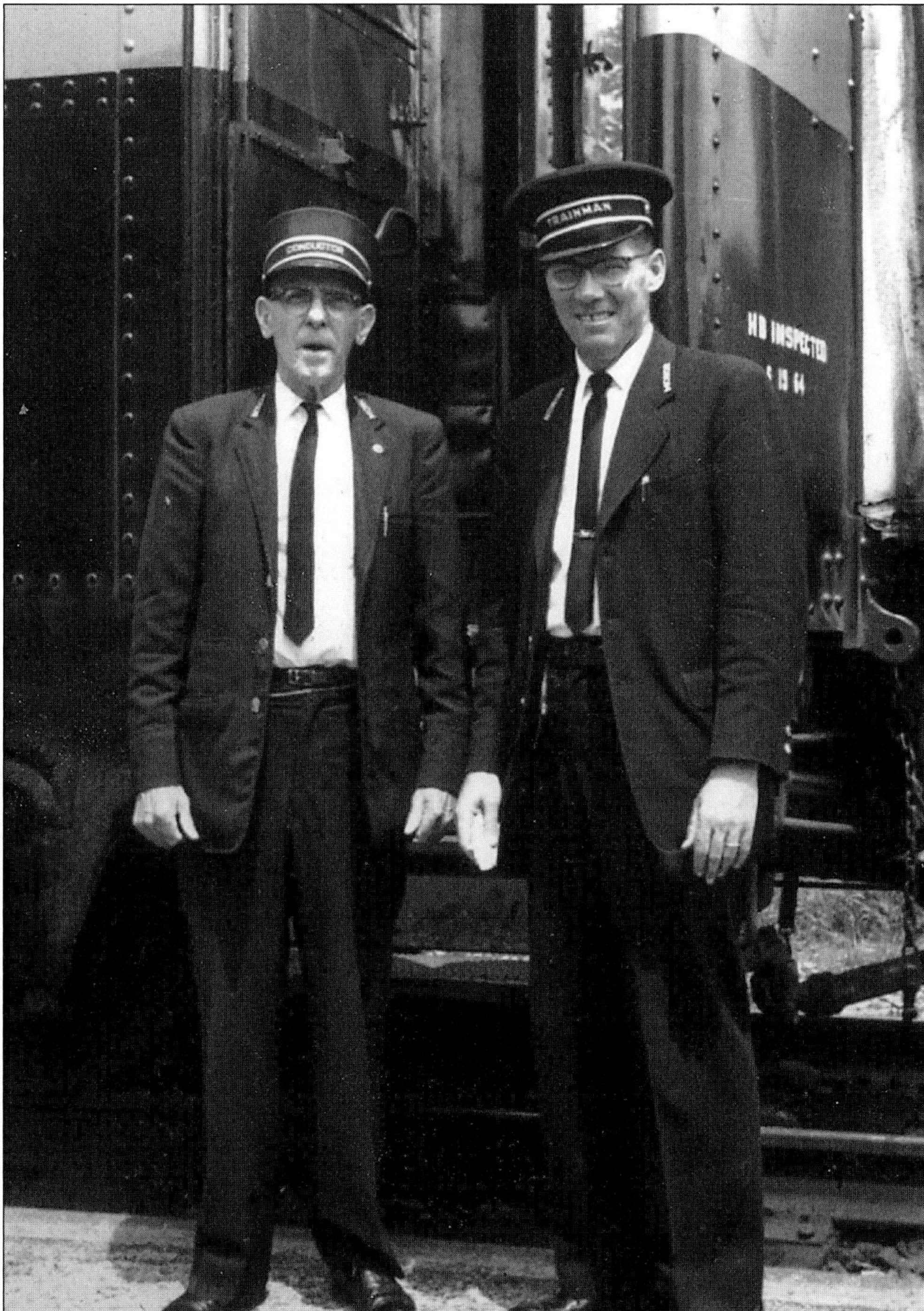

Passenger Crew at Mitchell Depot. A Monon passenger car stops at the Mitchell depot. The gentleman on the left was the conductor, Bill "Hickory" Cornwell, and the trainman to the right is Bill Hessler. The last Monon passenger train went through Mitchell in September 1967. This photograph was taken on July 15, 1964, by Charles Huffer. (Courtesy MRHTS Collection.)

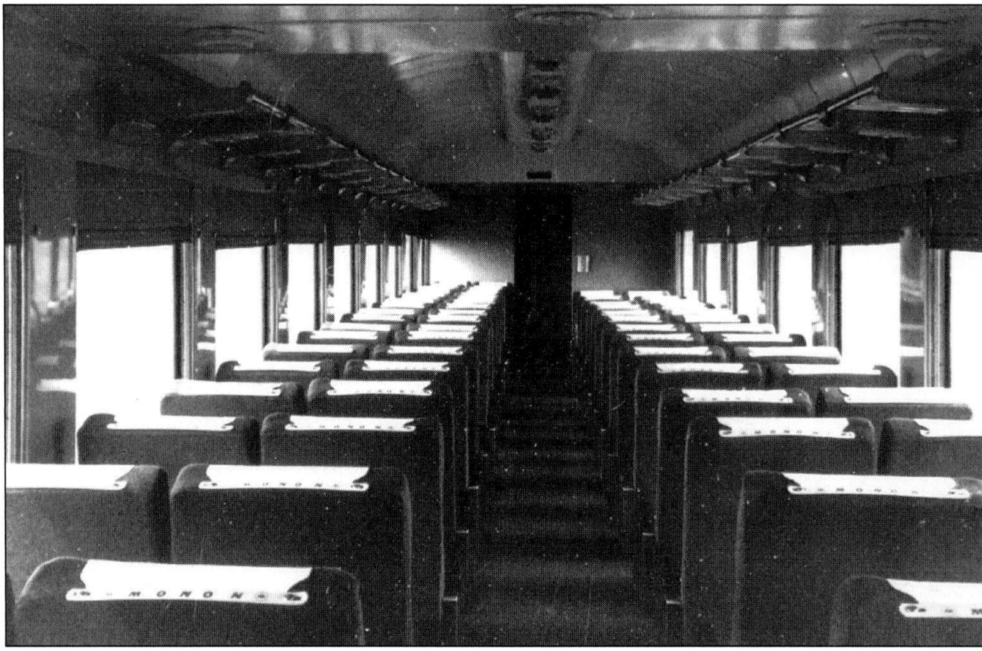

MONON PASSENGER CAR. Above is the interior of a Monon passenger coach. The photograph was taken on August 8, 1965, by Charles Huffer. By that time, the use of passenger trains had been greatly reduced due to the increased use of automobiles. Most coaches were equipped with benches that had backs which could be flipped, so passengers could always face the direction the train was traveling. (Courtesy MRHTS Collection.)

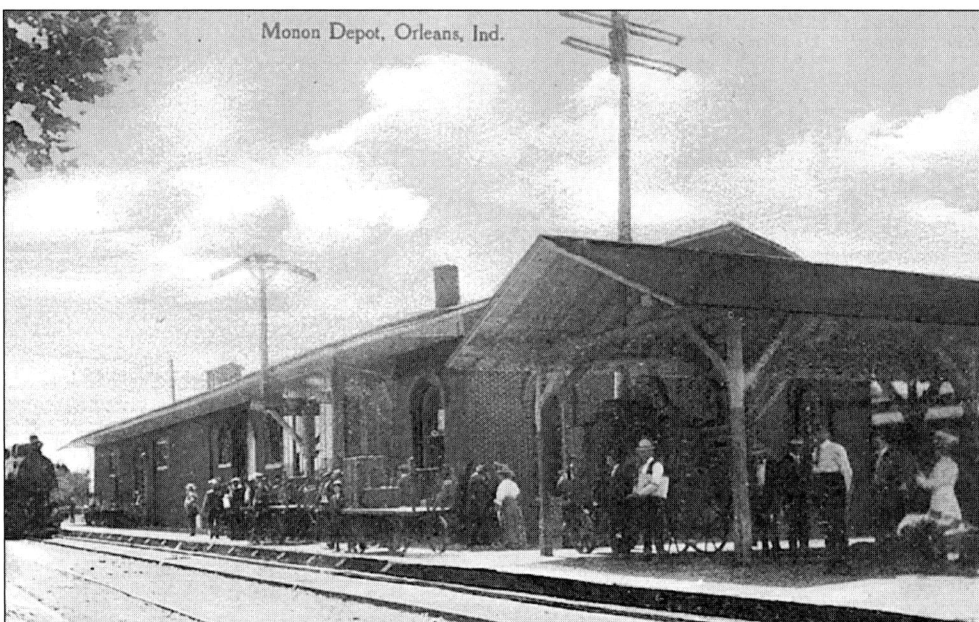

MONON DEPOT AT ORLEANS. This postcard shows the old Monon station in Orleans, about 10 miles south of Mitchell on SR 37. The hustle and bustle common at the train station is well depicted. (Postcard by Van de Walle Music Co.)

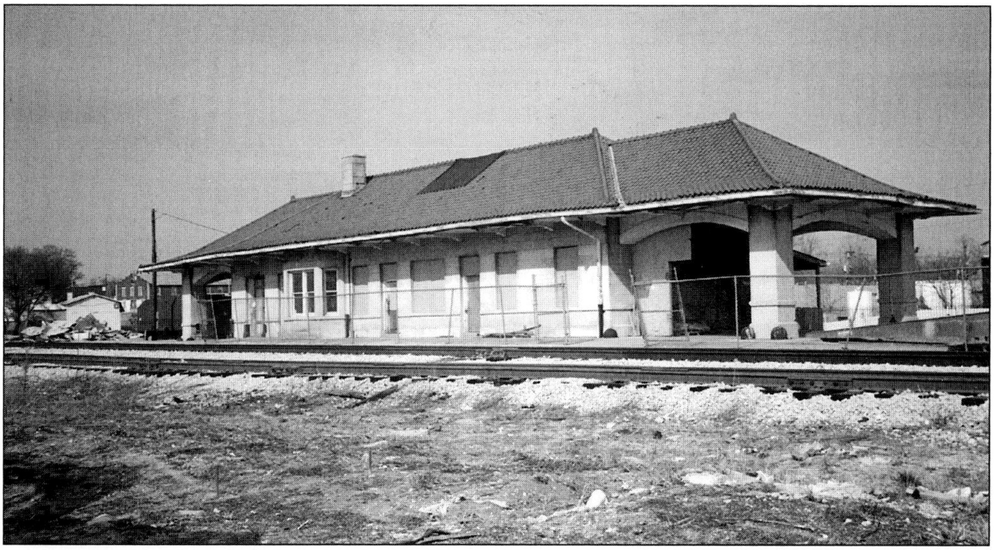

Monon Depot at Bedford. The Monon depot is still standing and currently in use as a recycling center. This passenger depot was constructed of stone in 1926 and is located on J Street. The area surrounding Bedford once prospered with many stone mills. The city is bordered by valleys to the north and south, which meant that the railroads had to deal with steep grades. The Monon hauled many tons of Indiana limestone from this region. A 2005 visit to the depot revealed that interior walls have been installed to provide office space for the recycling center.

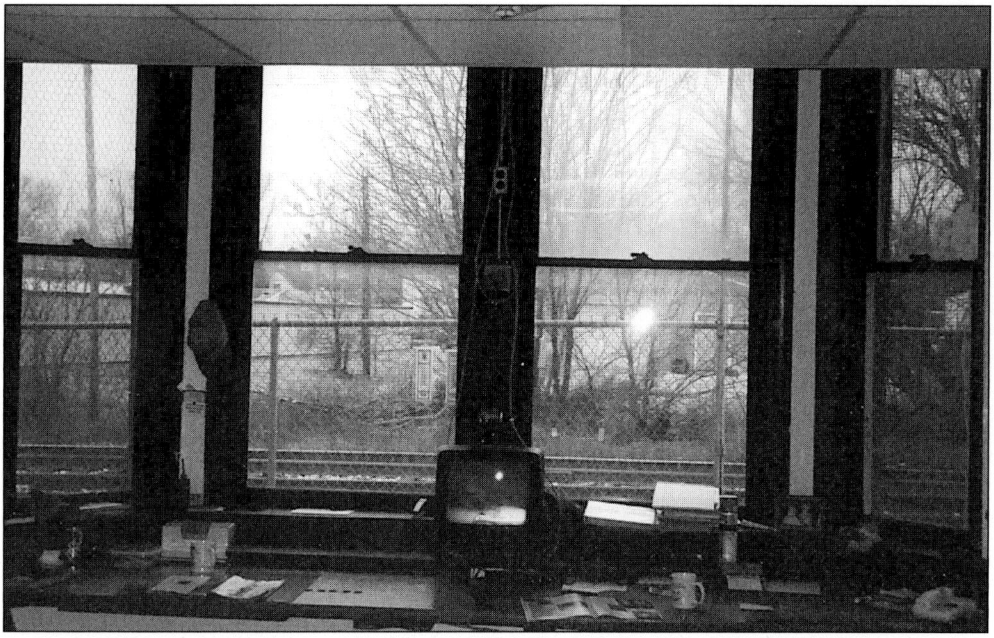

Bedford Depot Bay Window. This photograph shows the inside of the Bedford Monon depot bay window as seen today. In this spot, agents completed various forms as trains arrived or departed. The recycling center has reconstructed the interior, dropping the ceilings and adding some walls. Jamie Harris, director of Bedford Urban Enterprise, allowed entrance to this depot and the Milwaukee passenger depot. Both depots are owned by BUE.

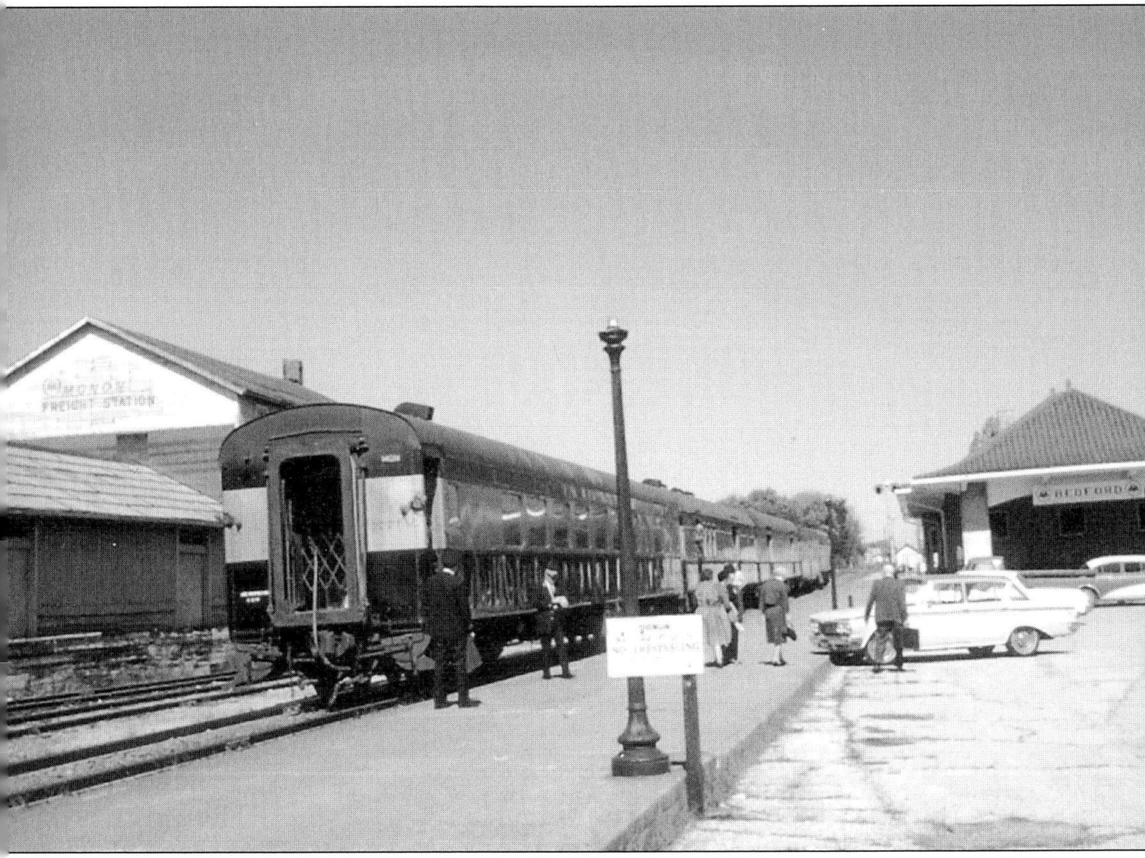

PASSENGER TRAIN AT BEDFORD. Pictured here is a Monon Passenger train stopped at the depot in Bedford. The photograph was taken on October 3, 1964, by Charles Huffer, and shows coach #42. The depot is located north of downtown Bedford. The city caused the Monon line great safety concerns because the tracks went down the middle of busy streets. New Albany, Bloomington, and Lafayette all presented a similar challenge to engineers. Note the Monon freight house to the left of the rear passenger car. (Courtesy MRHTS Collection.)

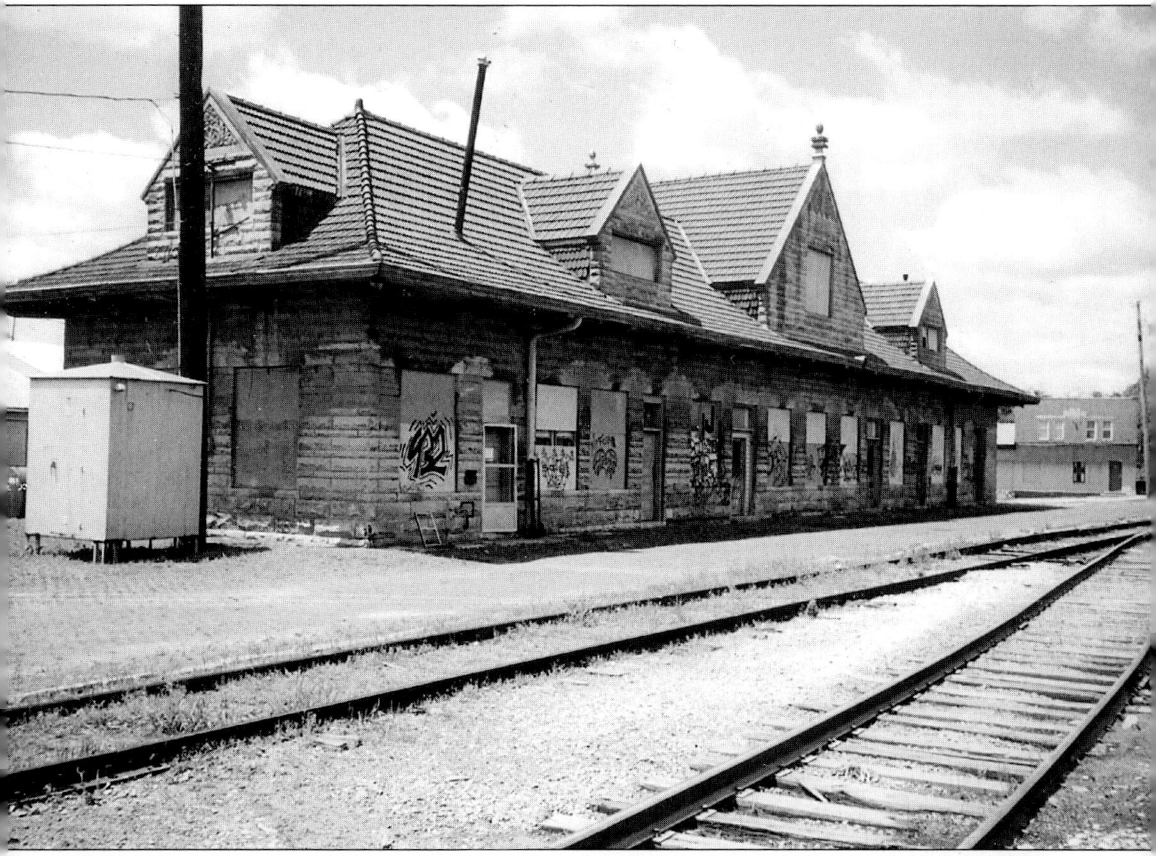

MILWAUKEE PASSENGER DEPOT AT BEDFORD. Also in Bedford stands the old Milwaukee passenger depot, built in 1899 by the Southern Indiana Railway. The depot features limestone construction, a tile roof, and gabled dormers on the sides and ends. Funds have been acquired from various grants to begin refurbishing this fine stone structure, located between I and J Streets. A recent tour of the depot reveals great roof damage, contributing to internal damages. However, the wood coffered ceilings and walls are still impressive.

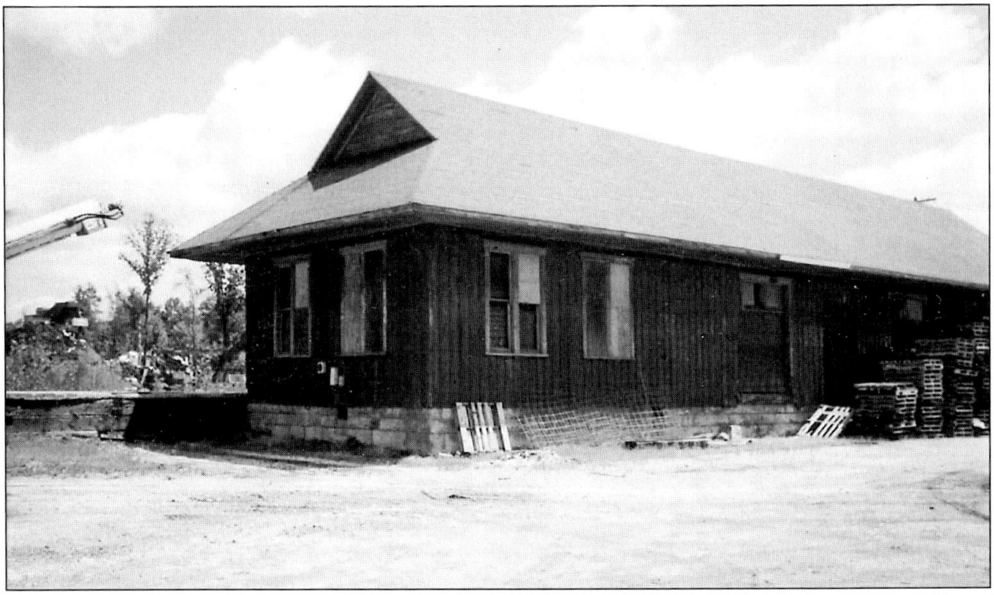

Milwaukee Freight Depot at Bedford. This wooden frame freight depot features board and batten siding and was built by the Southern Indiana Railway in 1899. It is located on I Street. The Milwaukee Road line ran from Westport through Seymour and Bedford and on to Terre Haute. Standish Farm Supply now uses the building.

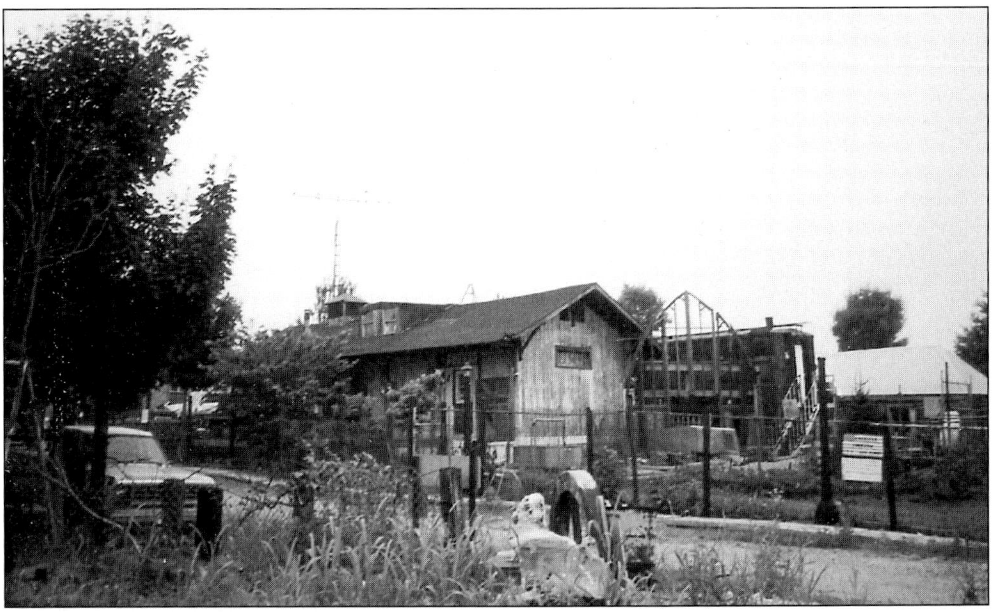

Ellettsville and Clear Creek Depots. A gentleman who lives south of Bloomington has acquired both the Ellettsville and Clear Creek depots. The Ellettsville depot was a combination depot built in 1907, while the Clear Creek combination depot was constructed in 1893. The current owner used them in the creation of this dwelling. Both were of frame construction, though with different types of siding, and were moved from their original locations to this site southeast of Smithville. Numerous pieces of railroad equipment, including rolling stock, are stored on the property.

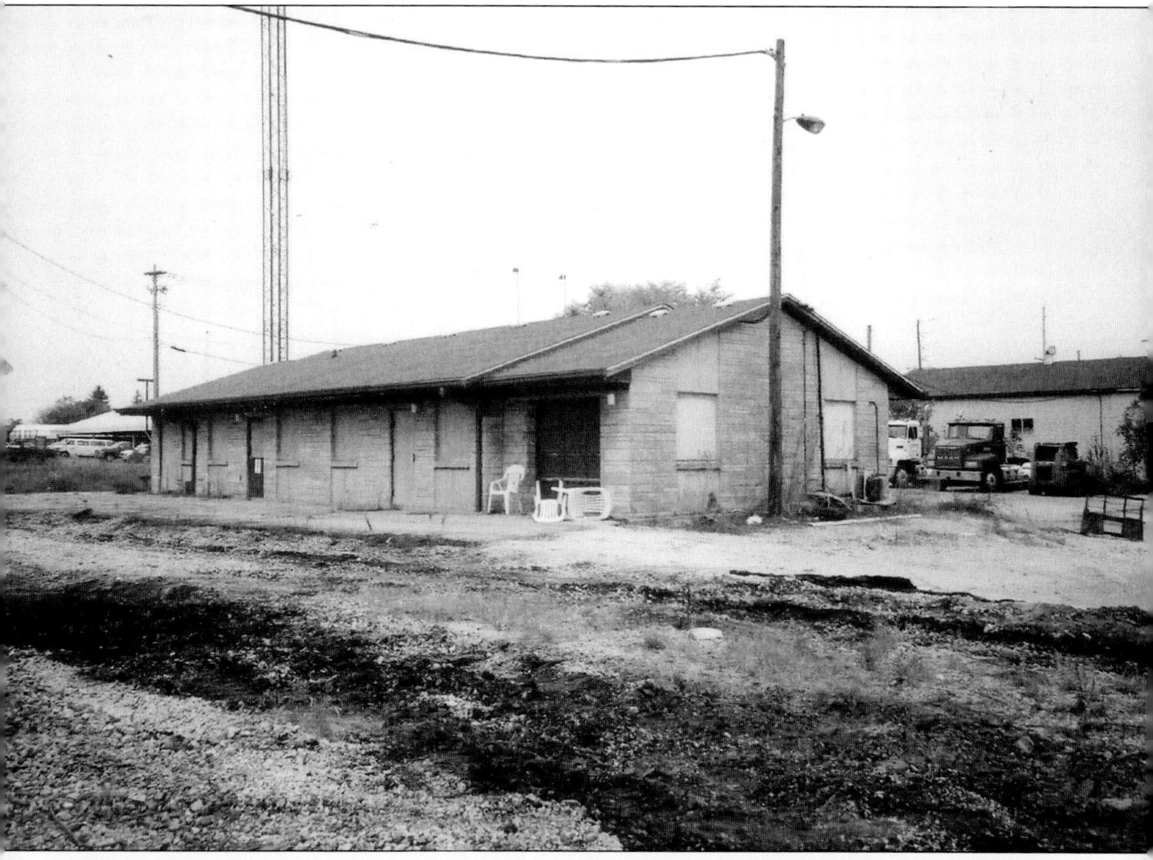

McDoel Yard Office in Bloomington. The McDoel Yard was named for Monon President W.H. McDoel, who served from 1899 to 1909. While under his leadership, the Monon shops were moved from New Albany to Lafayette. This photograph was taken during the Monon Railroad Historical-Technical Society's annual tour in October 2004. At that point, most of the rail had been removed, and there were plans to demolish the yard office shown here. At one time, the yard had a 14-stall roundhouse.

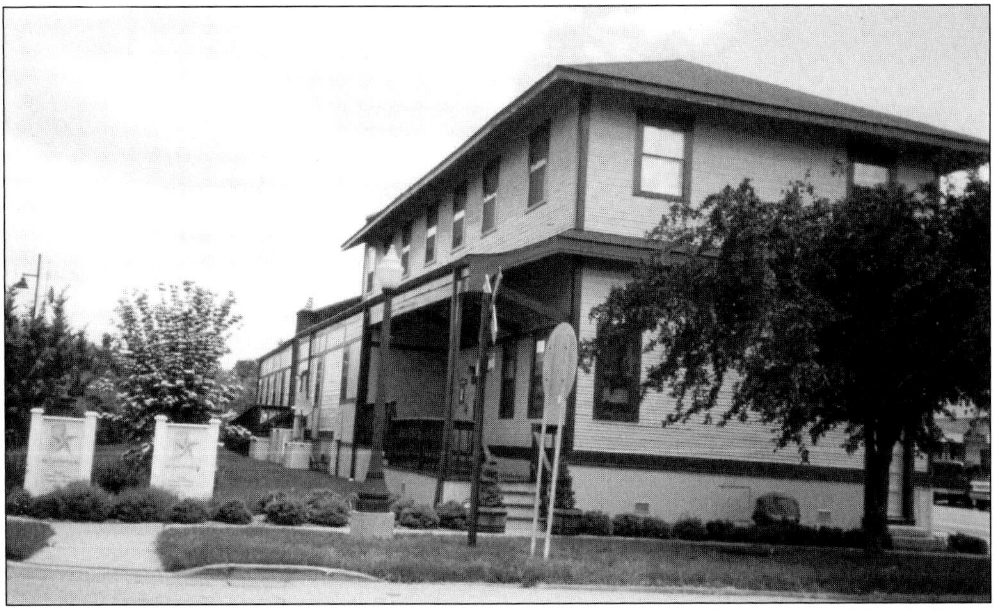

Bloomington IC Freight. While in Bloomington, you may visit the Illinois Central freight house located downtown at 301 North Morton Street. The IC, like the Monon, hauled limestone from local quarries years ago. It is fine-looking wooden building, nicely restored, which houses various businesses. The depot was placed on the National Register of Historic Places in 1983. The Indiana Railroad still serves Bloomington, but the depot is for non-railroad use.

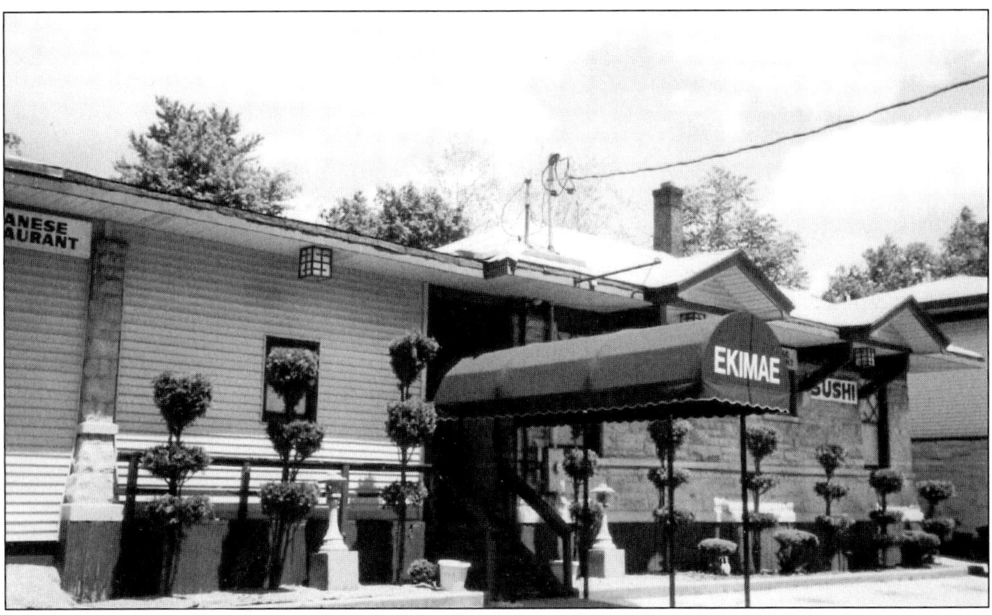

Bloomington IC Passenger. The passenger depot of the Illinois Central in Bloomington is now a Japanese restaurant, located at 825 North Walnut. This passenger train was important years ago for college students traveling to and from Indiana University. The former IC line tracks nearby are still in use by the Indiana Railroad. The stone section on the right is the original depot..

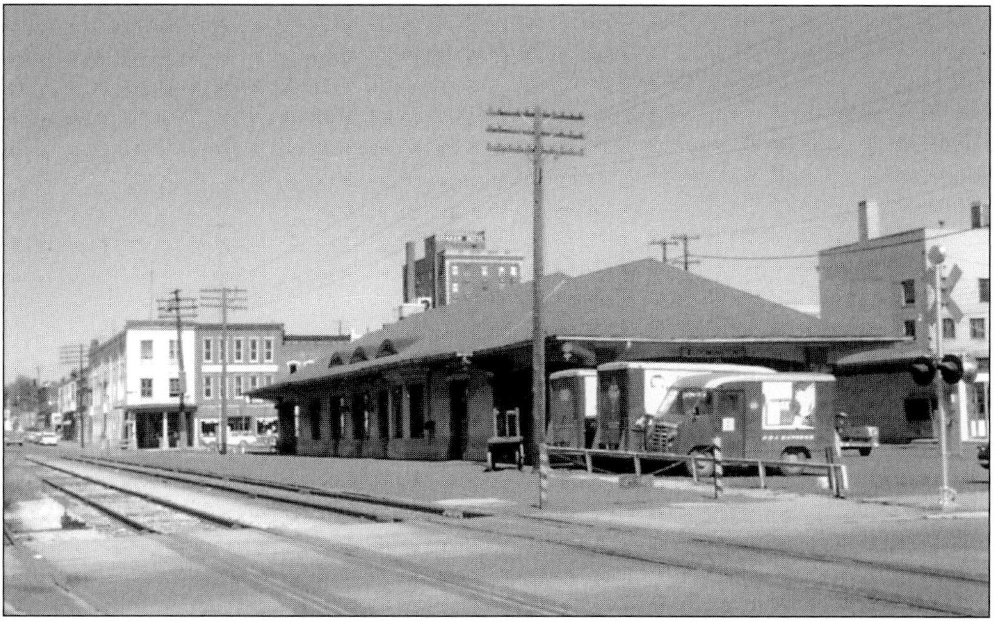

Bloomington Monon. This building was torn down years ago, but is a great example of the limestone depots built by the Monon, which also built these sturdy limestone depots at French Lick, Bedford, Frankfort, and Lafayette. Of these four, only the depots at Lafayette and French Lick are still standing. (Courtesy MRHTS Collection.)

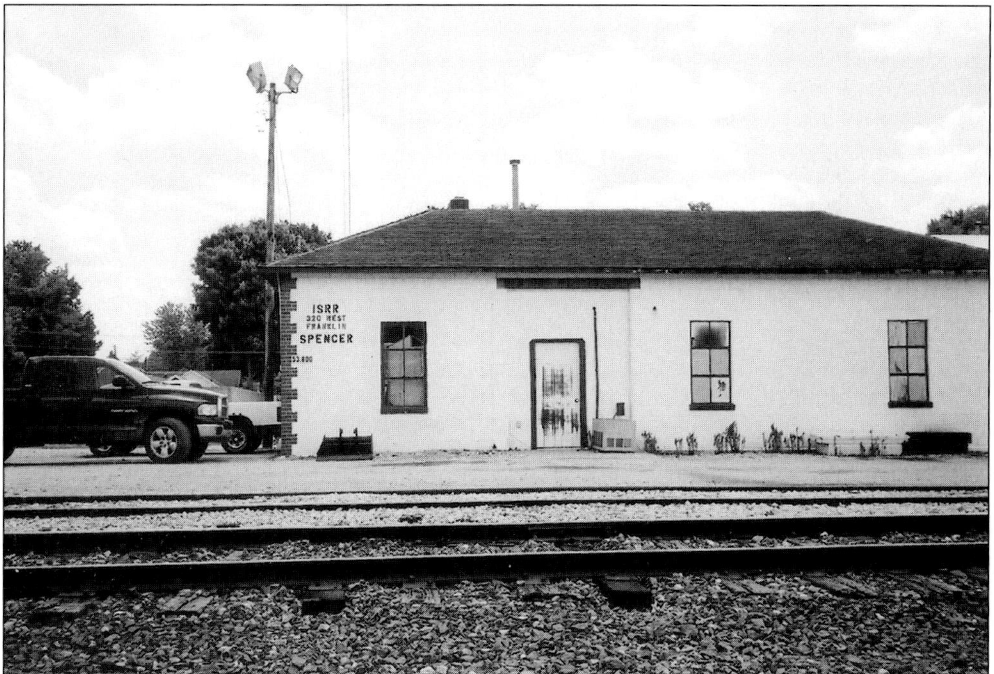

Owen County. Spencer has a small Pennsylvania depot at the intersection of Wolfe and Franklin Streets. Constructed in 1928, this depot still stands right next to the tracks, at 320 West Franklin. Today it is used by Indiana Southern Railroad (ISRR).

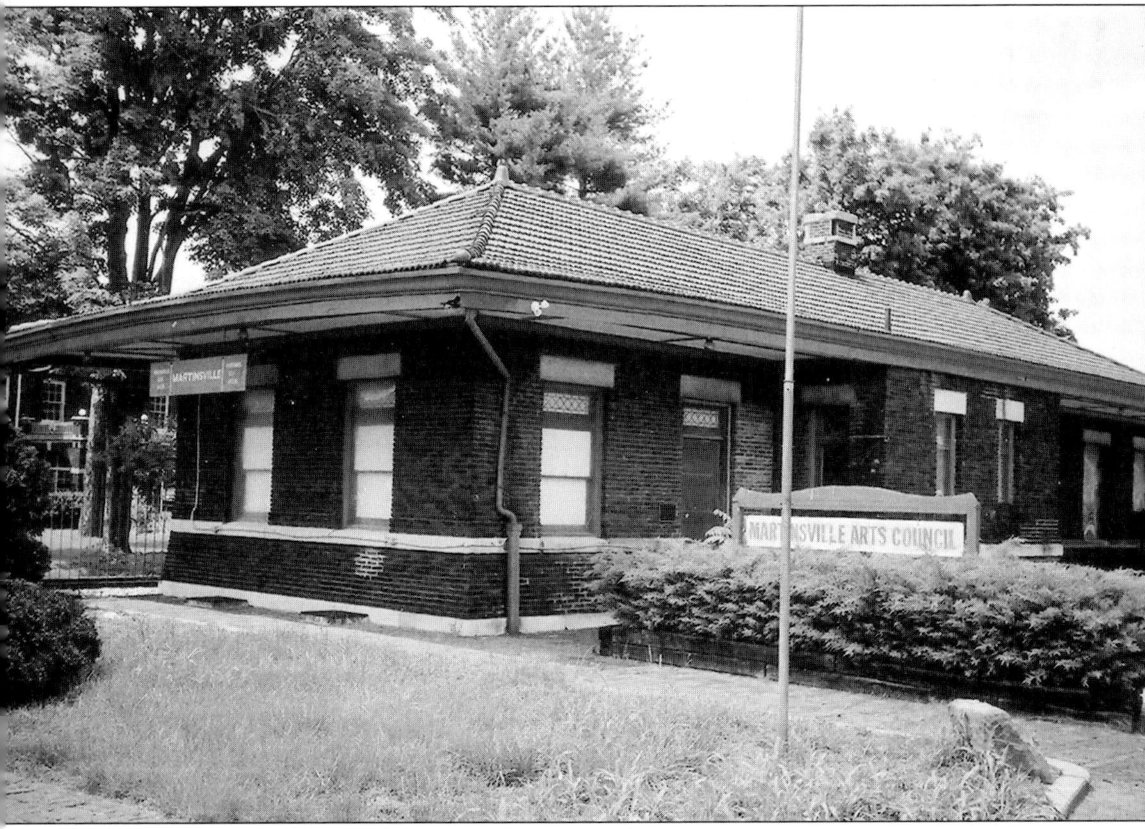

Martinsville Vandalia Depot. This 2000 photograph shows the restored depot located in Martinsville. Built in 1911, this brick PRR (Vandalia) passenger depot is located at 210 North Marion Street along the old PRR railbed. It is used by the Martinsville Arts Council. An article in the *Indianapolis Star* in January 1999 tells of the Martinsville Chamber of Commerce fighting roof leaks while they met in the depot. However, a brighter future for the structure came into being as members of the Martinsville Arts Council launched a project to restore the red-clay tile roof. The depot was placed on the National Register of Historic Places in 1991.

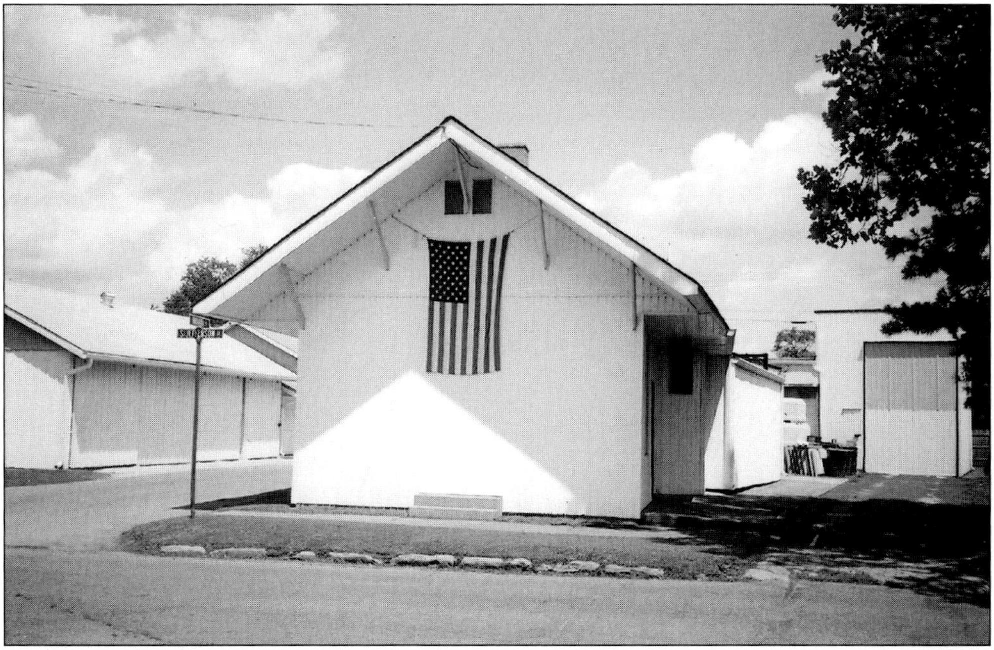

MARTINSVILLE DEPOT. This wooden frame depot was used by CCC&StL as a combination depot. It was built in 1881 by the Cincinnati, Indianapolis, St. Louis & Chicago. Somewhat altered, it does not immediately appear to be a depot. It now operates as a storage building, standing at the corner of Jefferson Street and Indiana Street with no tracks nearby.

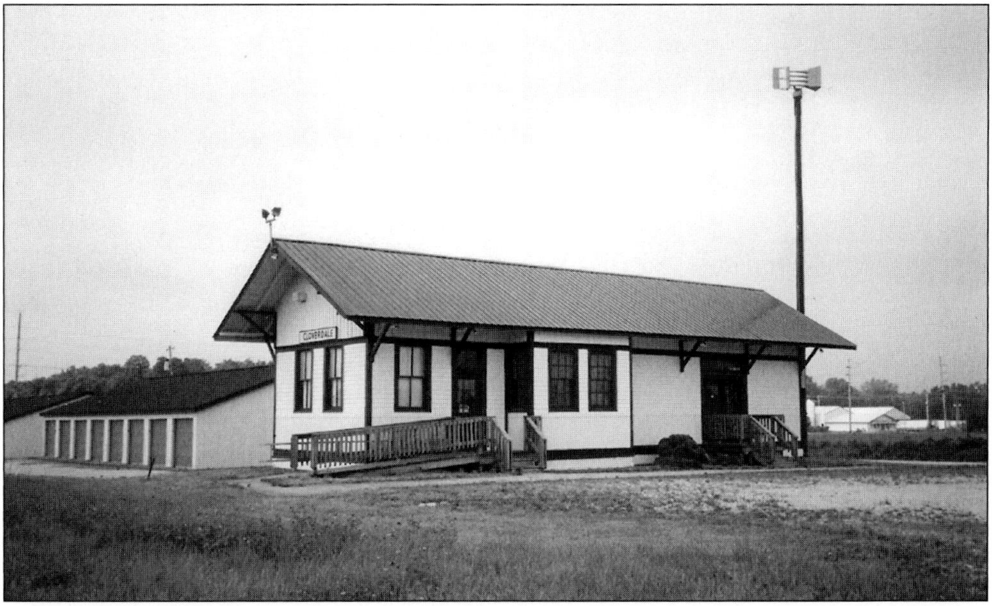

MONON IN CLOVERDALE. The Monon had a small wooden depot in Cloverdale that was moved north of town several years ago. It is now located off the road on U.S. 231 near the Interstate 70 juncture, behind some fast-food restaurants and businesses. Cloverdale was named after the fields of clover in the area. Built in 1885, this combination depot has been restored and is home to a business.

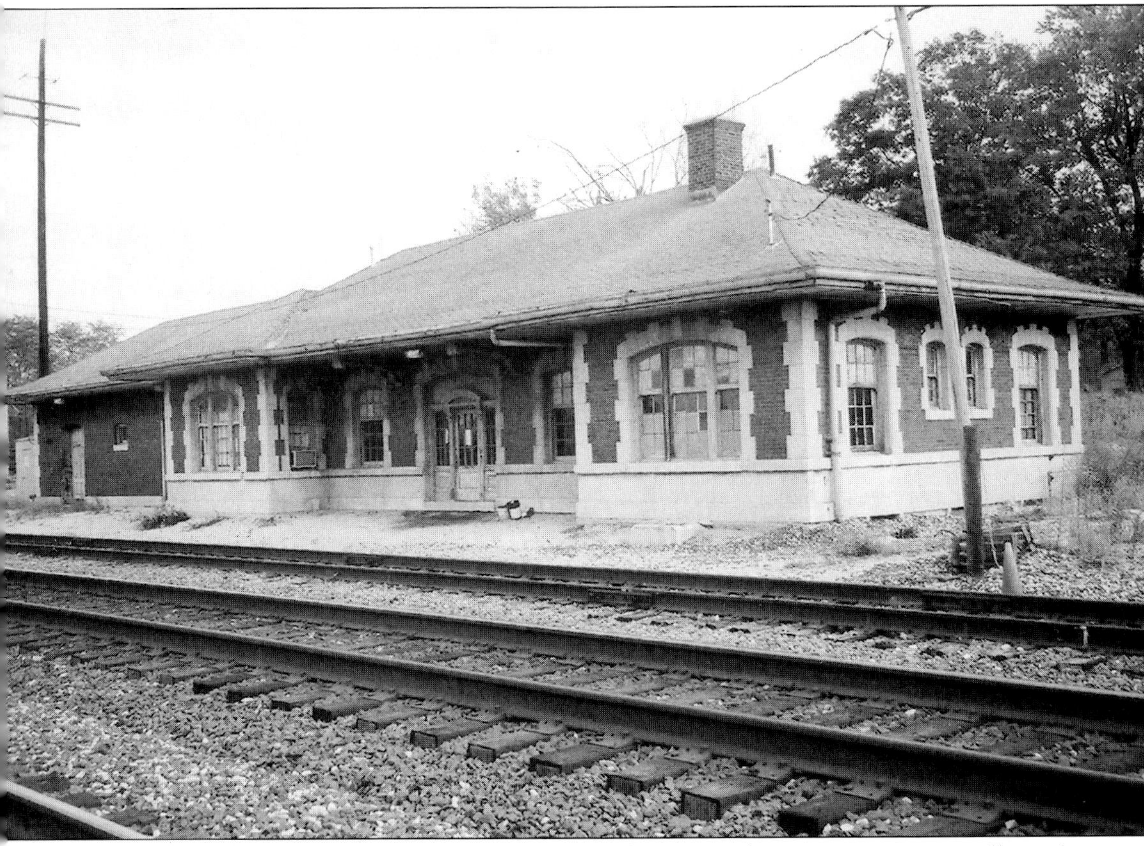

Greencastle Passenger Depot. The "Big Four" (CCC&StL) passenger station is still standing and in use by CSX for maintenance work. Located at Depot and Madison Streets, it is a significant brick structure. The Monon Grill, a restaurant on U.S. 231 near this depot, has been in business for a long time. It once was located next to the old Monon depot before that building was demolished several years ago.

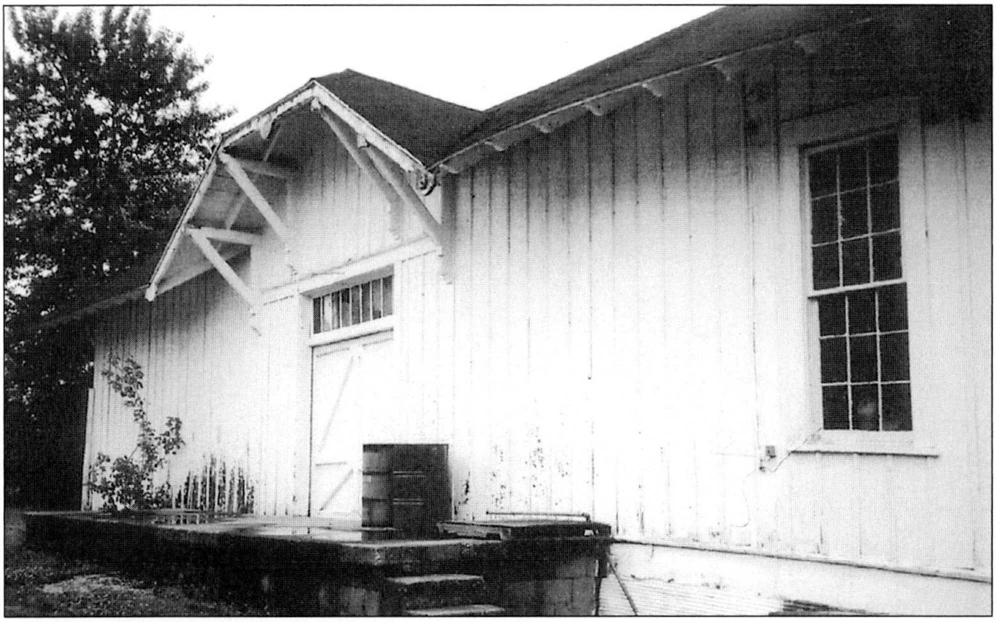

Vandalia Freight Depot. While in Greencastle, you may also locate the PRR wooden freight station at Berry and Crown Streets. It was built in 1894 for the Terre Haute & Indianapolis, but is currently being used for storage. Home to DePauw University, Greencastle is one of many college towns up and down the Monon.

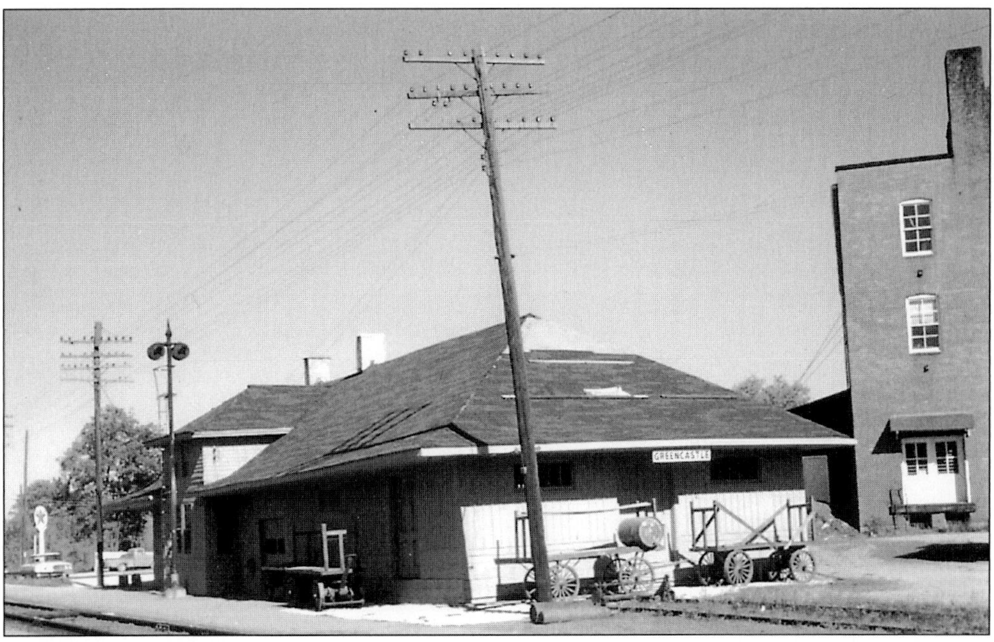

Greencastle Monon Depot. At the north edge of Greencastle stood the Monon Depot. Depauw University students often rode the Monon to and from school. The Monon Grill is still located next to the place the depot used to stand. Inside, the restaurant features multiple walls covered with railroad history related to Greencastle and the Monon. (Courtesy MRHTS Collection.)

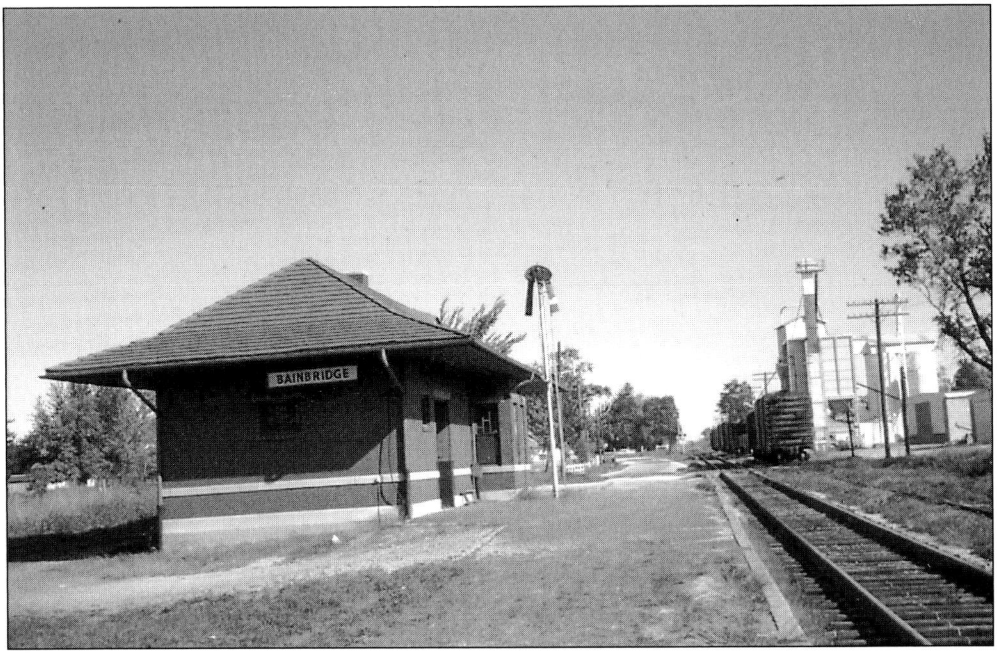

Bainbridge Depot. Built in 1912, the Bainbridge depot belonged to the Monon Railroad. It was a brick combination structure. There is a certain amount of urgency in dealing with these old buildings; this photograph was taken in 2001 and by 2003, the depot had been torn down. It is a sharp reminder that we need to keep our cameras with us and loaded because these structures are quickly disappearing. The rail line is still used by CSX. (Courtesy MRHTS Collection.)

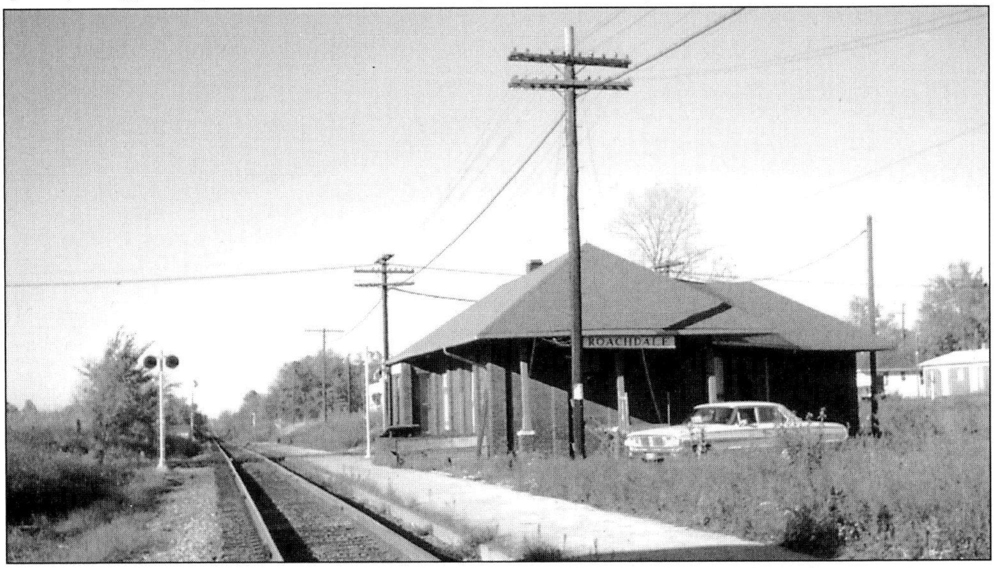

Roachdale Depot. Also used by the Monon, the Roachdale Depot was a combination junction depot with the CH&D railroad. Built in 1916, it was an L-shaped depot, which allowed it to have visual approaches for both railroads. Looking closely, you can see the junction of the CH&D at the edge of the building. The depot was destroyed in 2003, as was the Bainbridge depot. The rail line is still used by CSX today. The photograph was taken in October 1964 by Chares Huffer. (Courtesy MRHTS Collection.)

Six

West Central Indiana

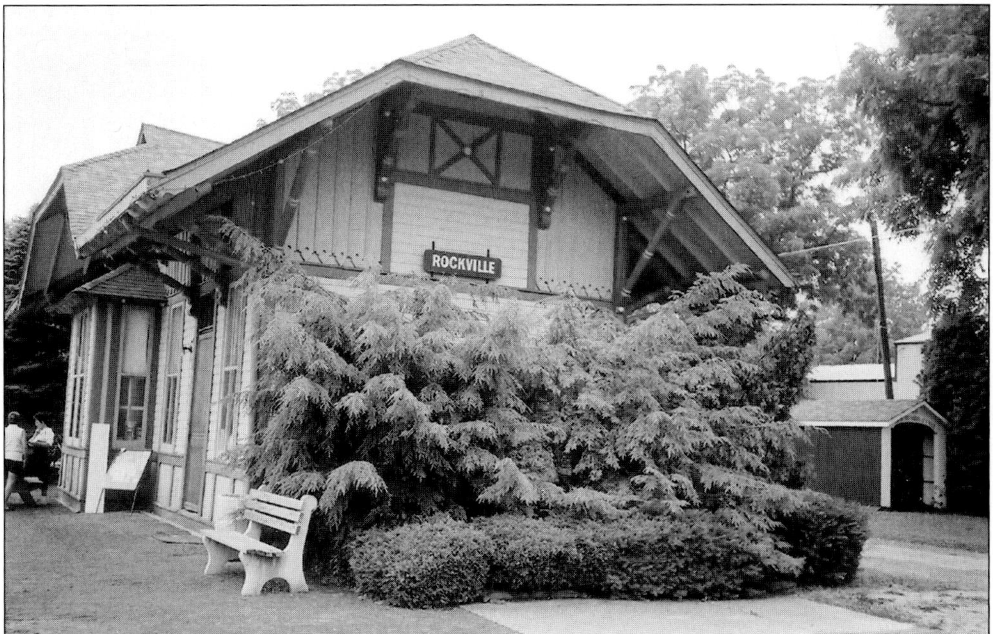

Rockville Depot. Rockville is the county seat of Parke County, noted for its many covered bridges, but also boasting a wonderful old wood depot. This Pennsylvania combination depot is located on U.S. 36. It was built for the Terre Haute & Logansport Railroad in 1884. It has been relocated and restored and is now used as a tourist center.

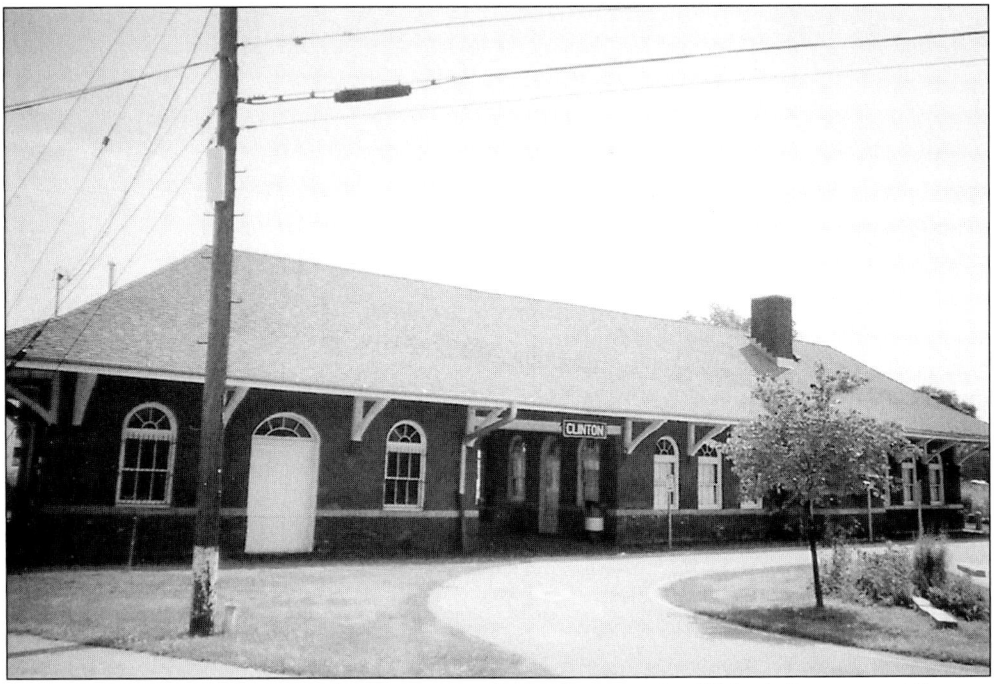

Clinton Passenger Depot. When you cross the bridge over the Wabash River into Clinton, it appears you are leaving the state. Actually, though, the river meanders even farther west before it becomes the western boundary of Indiana. There are two depots in Clinton, both on Vine Street in close proximity. The Chicago & Eastern Illinois (C&EI) passenger depot is in very good condition following a restoration. It is now a museum and was added to the Clinton Downtown Historic District in 2000.

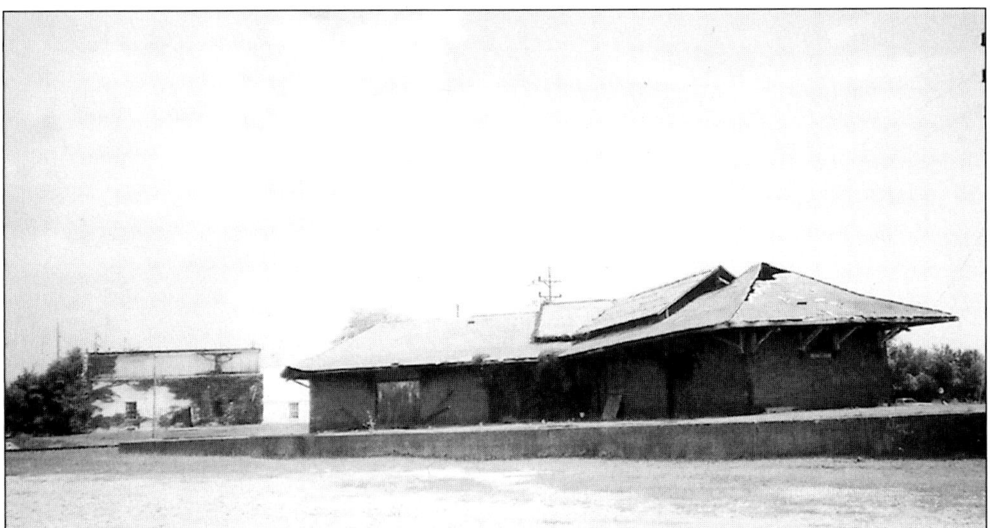

Clinton Freight Depot. The C&EI freight house in Clinton has not been restored, but is unique in its shape. You will take note of the Y shape of the building. It was constructed in 1912. CSX still uses this rail line. If you look east down the tracks, you can get a pretty good view of the rail bridge that crosses the Wabash river.

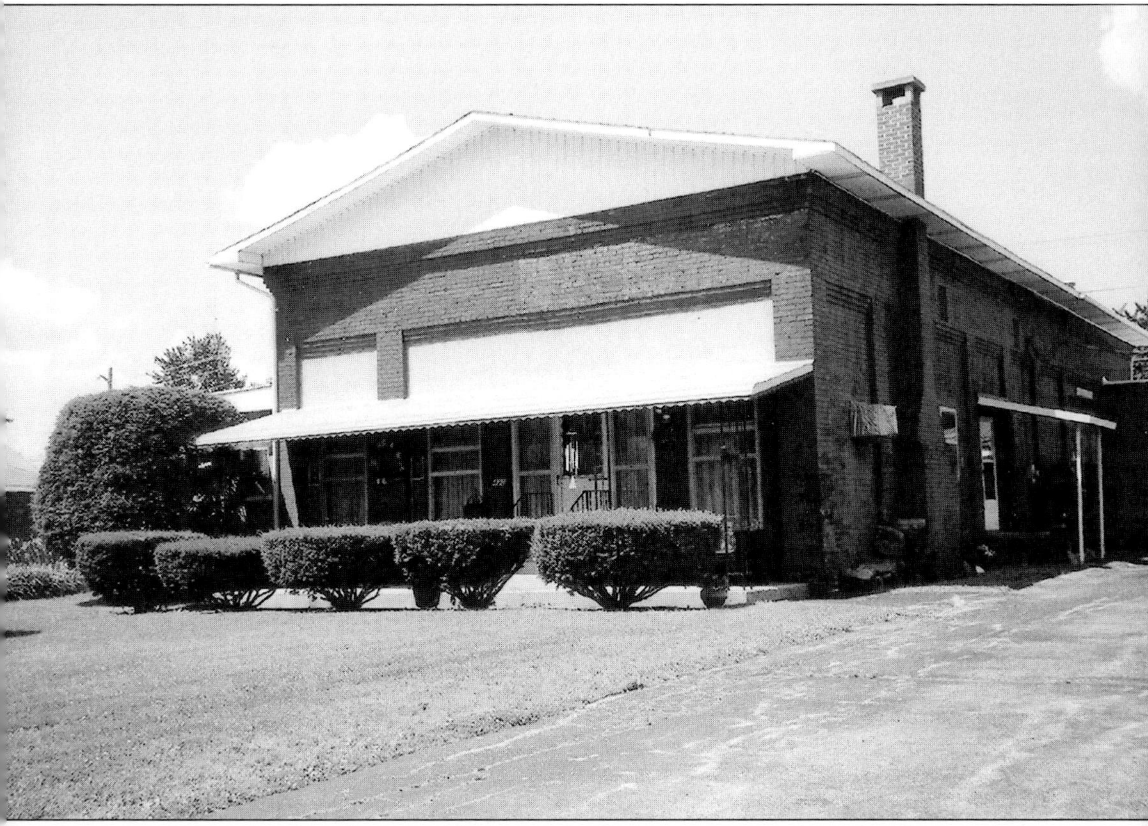

SULLIVAN INTERURBAN. Sullivan is like many smaller towns across the state that needed a connection with a nearby city, resulting in the popularity of interurbans from 1900 to the 1930s. The interurban linked towns like Sullivan with cities like Terre Haute, providing them with goods and employment. Sullivan also had need for rail connections because of the prominent seams of coal throughout the neighboring region. One of the interurban passenger stations still stands at the corner of Court and Wall Streets. This Terre Haute Traction and Lighting (THT&L) station is a brick structure, now occupied by a business.

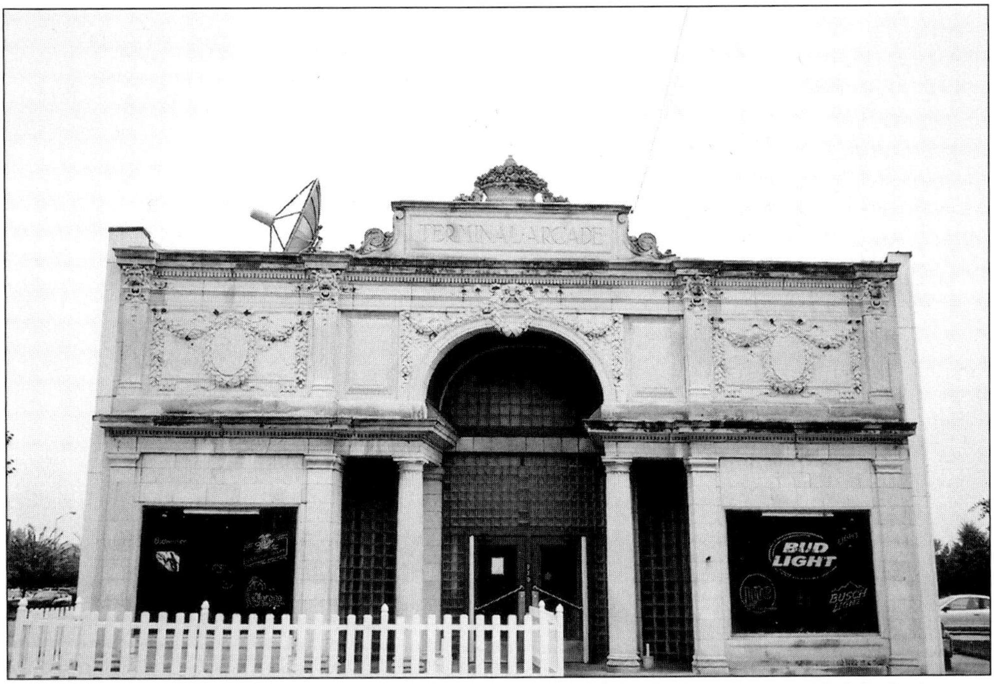

Terre Haute Arcade. Terre Haute has an interurban building downtown at 822 Wabash Avenue between Eighth and Ninth streets. It is an old structure with the words "Arcade Building" carved above the door and windows. Originally, it served a THT&L brick interurban passenger station, but housed a business at the time of this photograph. Designed by Daniel Burnham in the Beaux Arts style, this depot was placed on the National Registry of Historic Places in 1983. Burnham designed several outstanding railroad structures such as the PRR station in Richmond.

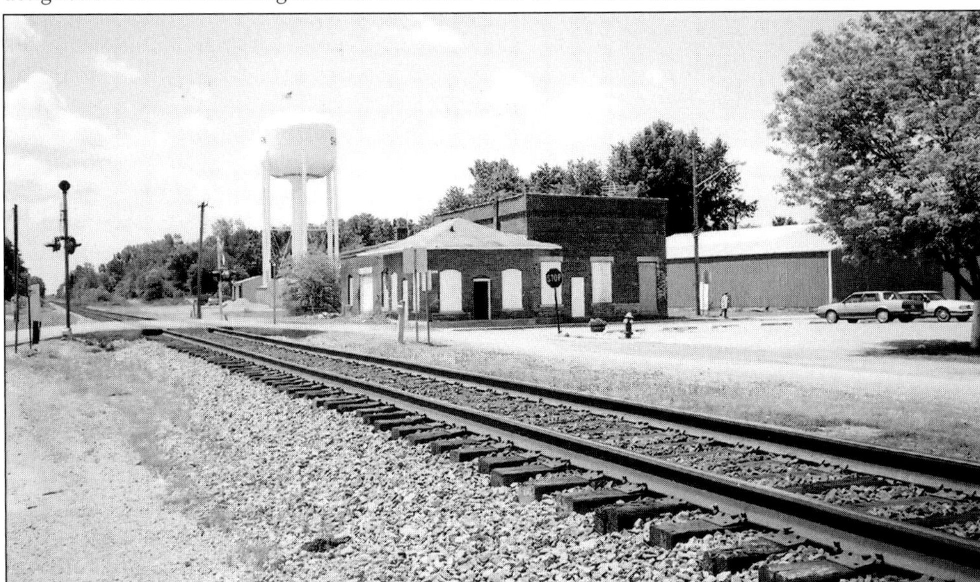

Shelburn Interurban. South of Terre Haute, off U.S. 41, is the small town of Shelburn. The THT&L had a scheduled stop at Mill and Interurban Streets, and the tracks are still there. This brick depot was a combination freight and passenger stop and is now a small business.

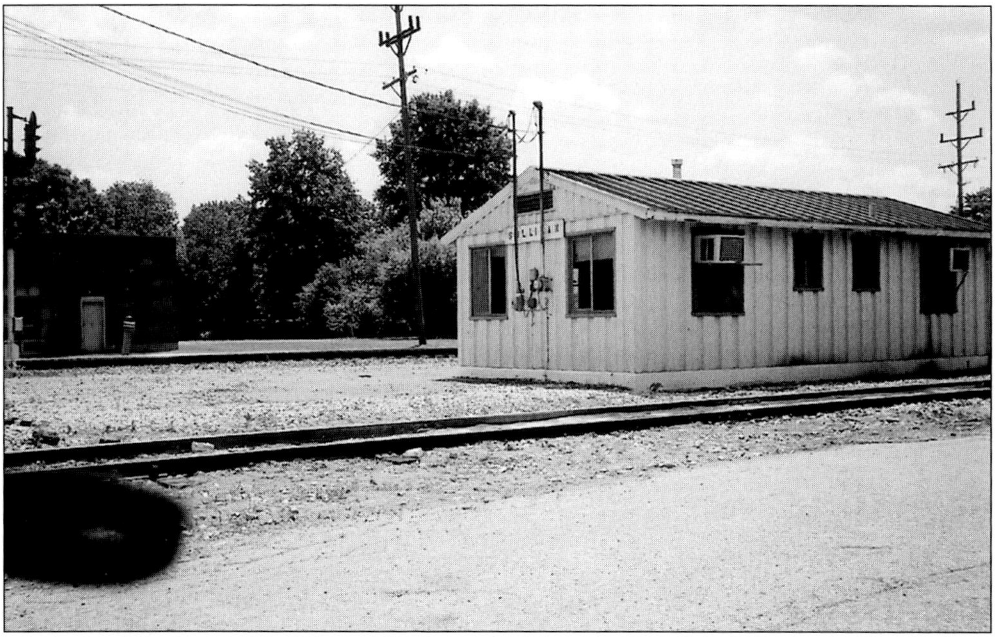

Sullivan CSX Shop. This newer-looking metal structure is a CSX shop building, located along the current CSX trackage on Depot Street in Sullivan. The street name hints that another depot probably stood near this location in years past. CSX and other class-one lines no longer have need for many buildings and use small structures such as this one for their work bases.

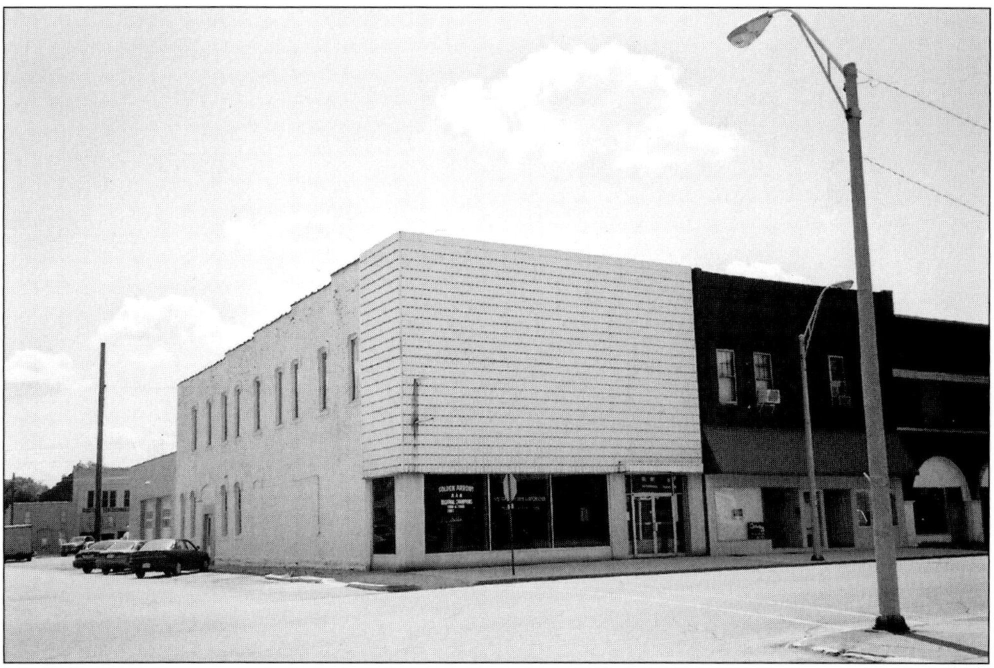

Sullivan Interurban. This THT&L interurban depot in Sullivan is located at the corner of North Court and Wall Streets. Many interurban depots were simply storefronts, so once the interurban went out of business, they reverted to their former uses. This building has obviously been altered over the years.

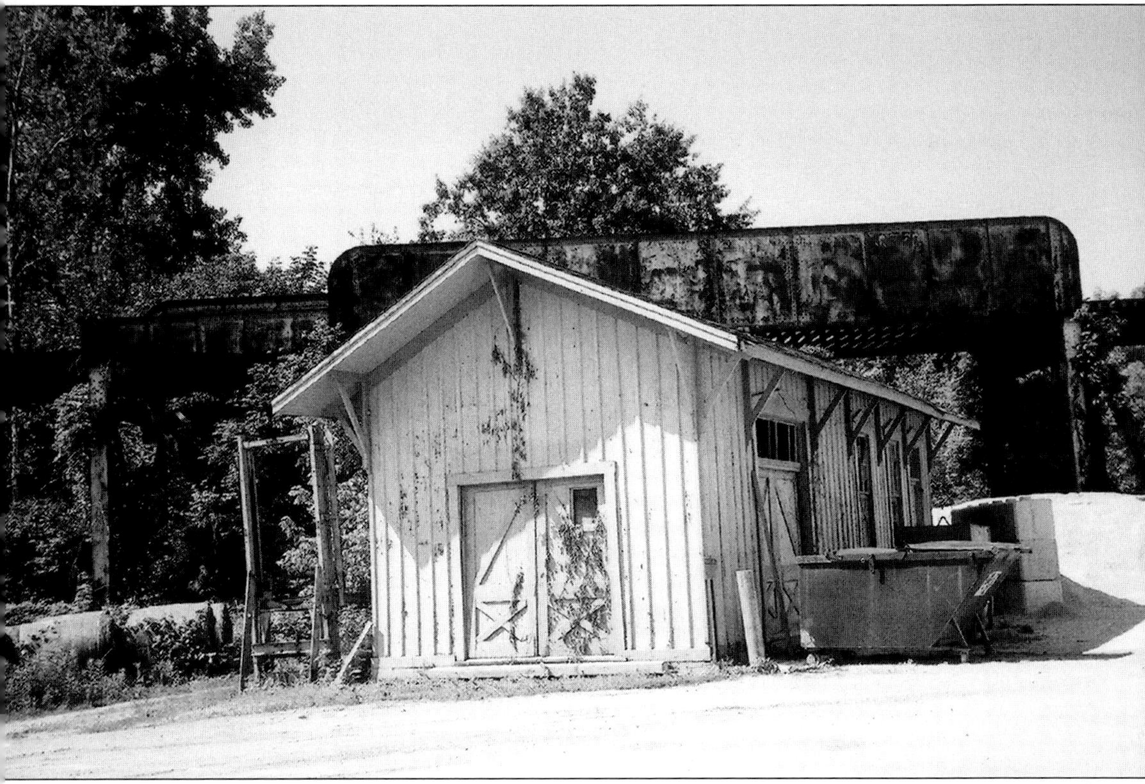

ELLISTON CROSSINGS. When in Elliston, look for a road on the left leading to the tracks south of SR54. The Evansville & Indianapolis (E&I) station still stands below the bridge, though the depot is no longer in use. The location is quite unique as it stands at the intersection and crossing of three rail lines. You will see an Illinois Central (IC) bridge above what was once a crossing diamond of the Monon's Bedford & Bloomfield (B&B) branch and the E&I. Both of the roadbeds have been removed, but the bridge is still is use by the Indiana Railroad.

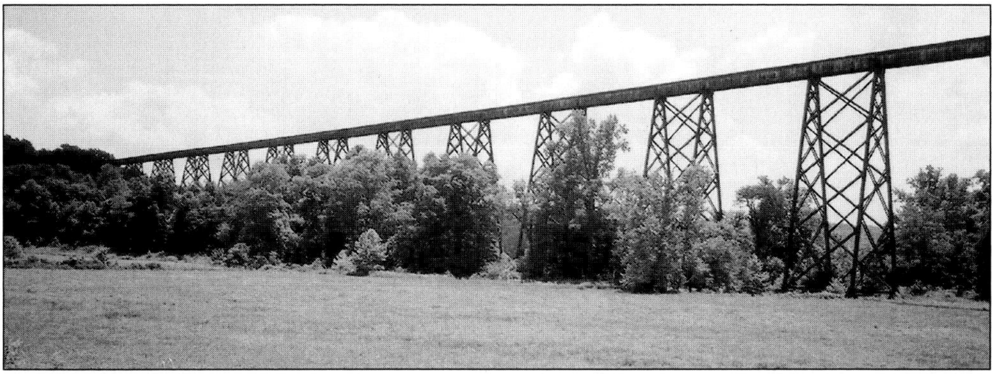

SPANNING RICHLAND CREEK VALLEY. According to some historians, Tulip Trestle is the third longest bridge of its type in the world. One of the longest railroad trestles in the United States, it boasts a length of 2,295 feet. It was built in 1906 by the Indianapolis Southern Railroad a few years before it merged into the Illinois Central in 1911, and is located about eight miles northeast of Bloomfield in Richland Creek valley. Visitors must travel along SR 157 north out of Bloomfield for 3.2 miles, turn right on County Road 325N and travel for 1 mile. Drive through a railroad underpass and pass the Tulip Church of God on the right. Continue on this road for another mile and bear right at the Beechwood Lake Baptist Youth Camp. There is another railroad overpass .6 miles farther along the road. On the left, within .5 miles, is a white frame Wesleyan Church. One mile past the church, turn right onto County Road 480 East. Travel half a mile to reach one of the towers of the viaduct.

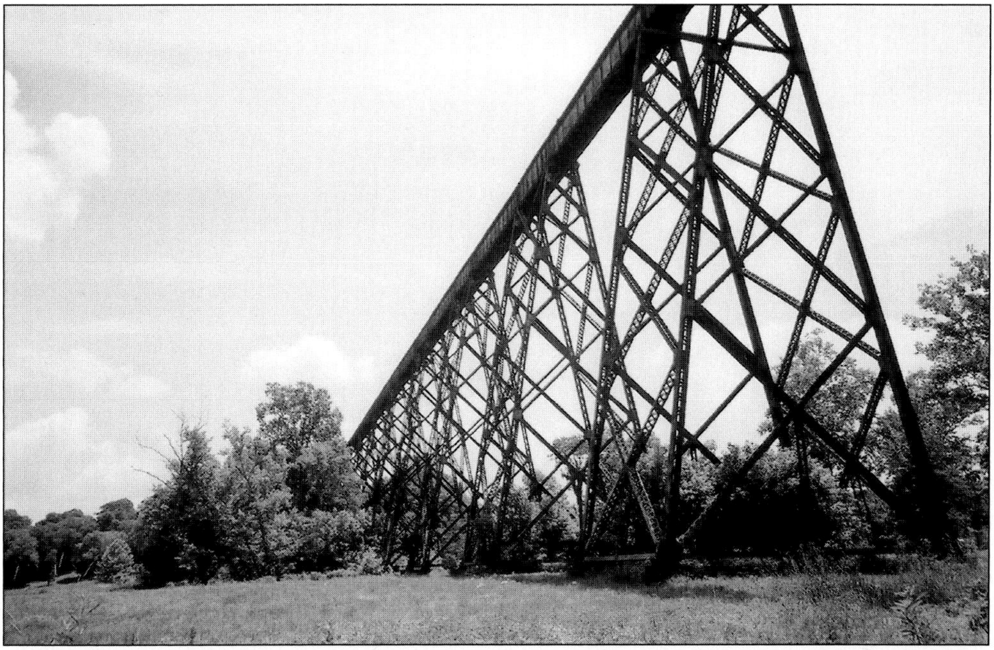

TULIP TRESTLE. This photograph better shows the 157-foot height of the trestle, also called Richland Creek Viaduct. The Indiana Railroad (IRR) has used this trackage since 1986 and hauls great amounts of coal from the region for use in Indianapolis. The IRR also transports lumber, chemical, scrap metal, and even appliances. It is certainly an impressive sight and worth seeking. While the original cost of construction was about $245,000, a Chicago bridge engineer estimated that to build a bridge the same size today would cost around $20 million.

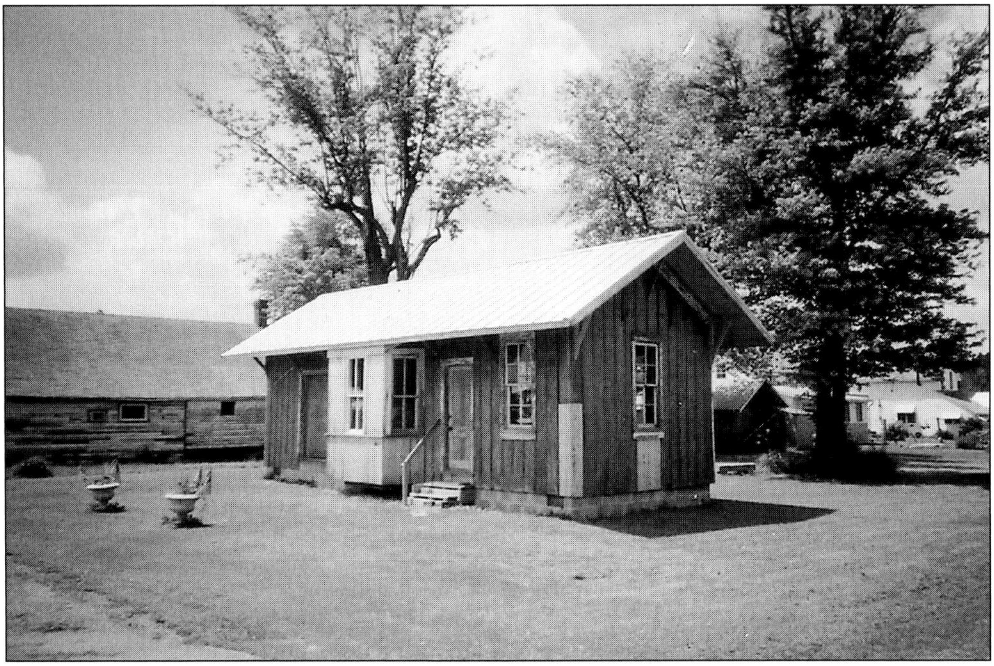

COAL CITY DEPOT. While on SR 157, go north to Coal City. A small wooden depot sits on the west side of the highway. This is the Coal City depot in Owen County. Well cared for, it appears unaltered and still retains the look of a depot.

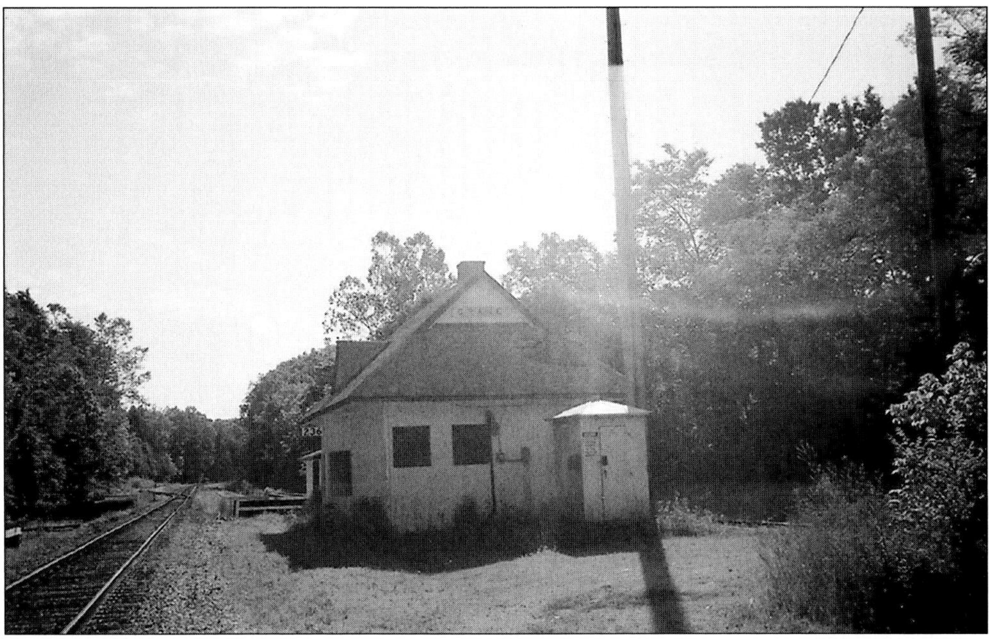

BURNS CITY. Return to Bloomfield and take U.S. 231 south to Burns City. This Milwaukee Railroad combination depot, built in 1898, is located on the northern edge of town, near the western gate of the Crane Naval Support Center. (Be sure to avoid the grounds of the center for security reasons.) For many years, the depot was instrumental in bringing materials and supplies to CNSC.

Seven

West on the Southern Line

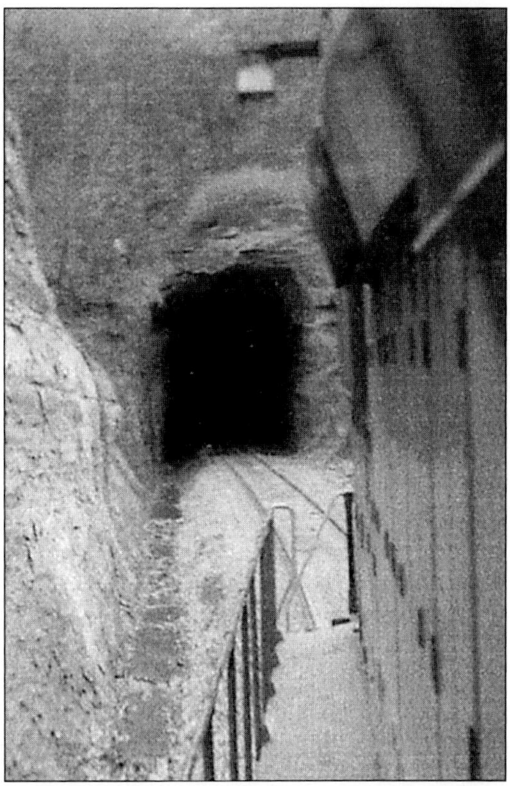

Duncan Tunnel East. The east entrance of the Duncan Tunnel is located west of New Albany on SR 62. Used for many years by the Southern Railway, it is now in use by Norfolk Southern. The Duncan Tunnel is also referred to as the Great Tunnel or the Edwardsville Tunnel. Extending for nearly a mile under the Edwardsville Hill, the tunnel was completed in 1881 and first used in 1882. It was built by the Air line, which first began between New Albany and St. Louis, and proved to be a huge job for several railroad companies. Many companies deserve credit for its construction, because one company would build a segment of track, go broke, reorganize, and then continue building.

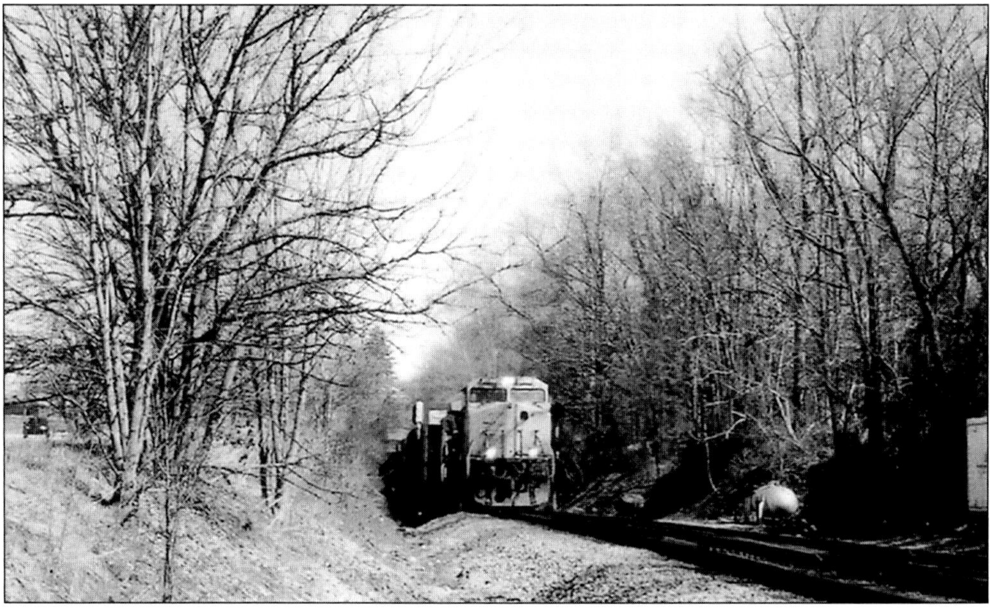

Duncan Tunnel West. This photograph shows a NS train exiting Duncan Tunnel, heading west toward Georgetown. The tunnel is 4,295 feet long and often requires an extra engine to boost trains up the hill. The rail line parallels SR 64 through much of southern Indiana. The Southern Railway also had responsibility for tunnels at English, Marengo, French Lick, and Unionville. Over half of the tunnels in southern Indiana were used by the Southern Railway.

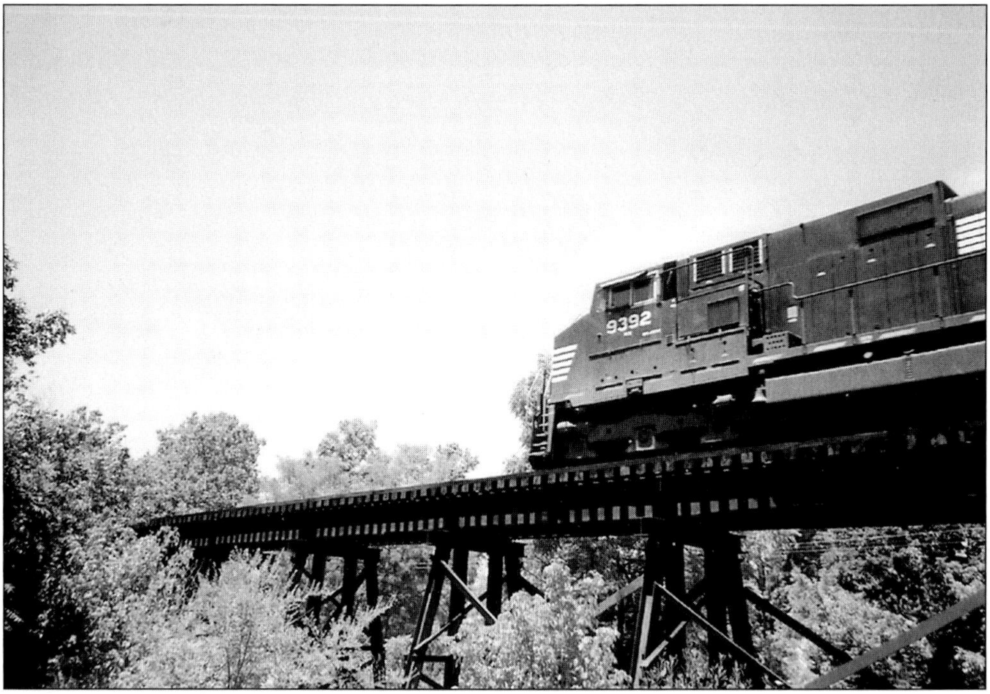

Georgetown Trestle. West of Georgetown is this small trestle shown with a train headed by NS #9392. It can be seen on the far left after passing through most of the town. The trestle passes over a Floyd County road; though not a large trestle it still makes for a scenic photograph.

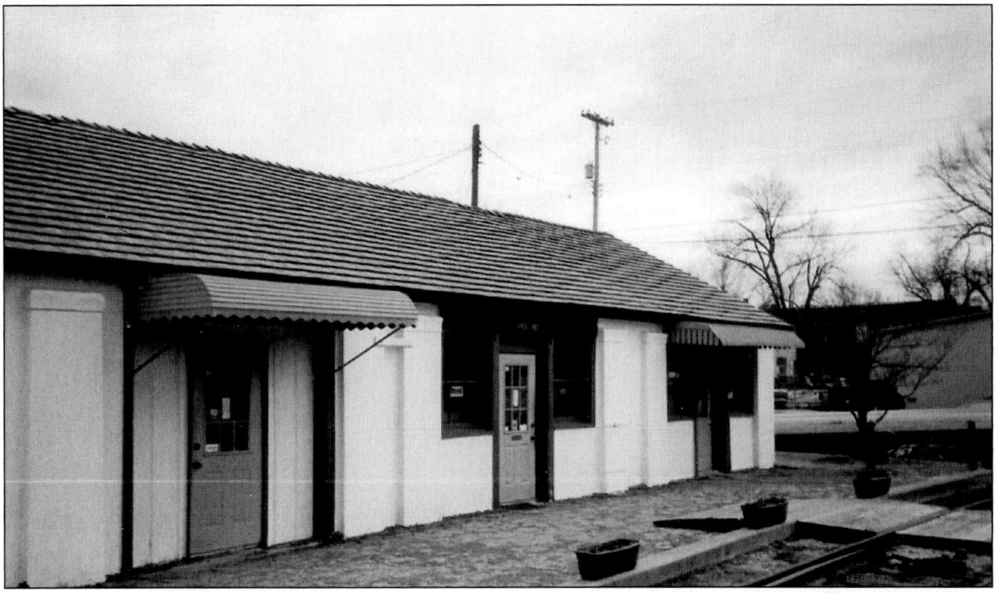

Corydon Passenger Depot. The Louisville, New Albany & Corydon passenger depot is located at 210 West Walnut Street on SR 62. It is a stucco/brick combination depot with a huge arched window. The LNA&C short line began in 1883, and once carried passengers and freight. More recently, the Corydon Scenic Railroad operated out of this building from 1989 to 2003. The excursion railroad announced in April 2003 that it was ceasing its operation for economic reasons. Today, the LNA&C uses this building for all of their business transactions.

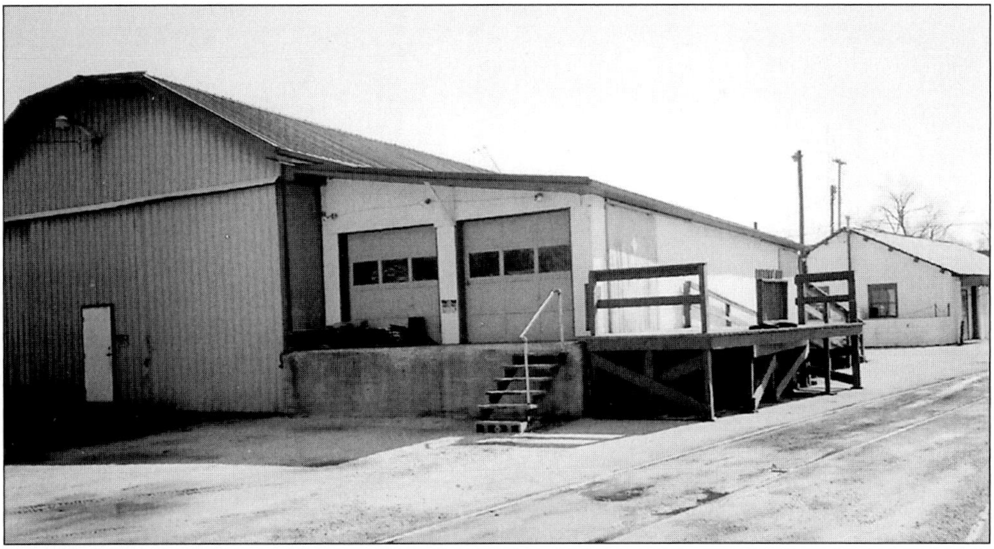

Corydon Freight Depot. Just north of the passenger depot is the LNA&C freight house. As the photograph shows, it still has the front dock. The interior of the freight house is now being used for storage, as freight is no longer handled there. The LNA&C operates its freight service over only eight miles of track. Today, the LNA&C still serves primarily as a freight service and works with the Norfolk Southern Railroad. They service many important industries in the Corydon area and connect with the NS at Corydon Junction. The passenger depot can be seen to the far right.

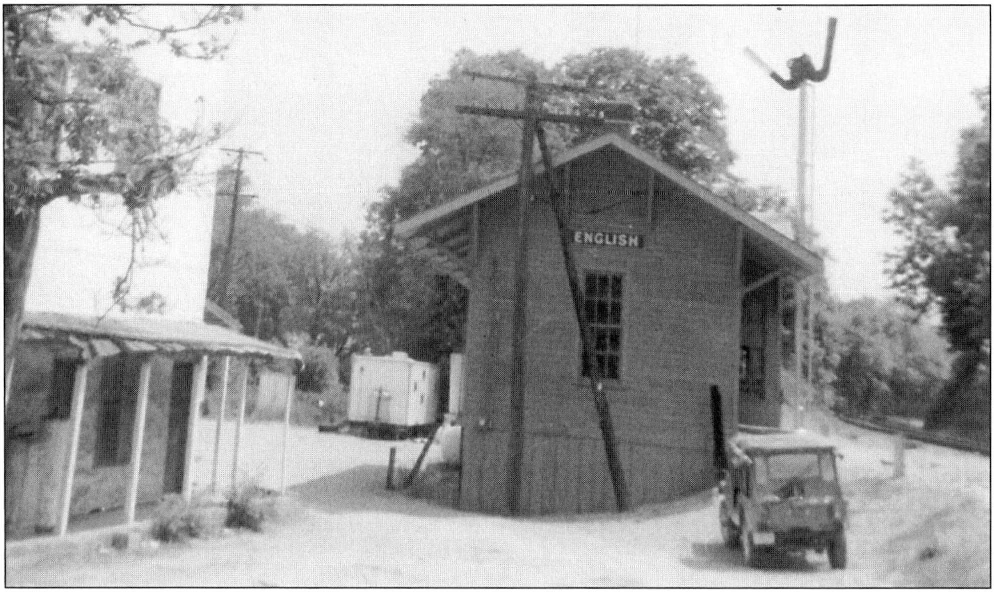

English Southern Depot. This 1977 picture shows the now-destroyed English combination depot. English is the county seat of Crawford County. This depot was located east of SR 37 in English. Much of English has been moved up to SR 64 because of the strong likelihood that flooding will continue to be a problem. The NS train still passes through the somewhat abandoned town. (Courtesy Maxwell D. Longest.)

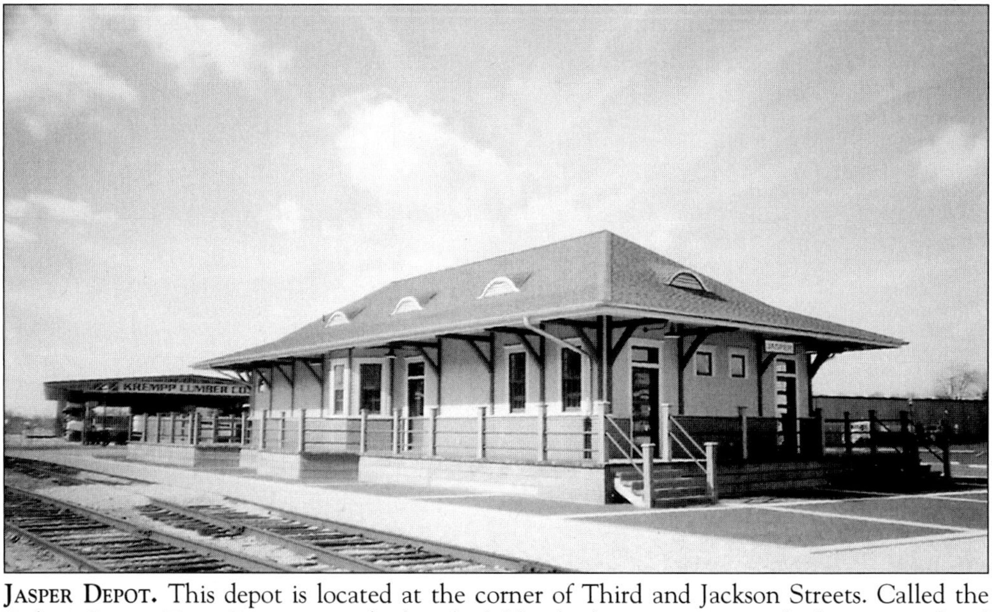

Jasper Depot. This depot is located at the corner of Third and Jackson Streets. Called the Dubois County Train Depot, it was built to look like the former structure, which was completed in 1906. The new depot was dedicated on August 3, 2004 and cost the Redevelop Old Jasper Action Coalition $400,000. By 2007, Jasper will have its own passenger rail line, tentatively called the Spirit of Jasper, to run between Jasper and French Lick by way of Huntingburg. The revitalization of this trackage is related to the recent acquisition by Orange County of a State of Indiana casino license.

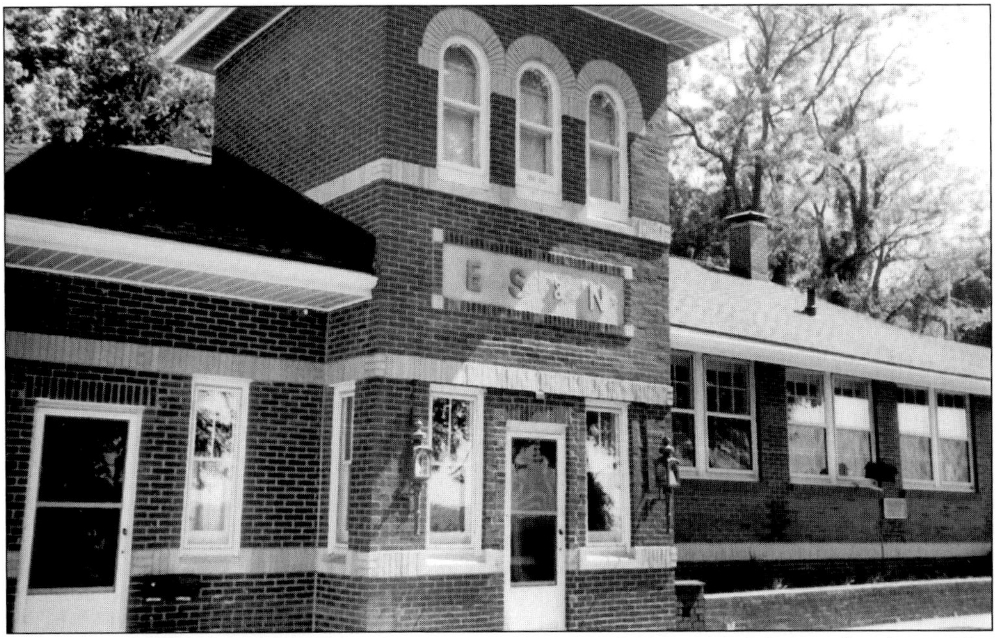

ES&N Newburgh Interurban. This quaint river town features several specialty shops. The brick depot is located on Water Street and was built in 1912 for the Evansville, Suburban & Newburgh (ES&N) Railway as a passenger and freight depot. Cars brought merchandise to local businessmen daily. The tower was used by the agent as a bedroom. Passengers and coal were transported by the ES&N until 1930, when operation ceased. In 1952, the depot was remodeled as a home by Leon and Jane Crenshaw. Note the "ES&N" on the face of the building above the doorway. The building has been part of the Newburgh Historic District since 1983.

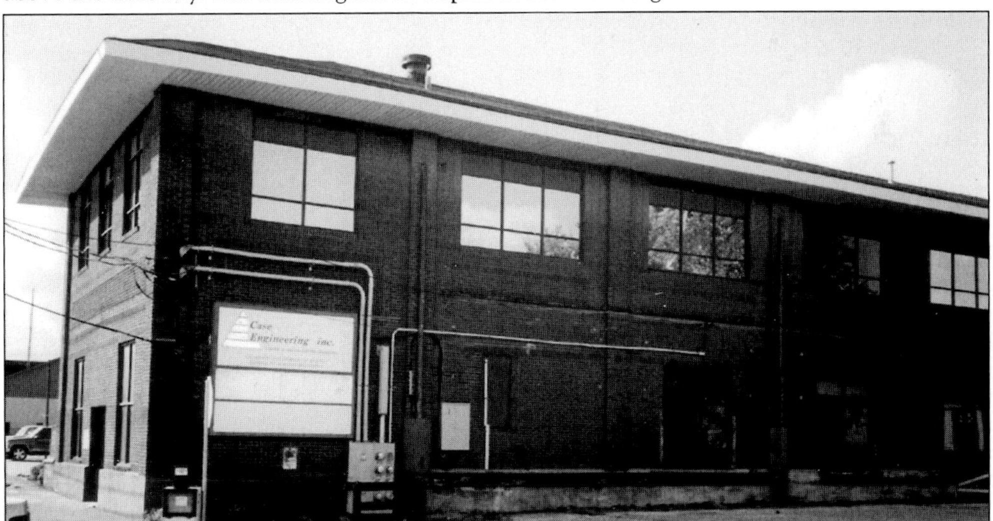

Evansville C&EI Freight House. Travel further west to Evansville on SR 66. The brick C&EI freight house, located at 1401 Franklin Street, is now used for storage. Franklin Street runs parallel to SR 62, three blocks to the north. A noted river city, much historic architecture remains. Mesker Park Zoo and the Botanic Gardens are attractions of note. The Evansville Museum of Arts, History, and Science, located on Riverside Drive, offers something for everyone.

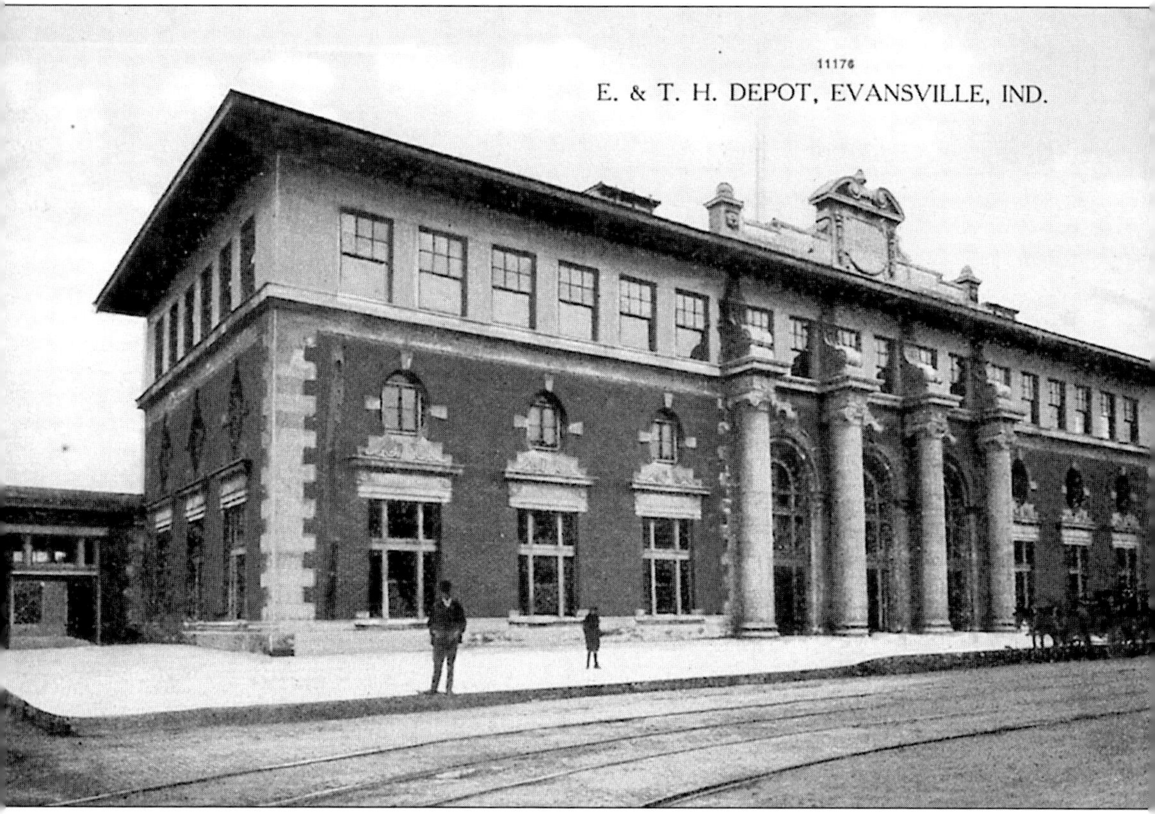

EVANSVILLE & TERRE HAUTE RAILROAD STATION. This postcard shows one of the classic depots in Indiana rail history. Built in 1905, the depot was designed by Chicago architect Daniel Burnham, who was also noted for the design of the Arcade Building in Terre Haute. It serviced the Evansville area until the start of World War II and was later used by the Chicago & Eastern Illinois (C&EI). The depot was demolished in 1966, although the columns were salvaged and are now part of the Evansville Four Freedoms Monument along the Ohio River. (Postcard by Curt Teich & Co., Chicago.)

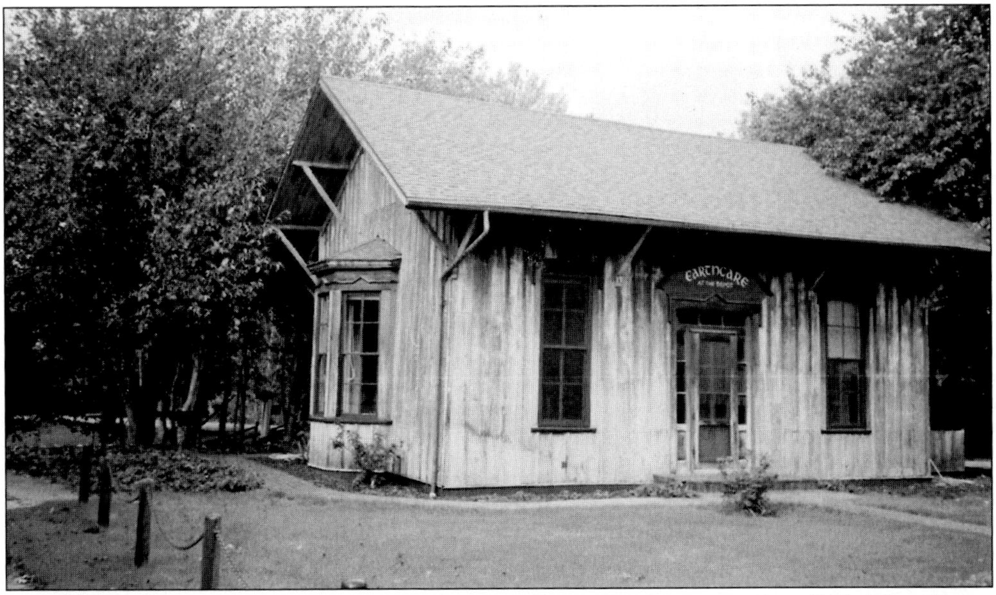

New Harmony Depot. Take SR 66 out of Evansville to New Harmony State Park. This Illinois Central wood combination depot is east of downtown, on Raintree Street. Built in 1881, it now houses a business. The history of the community is quite fascinating. A German religious group settled here in 1814 and built a planned commune. In 1825, Robert Owen, a wealthy Welshman, bought the settlement from owner George Rapp and tried to organize a community for educational and social equality. There is a play each summer that commemorates this social experiment. In 2000, the depot was recognized as part of the New Harmony Historic District.

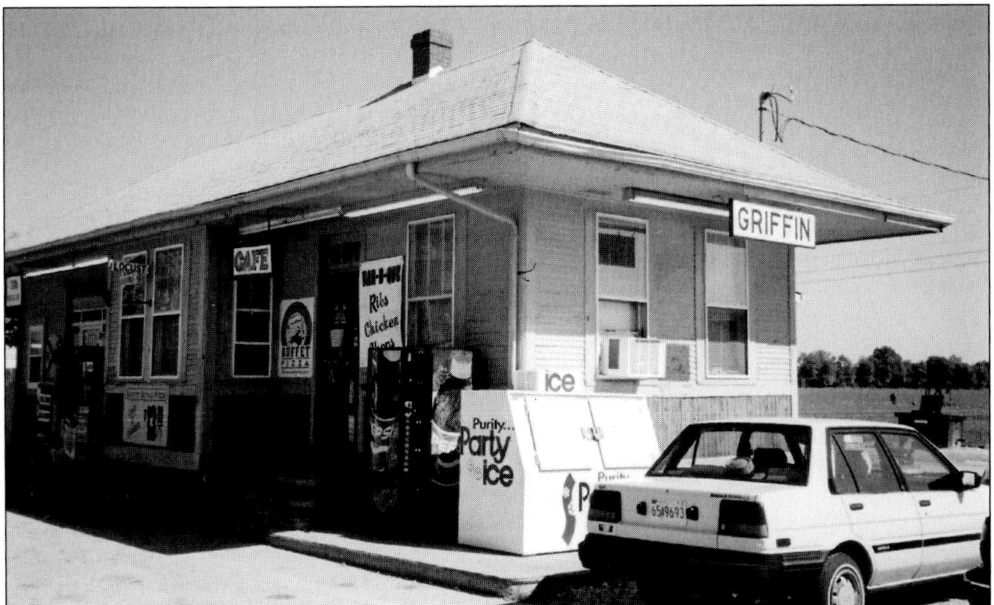

Griffin Depot. This depot has been converted to a service station and cafe. It was originally an Illinois Central combination depot, built in 1925 with a wooden frame and horizontal siding. It stands at 232 Main Street, and with the long overhanging roof, still maintains the appearance of a depot.

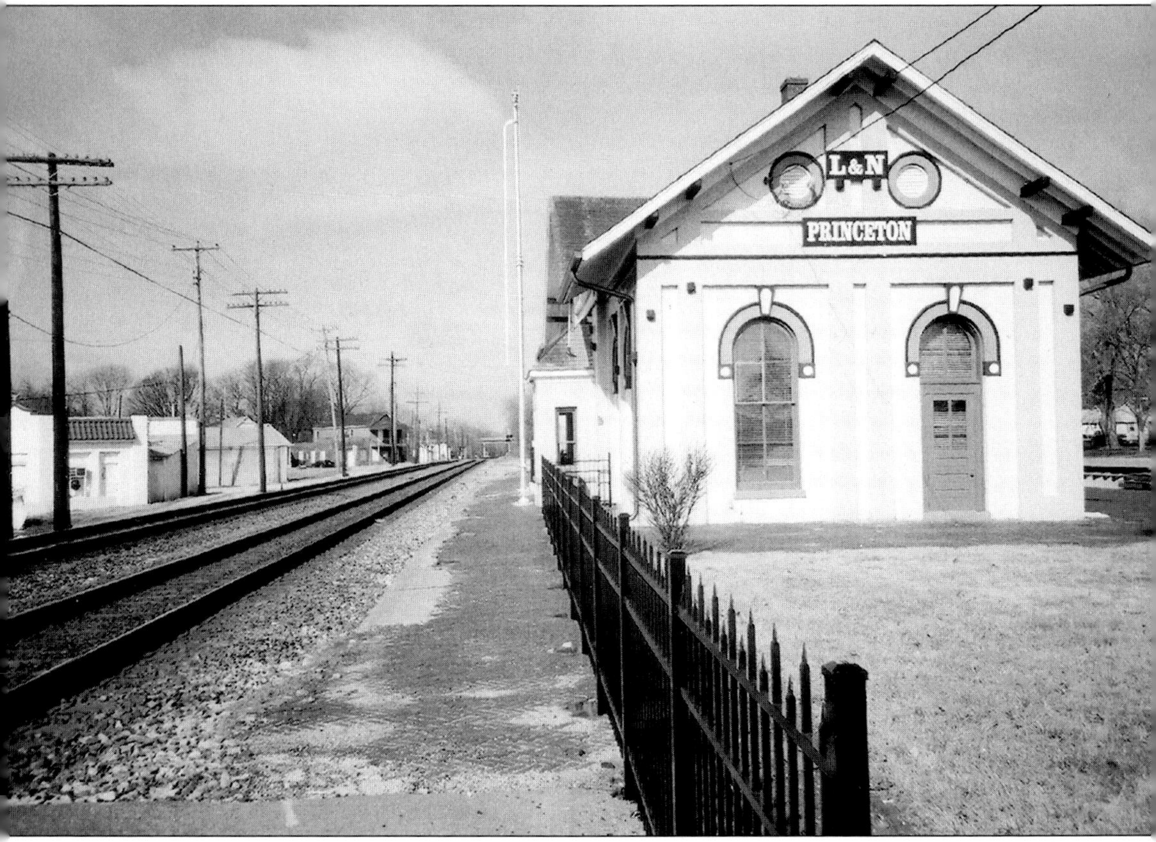

Princeton Depot. Located at Broadway (SR 64) and Second Streets, the brick C&EI depot in Princeton has been refurbished and well cared for. The tracks are still in use by CSX. Constructed in 1875, this was an active station until 1967, when the C&EI ended passenger service here. Years past, this line presented local patrons the option of going north or south on shopping adventures. In more recent years, the depot was used by the railroad for storage of maintenance equipment. It was scheduled for demolition, which was prevented when a local restoration group intervened.

PRINCETON DEPOT TODAY. This photograph shows a converted room in the depot that now houses the office of the Gibson County Visitor and Tourism Bureau. Note the sliding door and large brackets behind the desk; the opposite wall also had these doors. This area was used as the mail and baggage room. At one time, mail was transferred to and from passenger trains that had a Railway Post Office in the train. The Railway Express Agency (REA) also transferred shipments to and from REA cars. Passenger trains were once a primary means to transport mail and packages. Newspapers from cities like Chicago were dropped off at the depot from southbound passenger trains.

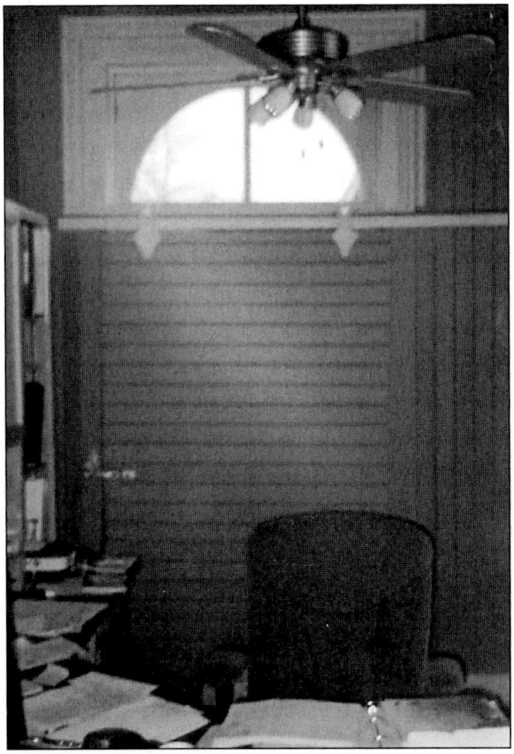

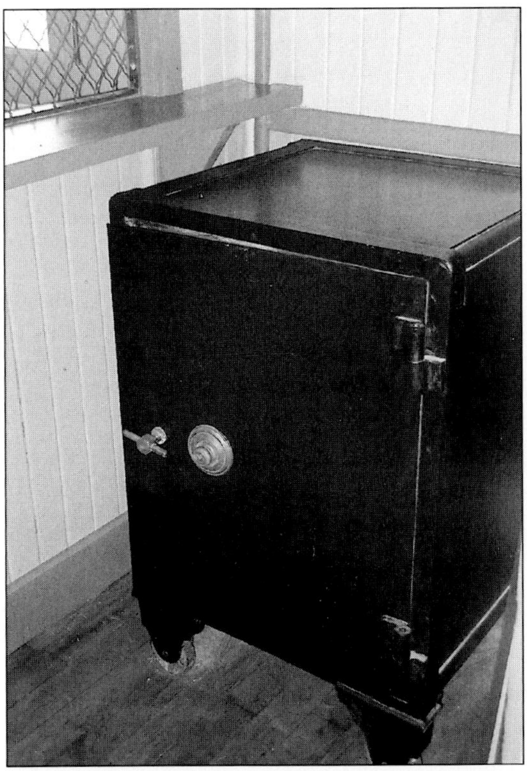

PRINCETON DEPOT SAFE. Depots had safes so that important papers, money, other valuables, and even company payroll could be protected. This safe was located in one of the more secure areas of the depot, and the railroad agent was responsible for the safe and its contents. This safe was in the building when the depot was procured and was probably used by the station agents to store money from the sale of tickets and package shipping. The age of the safe is unknown.

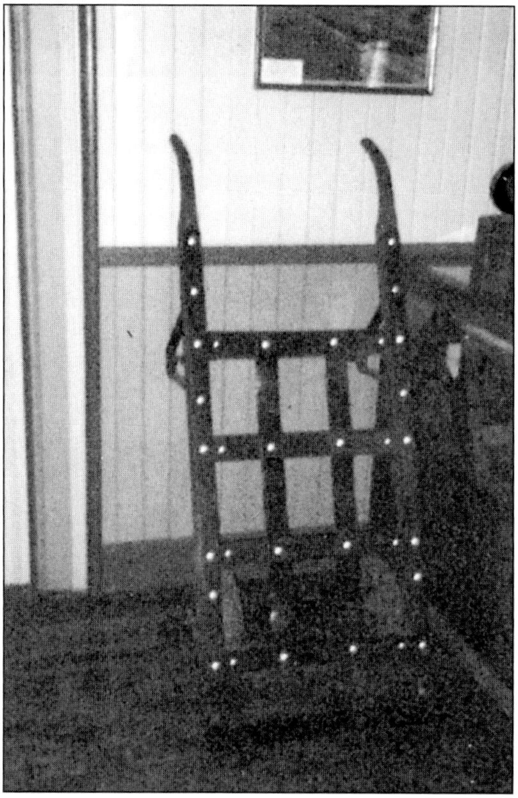

PRINCETON TWO-WHEEL FREIGHT CART. This was a very common sight in freight depots. Boxes, crates, and other packages would be unloaded from a coach and stacked vertically. A cart such as this one could be pushed under the load in order to transport it into the proper area inside the depot. There used to be a freight station building just north of the depot, more adequate for larger shipments. In years past, flat cars would bring farm implements such as tractors, plows, and other machinery by rail. They were unloaded at the loading dock.

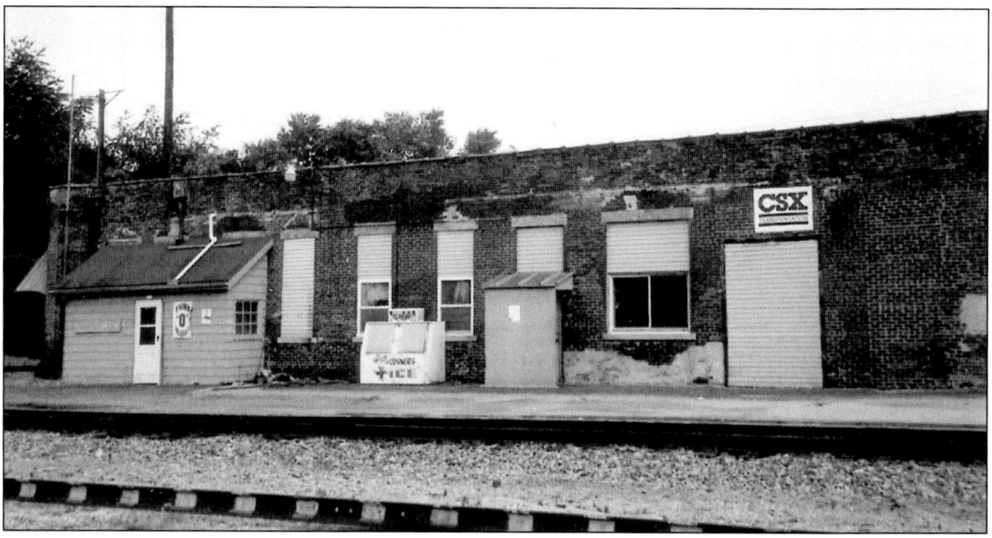

B&O DEPOT AT VINCENNES. This photograph shows the Vincennes passenger depot as it is today. It was originally a two-story building, the Vincennes Union Depot Hotel. About 1937, the top floors were removed, as well as a long extension to the east. Today, only a portion of this once fine depot hotel stands at the junction of the CSX tracks. Vincennes once had an extensive railroad system. Passenger service was provided by the B&O Railroad, moving from east to west, and the C&EI Railroad, moving from south to north. Vincennes was the crossing point for these two railroads.

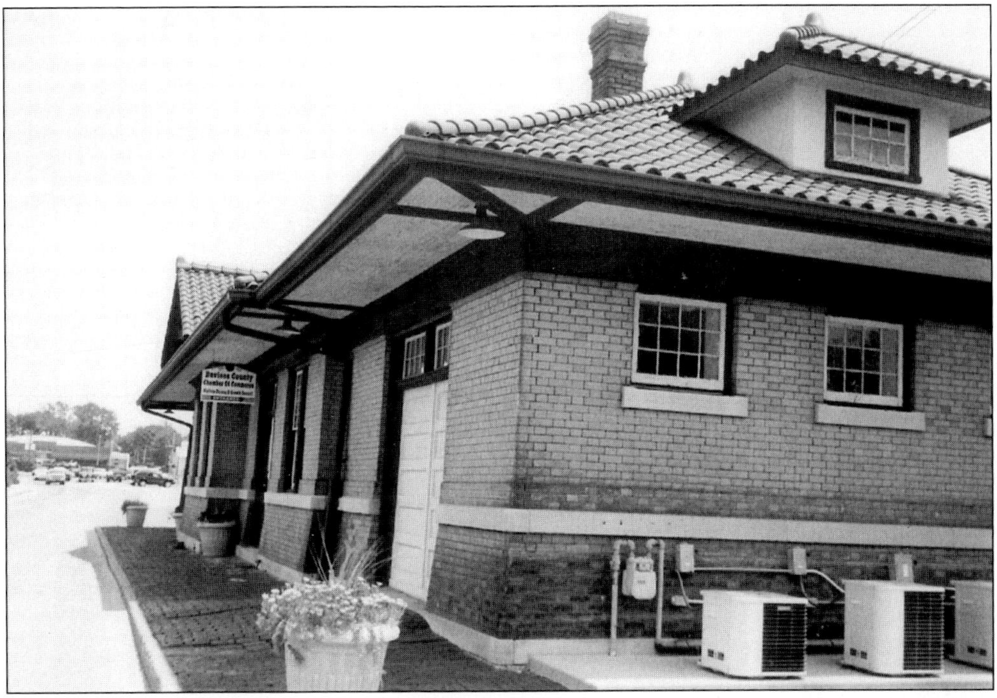

Washington B&O Depot. The Baltimore & Ohio depot pictured here stands east of Meridian Street. Built in 1906 and restored in 1990, this brick, Mission Revival-style building is currently in use by the Chamber of Commerce. The depot was added to the Washington Commercial Historic district in 1990, boasting links to the city's trading and industrial history, with railroad machine shops and car works. Nearby tracks are still in use by the CSX Railroad.

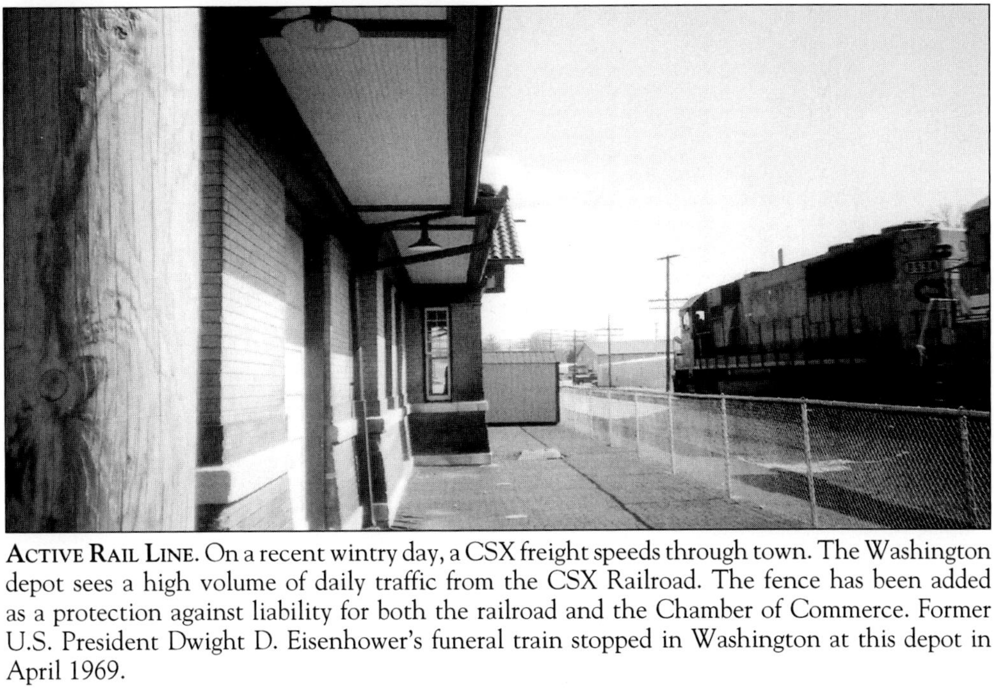

Active Rail Line. On a recent wintry day, a CSX freight speeds through town. The Washington depot sees a high volume of daily traffic from the CSX Railroad. The fence has been added as a protection against liability for both the railroad and the Chamber of Commerce. Former U.S. President Dwight D. Eisenhower's funeral train stopped in Washington at this depot in April 1969.

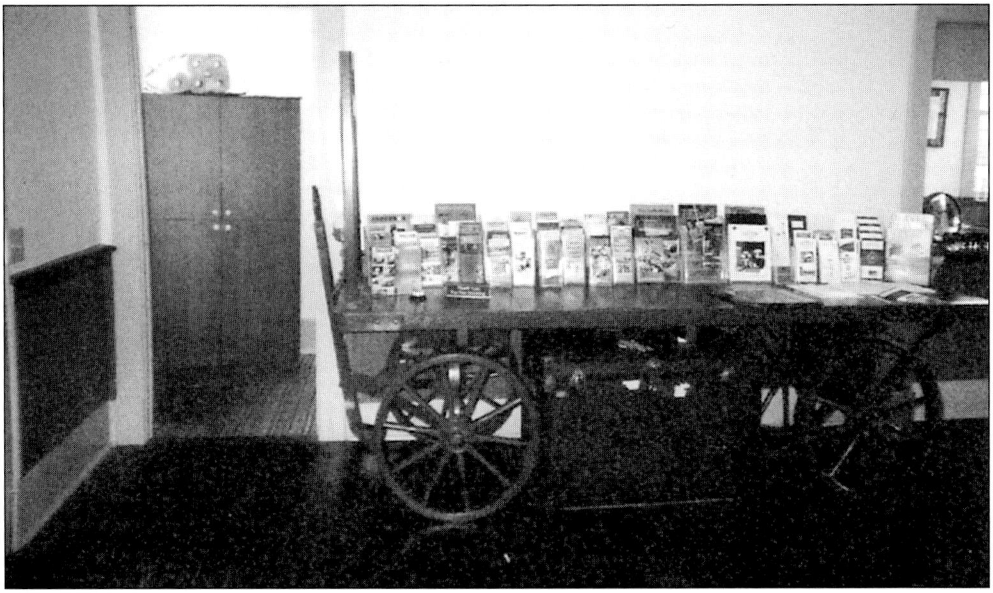

Chamber of Commerce. The Washington Chamber of Commerce has found a nice use for an old railroad transport wagon. The wagon is full of brochures of local sponsors and businesses, in addition to regional tourist attractions. Across the room, a converted heating stove serves as the base of a water dispenser with a big glass jug. Another area of the depot is used by various community groups as a meeting room.

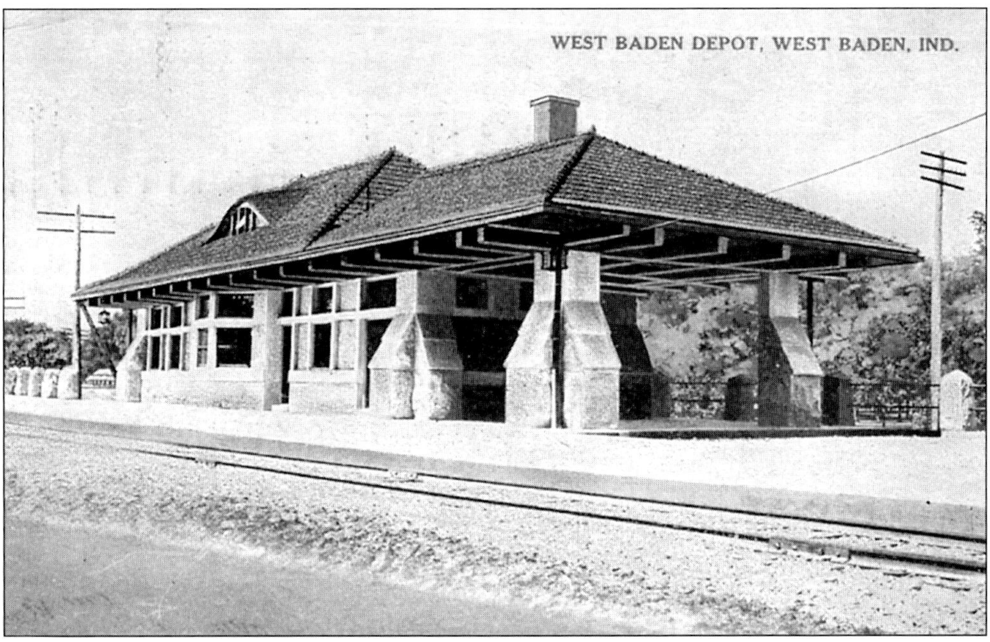

West Baden Monon Depot. The Monon depot shown in the 1910 postcard was demolished years ago. Wealthy travelers from cities like Louisville, Chicago, Indianapolis, and Cincinnati routinely made their way to West Baden via the Southern and Monon railroad lines. On the first Saturday in May, the Kentucky Derby brought hoards of visitors to West Baden and French Lick. (Postcard by Baker & Meyer Publishers.)

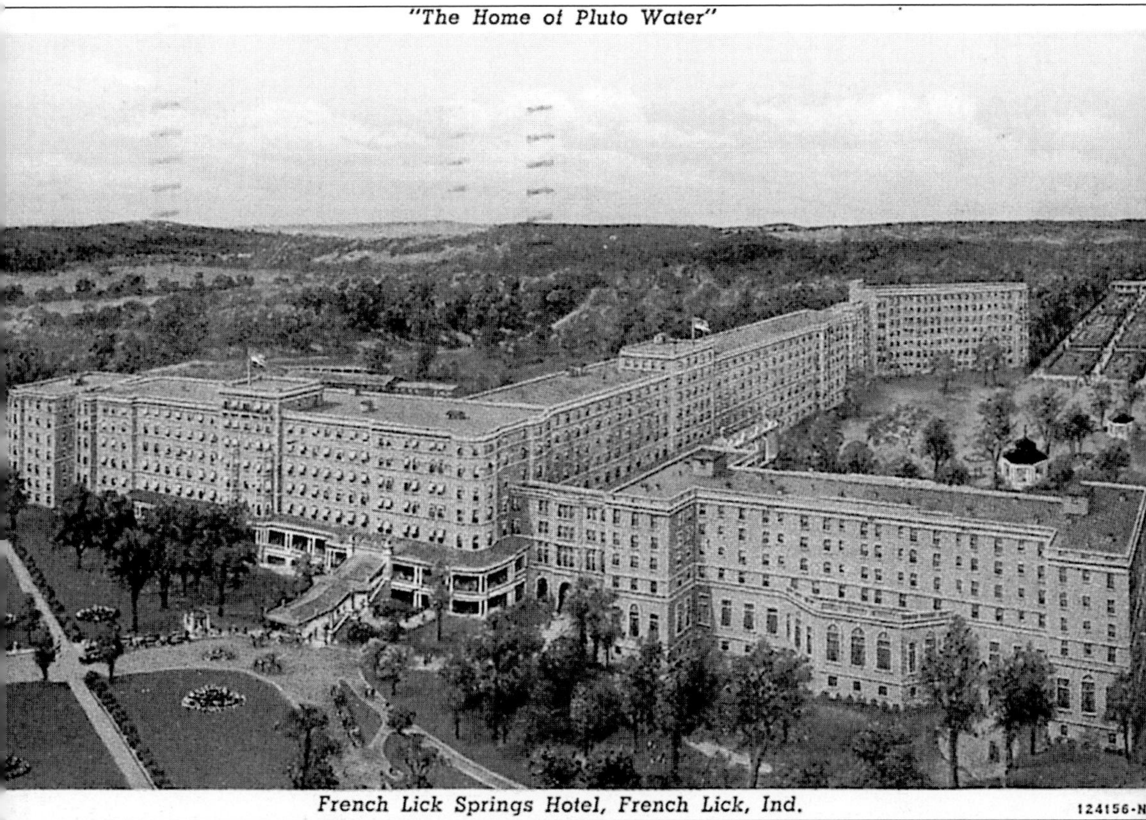

French Lick Springs Resort. Both French Lick and West Baden are quite famous for their tourist resorts, which grew out of the popularity of the local spring water, often called "Pluto Water." French Lick's name is derived from the early French settlers and the local "mineral licks" used by area wildlife. The French Lick Springs Hotel, shown in this postcard, was especially noted for its entertainment and gambling. It was a favorite escape for horse players who attended the Kentucky Derby. The Monon ran "Derby trains" from Louisville to French Lick until May 1971. French Lick was accessible from the north by the Monon Railroad and from the south by the Southern Railway. (Postcard by C. T. American Art Postcards.)

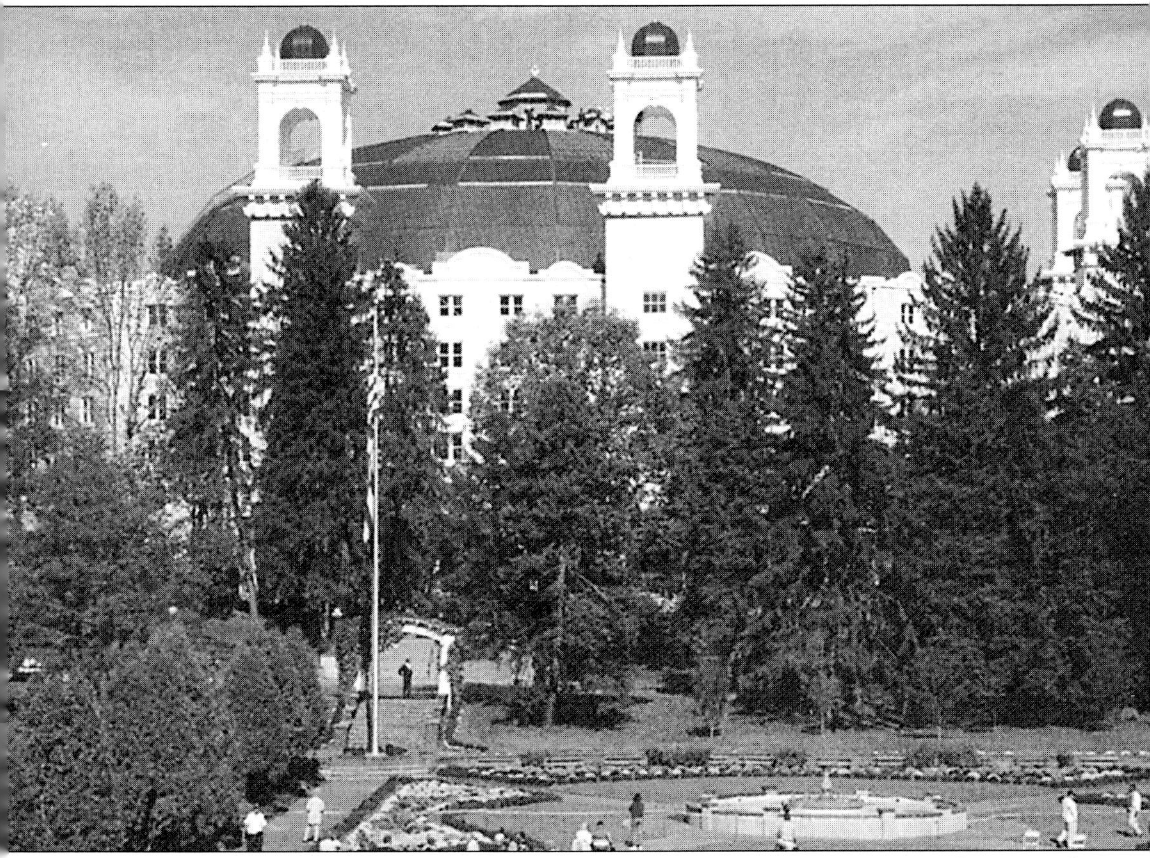

West Baden Atrium. While in West Baden, note the huge atrium rising in the west. This atrium is part of what was the once glorious West Baden Springs Hotel. Several years ago, a television news article showed college students flying "ultra-light" paper airplanes within the atrium. The interior air currents would cause these planes to float. The hotel is no longer in business, but its dome and grounds are so impressive that tours are given regularly. This postcard shows the sunken gardens, in the foreground, and the four towers, a trade mark of the hotel. (Postcard by Robert Denbo, 1999.)

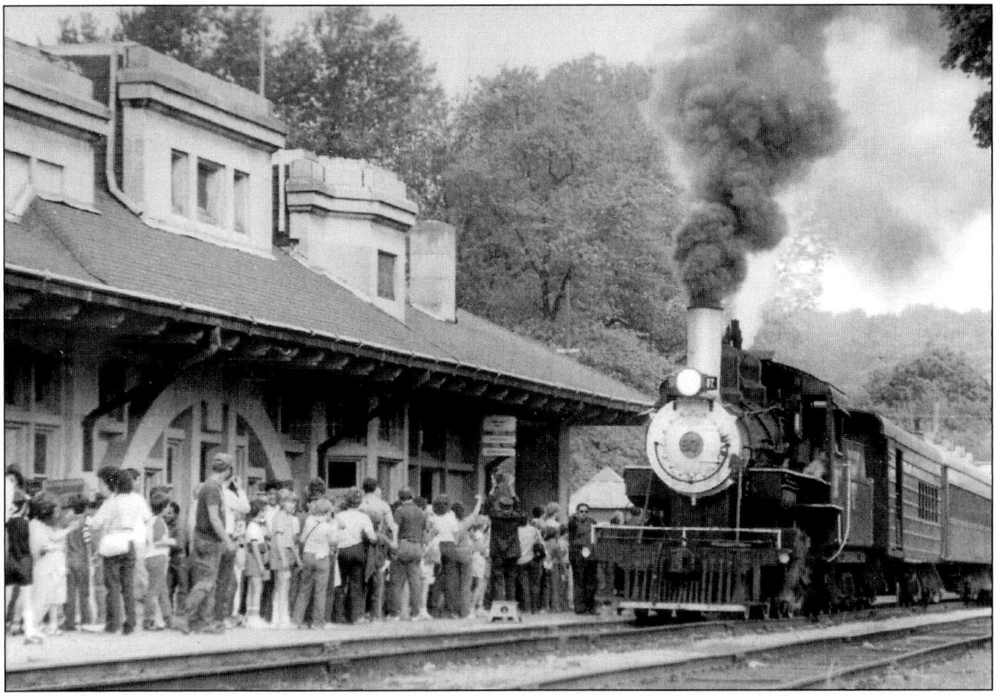

French Lick Passenger Station. The depot at French Lick was built in 1907 and was used by both the Southern and the Monon Railroads. This limestone station has been home to the Indiana Railway Museum since 1978. The Southern Railway Company granted the museum a total of 16 miles of track. The 1985 photograph shows school groups waiting for the French Lick West Baden and Southern tourist train. Steam locomotive #97 pulls the coaches and belches steam. (Courtesy Cecil Smith.)

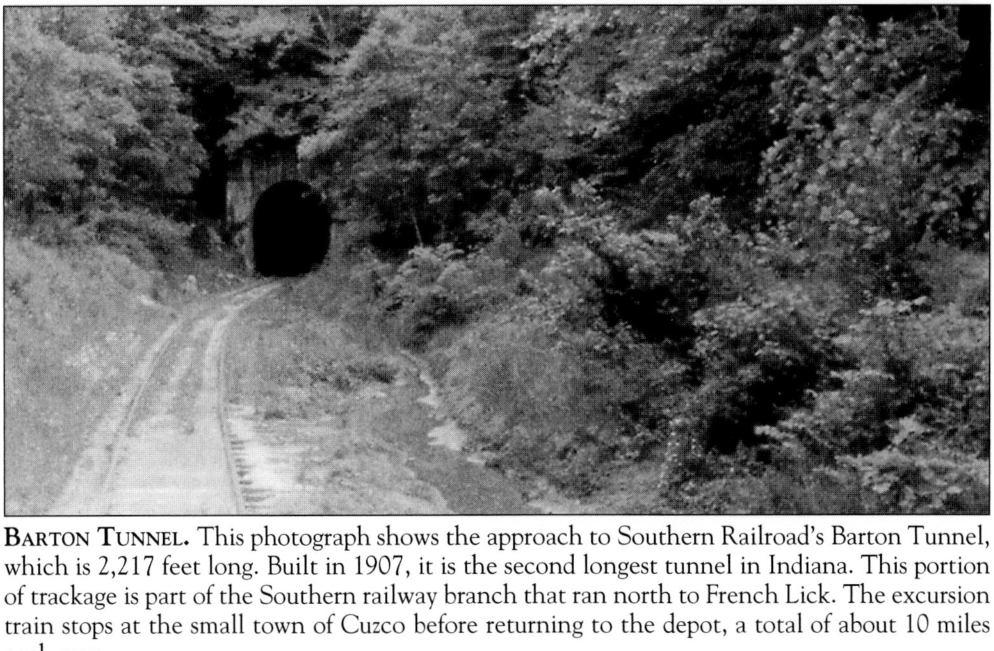

Barton Tunnel. This photograph shows the approach to Southern Railroad's Barton Tunnel, which is 2,217 feet long. Built in 1907, it is the second longest tunnel in Indiana. This portion of trackage is part of the Southern railway branch that ran north to French Lick. The excursion train stops at the small town of Cuzco before returning to the depot, a total of about 10 miles each way.

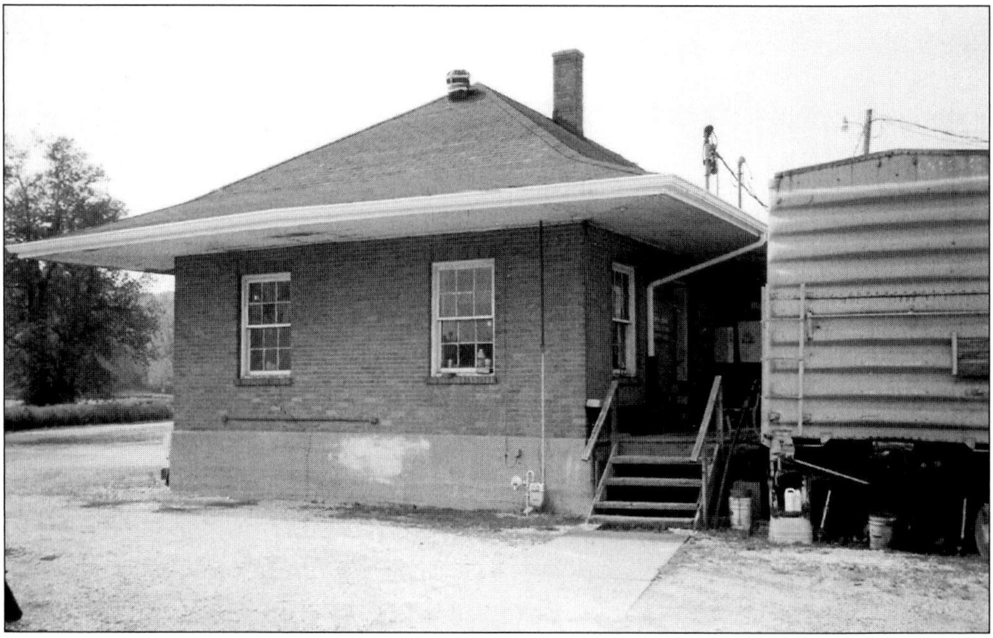

French Lick Monon Freight House. This photograph shows the Monon freight house at French Lick, located about a quarter mile north of the passenger depot. Today it houses the maintenance facilities for the FLWB&S tourist line. This brick maintenance facility helps to keep the tourist train running smoothly. It was built in 1929.

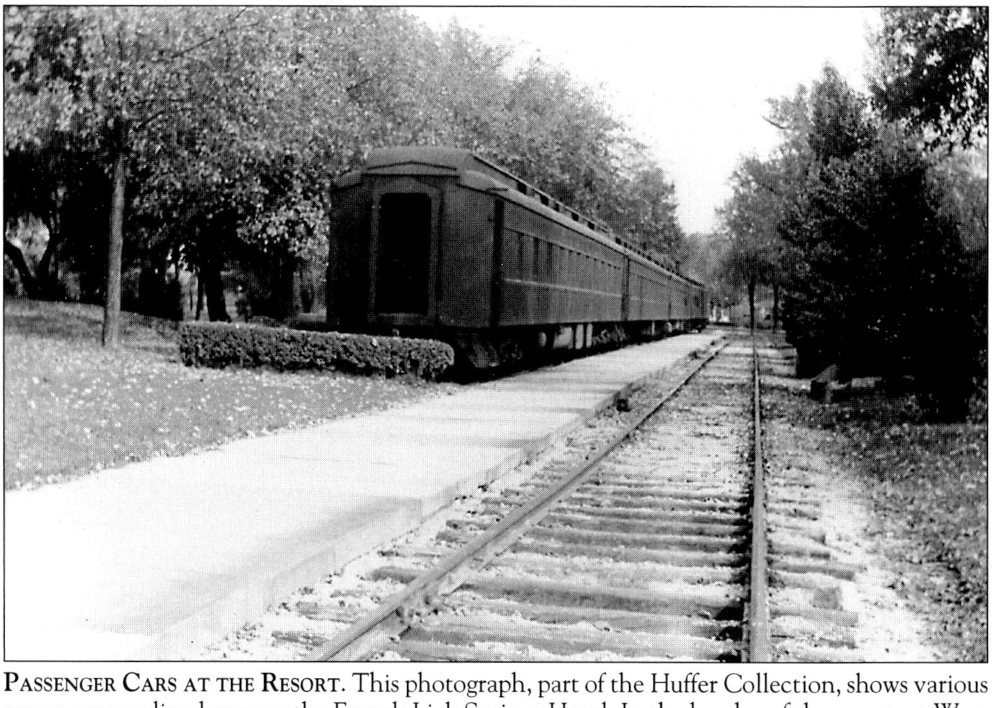

Passenger Cars at the Resort. This photograph, part of the Huffer Collection, shows various passenger cars lined up near the French Lick Springs Hotel. In the heyday of the resorts at West Baden and French Lick, it was not uncommon to see a half-dozen passenger cars queued up to serve the patrons. (Courtesy MRHTS Collection.)

Eight

A Local Class III Railroad (Short Line)

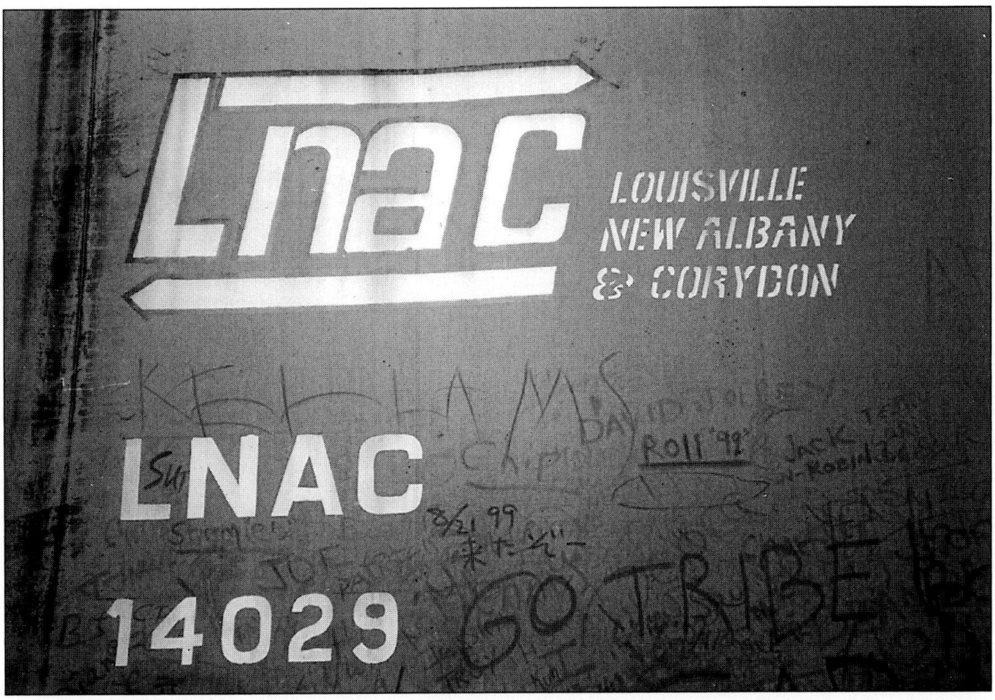

LNA&C Boxcar. The Louisville, New Albany & Corydon (LNA&C) railroad is a Class III railroad and has been operating since 1883. It ranks 10th of the 35 Indiana Class III lines (short lines) based on the volume of carloads handled. This photograph of one of the boxcars the railroad previously owned features the railroad name and logo. The present owners have been providing local freight service since 1987. The LNA&C operates daily according to needs of its customers. Presently, the crews are on duty 18 hours daily, 7 days a week, for switching. The line interchanges exclusively with Norfolk Southern at Corydon Junction, 7.7 route miles north of Corydon, 4 times a day. The Corydon Junction depot was demolished several years ago.

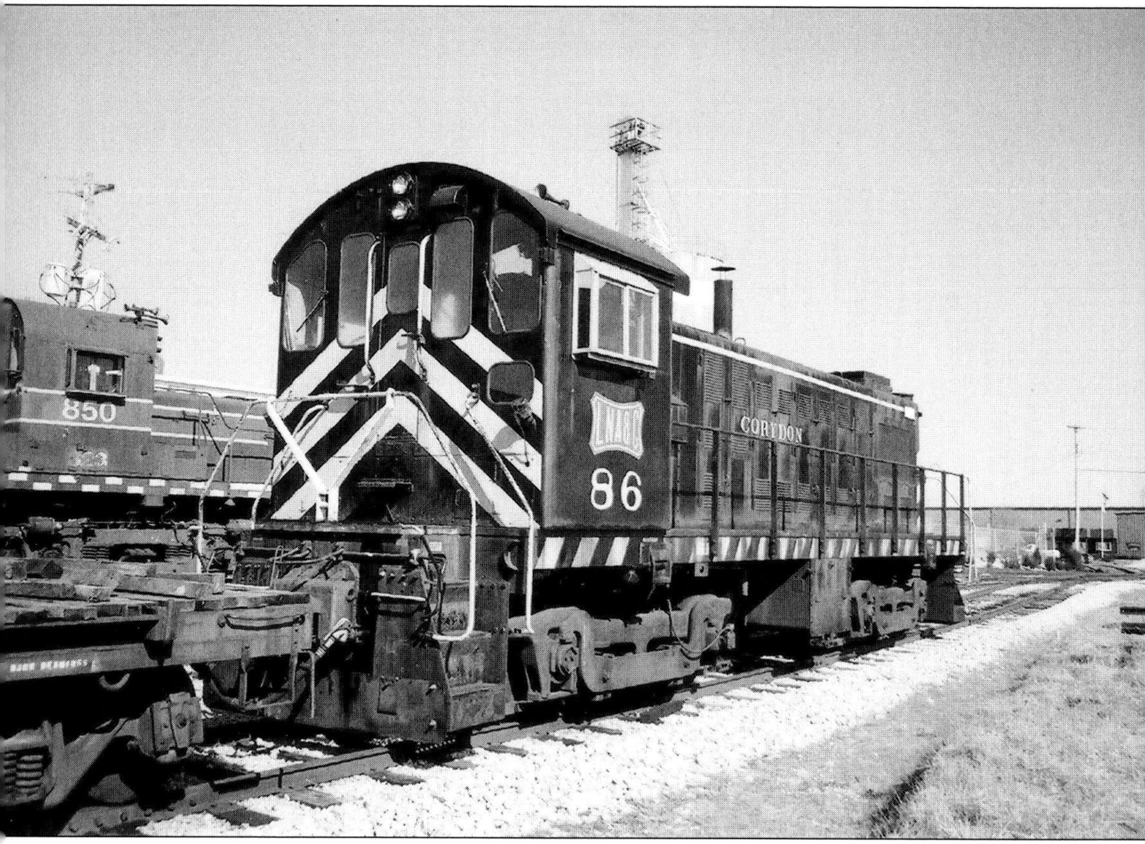

The LNA&C. The LNA&C was first envisioned in 1881 by Street John Boyle, and the first train ran in 1883. In 2000, the LNA&C handled nearly 3,400 carloads, moving automobile parts, silica, plastics, logs, popping corn, chemicals, and fertilizers. Recently, a company making automobile parts left the Corydon area, negatively impacting the railroad. This photograph shows one of the nine locomotives owned by the LNA&C, locomotive #86, an S-4 Alco engine that is currently in service. It was acquired from Grand Trunk Western Railway, and its original number was #1002. To its left is #850, also an Alco, that belonged to the I&HR Railroad as locomotive #27. It is a C-420, also in service. The engine is parked in the front of the engine house, located in the Corydon Industrial Park.

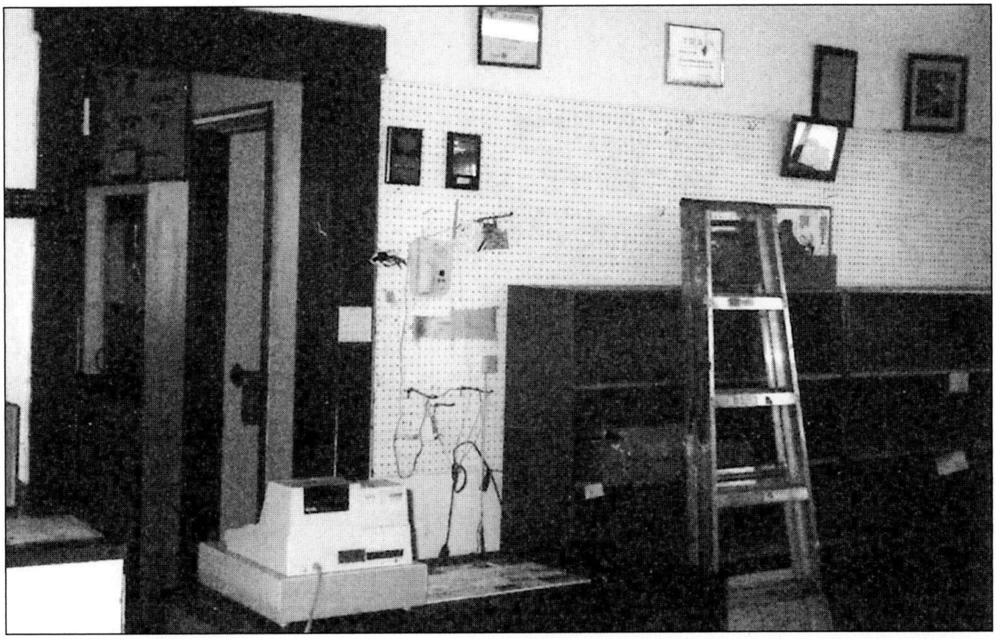

Ticket Counter. The LNA&C passenger depot has three separate rooms. This photograph shows the room used to sell tickets for the Corydon Scenic Railroad (CSR), which went out of business in 2003. It is now used for storage. The other two rooms include the general office, which is still in use, and a room previously used as a gift or souvenir shop for the excursion railroad. The excursion railroad began in 1989 and served more than 250,000 passengers over the years. The CSR recently sold its equipment, including the passenger cars, to the Cuyahoga Valley Scenic Railroad, an excursion railroad that operates along the Cuyahoga River and the Ohio & Erie Canal Towpath Trail between Cleveland and Akron, Ohio.

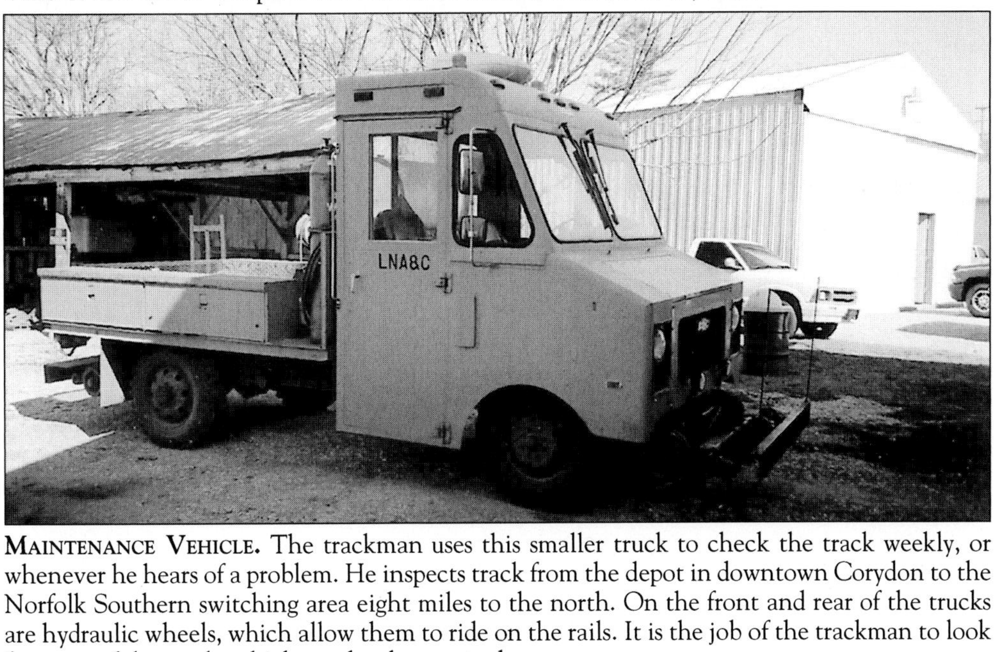

Maintenance Vehicle. The trackman uses this smaller truck to check the track weekly, or whenever he hears of a problem. He inspects track from the depot in downtown Corydon to the Norfolk Southern switching area eight miles to the north. On the front and rear of the trucks are hydraulic wheels, which allow them to ride on the rails. It is the job of the trackman to look for areas of the tracks which need to be repaired.

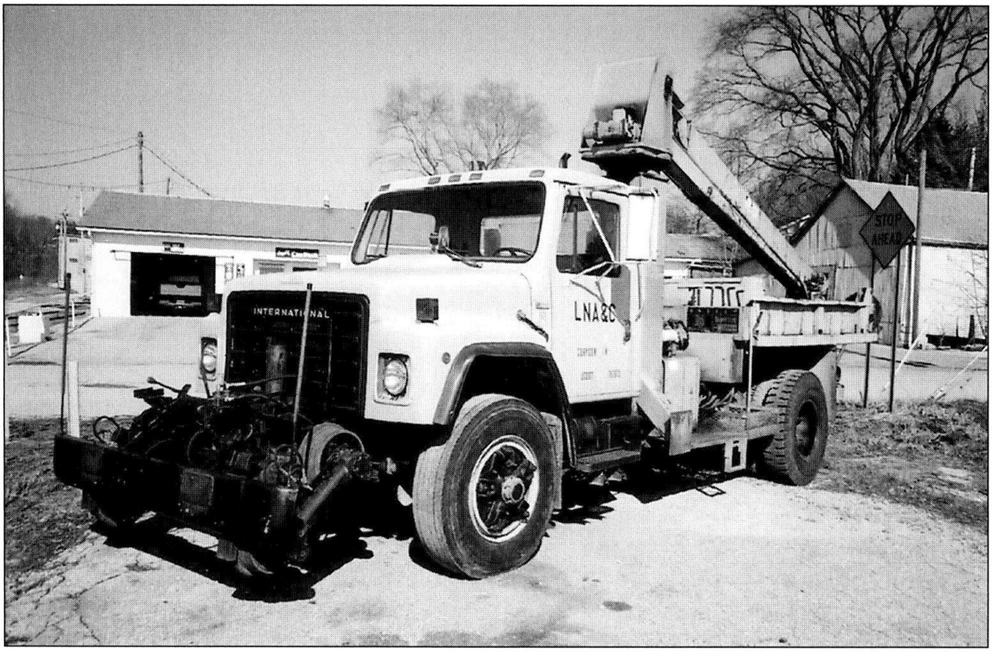

Track Maintenance Truck. This larger truck would be used for work on track sites that need repair. It is also equipped with track-running capability. On the rear is a back-hoe, which can be used to spread ballast, lift ties, and for other repair jobs. It can also be used to move gravel or ballast, and to create ditches when needed.

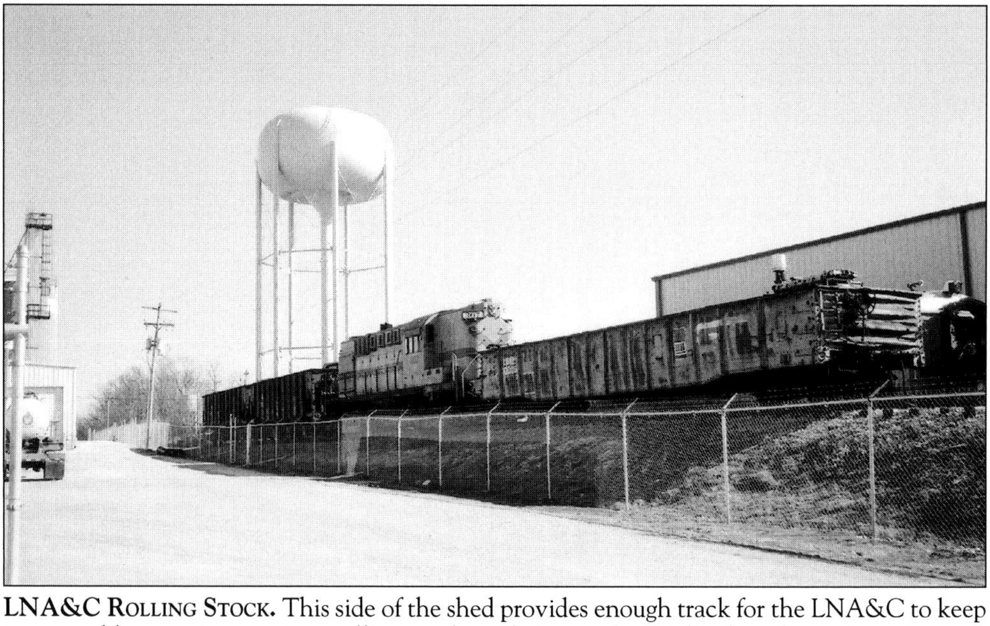

LNA&C Rolling Stock. This side of the shed provides enough track for the LNA&C to keep its unused locomotives, various rolling stock, and pieces of specialized track repair equipment. The white building is the locomotive shed. The building is too dark inside, and the equipment too large, to take quality photos. This area might be comparable to a larger railroad's train yard. Inside of the shed are several large pieces of rail equipment, including a ballast regulator, tie inserters, a tie crane, and two tie tampers.

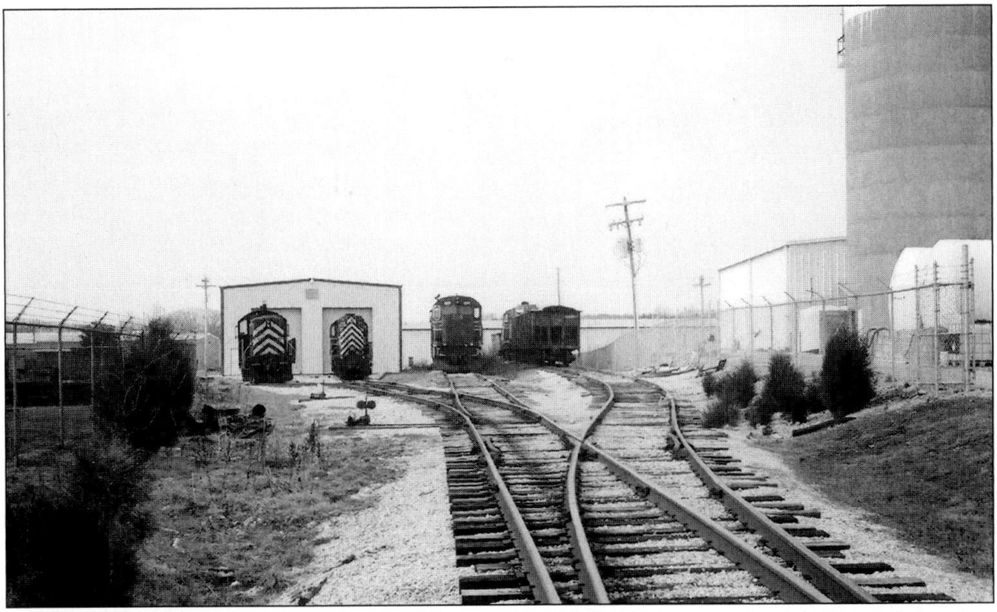

LNA&C Locomotive Shed. Pictured here are two of the engines parked in front of the shed doors. This photograph looks west; the LNA&C line is to the east where it connects with the main rail line. Engine #86 stands to the left, #850 is second from the right, and hopper cars are on the furthest right track. The shed is used mostly for protection from the elements and for storage of equipment that is not often used.

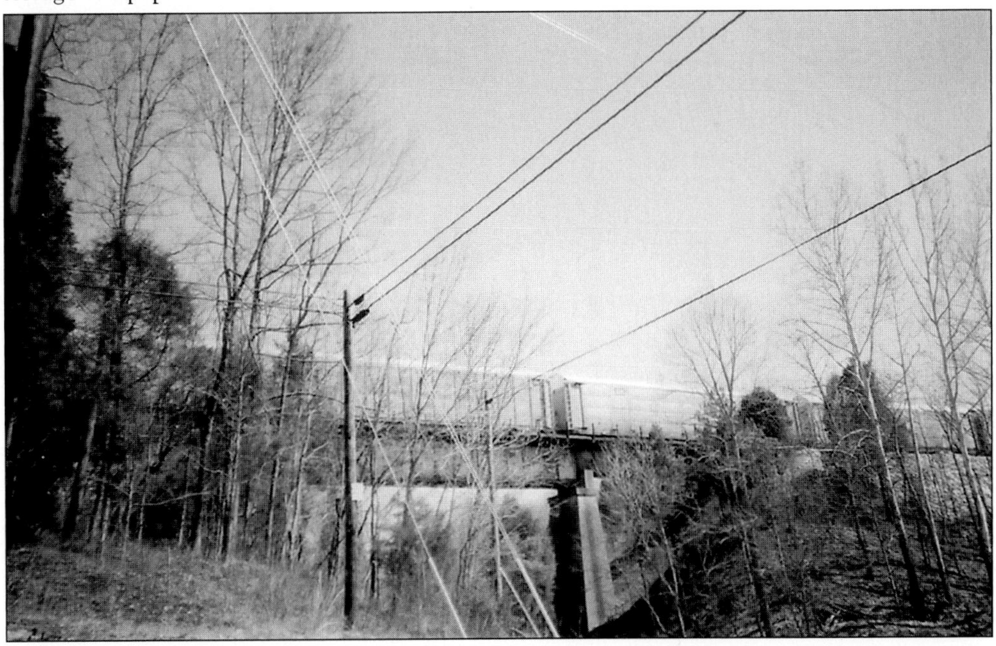

Norfolk Southern Trestle. This trestle is part of the Norfolk Southern line that runs west from New Albany into southwestern Indiana. It is located about an eighth of a mile east of what used to be the Corydon Junction depot. The trestle here crosses SR 135, just south of a little town called New Salisbury. The LNA&C connects with the NS just west of the trestle. The photograph shows an NS freight crossing the trestle and approaching Corydon Junction.

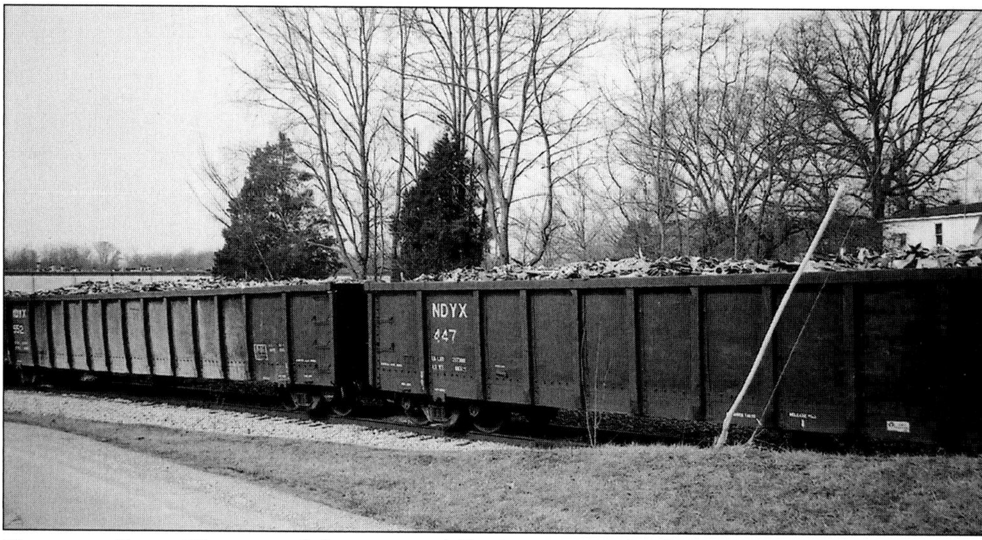

GONDOLA CARS. These gondola cars are full of scrap metal. There were four or five of them sitting outside a factory near the junction. One company that the NA&C railroad serves is Omni Sources, a company that deals with scrap metal. Other companies that the NA&C moves cars for include Lucas Oil and Natures Alpine. Michigan-based Tower Automotive, which has two plants near Louisville, was a customer of the railroad, but filed for Chapter 11 protection in U.S. Bankruptcy Court on February 2, 2005. The 700-employee Corydon Tower plant produced frames for Ford Explorers manufactured at the Louisville Assembly Plant.

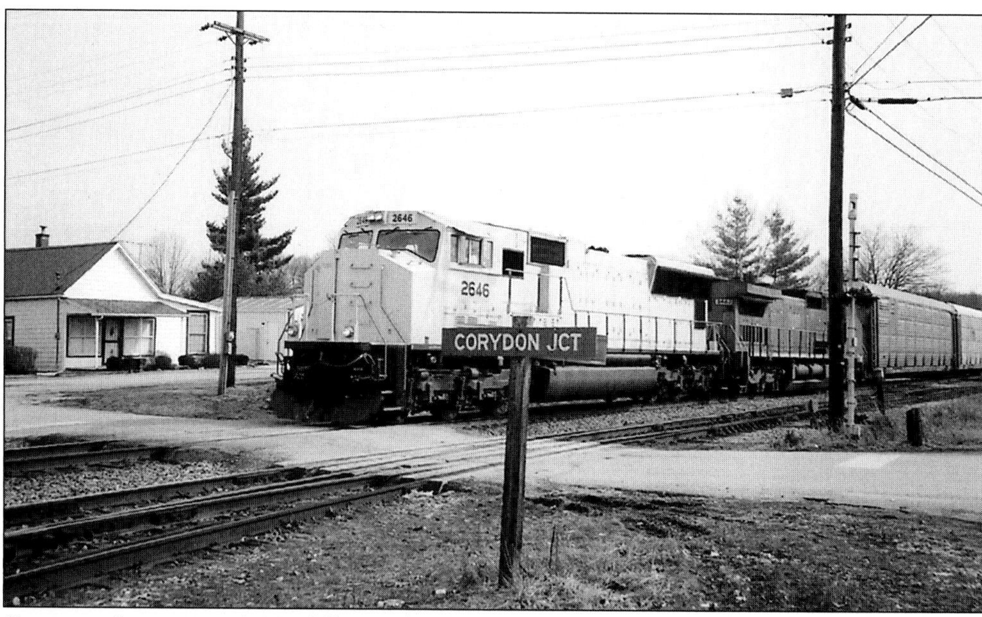

CORYDON JUNCTION. A Norfolk Southern freight pulled by two diesel locomotives has just crossed the trestle and approaches Corydon Junction, once a thriving depot site for the Southern Railway. Today, this location is the junction of the Norfolk Southern Railway line and the Louisville, New Albany & Corydon Railroad line. The NS runs four freights through every day so that the LNA&C can move cars to and from the Corydon area to factories and other sites.

Nine

Efforts in Preserving Our Rail Heritage

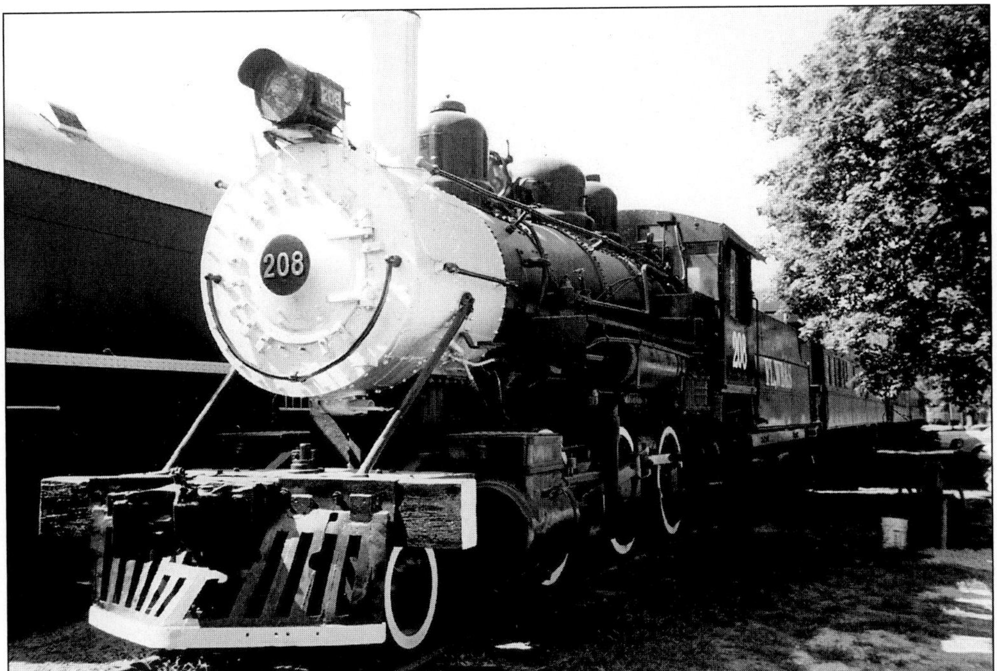

Locomotive #208. Southern Indiana has many communities and organizations that have made supreme efforts to retain railroad heritage. These include The Depot Railroad Museum in Salem, the Whitewater Valley Railroad in Connersville, the Carthage, Knightstown & Shirley Tourist Railroad in Knightstown, the Haley Tower Historical and Technical Society, and the Indiana Railway Museum in French Lick. Three of these groups have access to a rail line and run tourist excursions. This chapter will focus on each group's preservation efforts. The photograph above shows locomotive #208, built by Baldwin Locomotive Works in 1912 and currently on display at the Indiana Railway Museum. It has a 2–6–0 wheel alignment and is not currently operational. The railroad museum has continued to grow and currently boasts a roster of over 65 pieces of rolling stock and locomotives. In 2004, it carried more than 23,000 passengers.

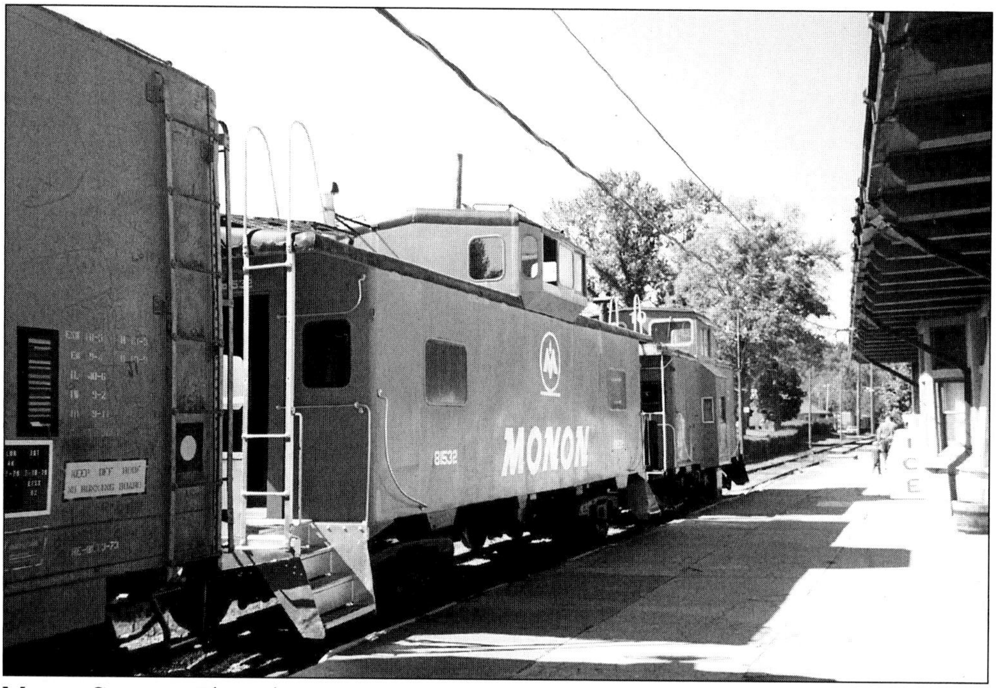

Monon Caboose. The Indiana Railway Museum is located on SR 56 in front of the French Lick Springs Resort. Caboose #81532 was built in 1956 for the Monon Railroad and is constructed of steel. It is currently on loan to the Museum from the Monon Historical Society and is open for viewing most days. The Museum is also home to several other interesting examples of rolling stock.

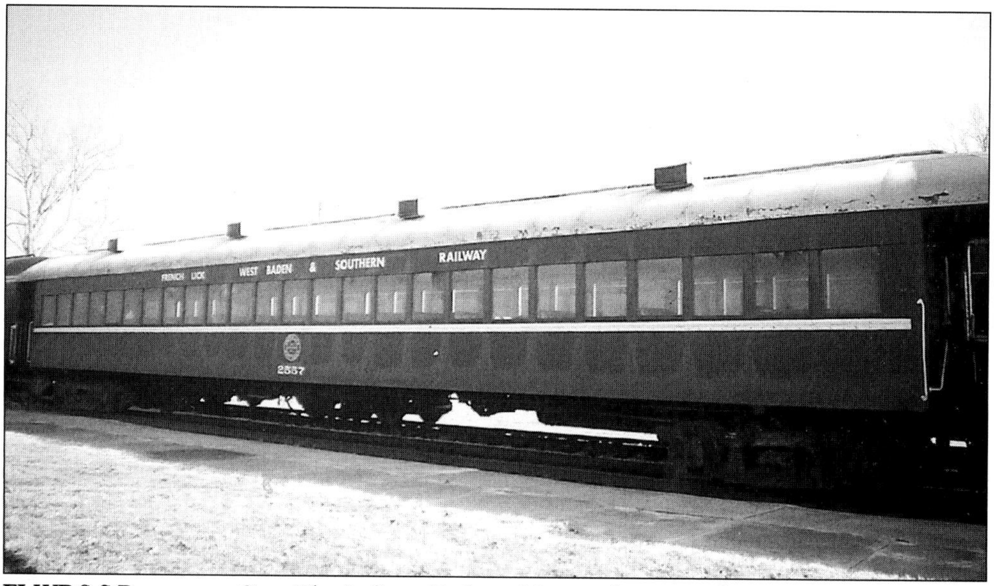

FLWB&S Passenger Car. The Indiana Railway Museum has several cars painted and lettered to show the excursion line's official name, French Lick, West Baden & Southern Railway. This photograph shows coach #2557 sitting near the depot during the off season. This coach allows 21st-century visitors a small taste of what was once "the only way to travel."

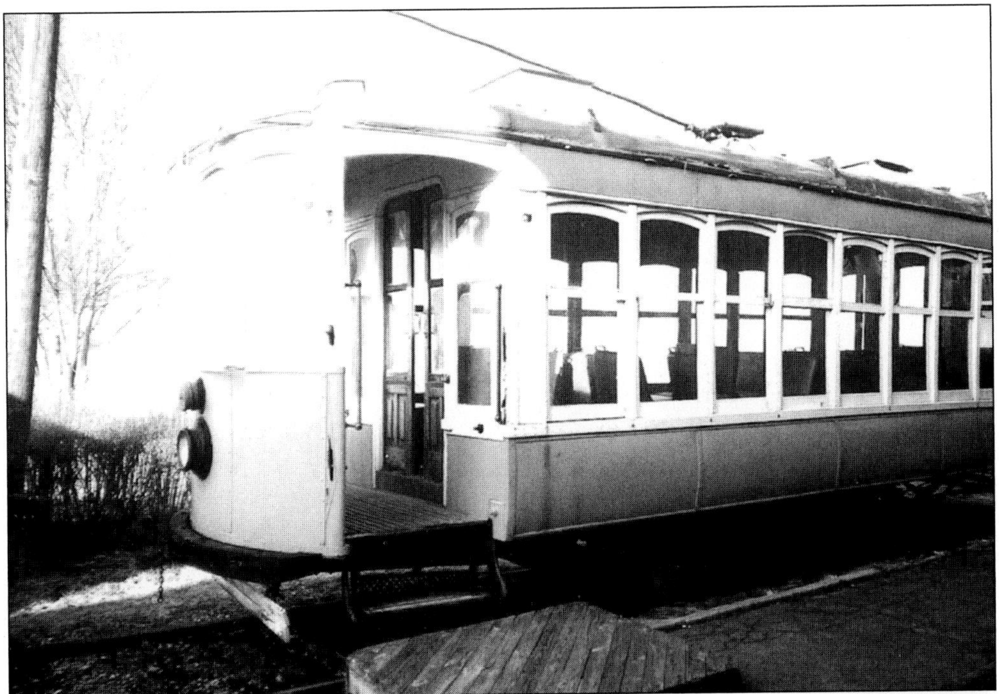

FLWB&S TROLLEY CAR. This car is part of the Springs Valley Electric Railway. Pictured here is trolley car #313, built in 1930 in Portugal. It operates between French Lick and West Baden. This car was acquired from a group in Toledo, Ohio. Note the cable above the car connecting it to the power source.

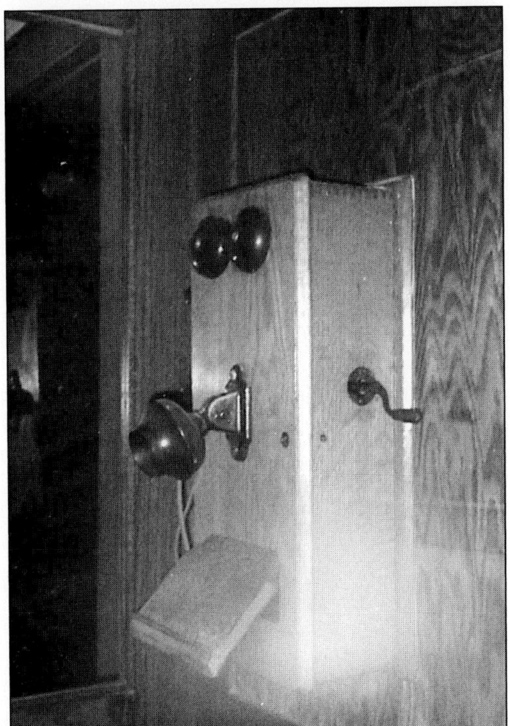

WOODEN TELEPHONE. Inside the museum depot lobby, many things that relate to rail travel of years ago can be found. In the center of the room sit long wooden benches used by the patrons. An authentic wooden phone booth, with a wooden telephone inside, stands against the wall. This phone booth is on loan from Vogel Smith, and this particular phone was manufactured for the Illinois Bell Telephone Company. On arriving at the depot, it may have been necessary for the passenger to make a call to request a ride from a friend.

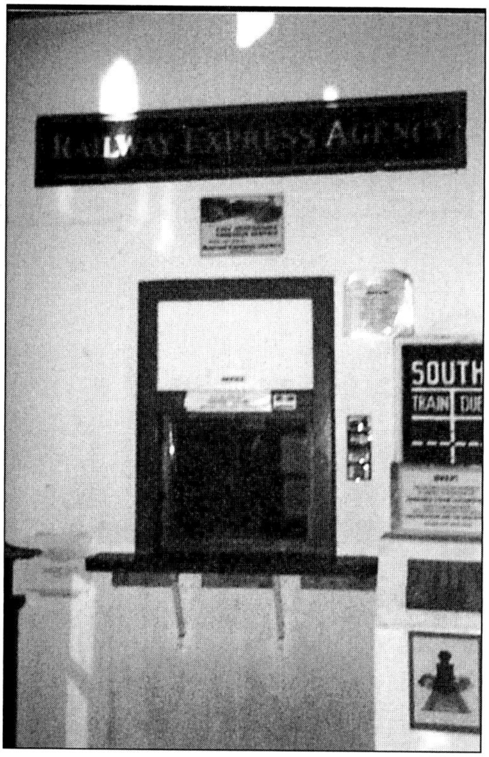

TICKET WINDOW. Plans for train travel began here at the window, where a friendly railroad agent sold tickets. The name above the window reads "Railway Express Agency." To the right is a chalkboard on which the agent provided information about arrivals and departures. Today, tickets for the French Lick West Baden & Southern excursion are sold here.

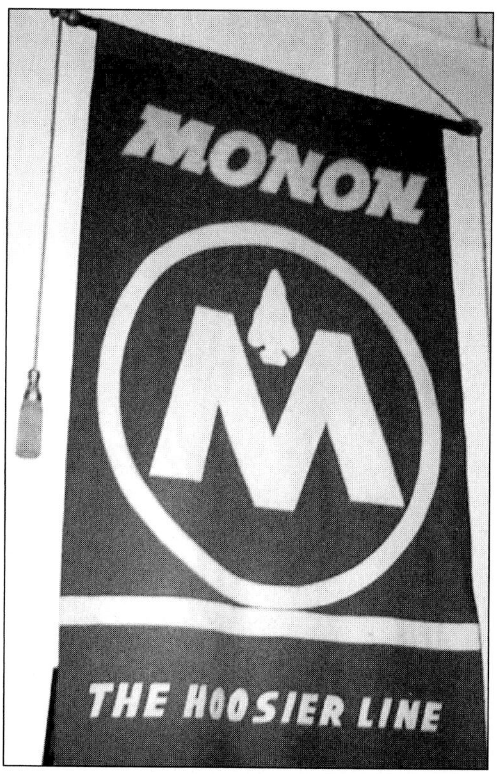

MONON BANNER. The Monon banner seen in the photograph tells a story about the rail line. The "M" stands for two teepees with an arrowhead in the center. The Monon began in Indiana, "land of Indians." The outer circle represents the railroad wheel, and the bottom line represents the rail the wheel rides upon. This banner currently hangs in the general office area of the FLWB&S Railroad. The logo represents the Monon line quite effectively. General Manager Alan Barnett graciously allowed this photograph to be taken in the office.

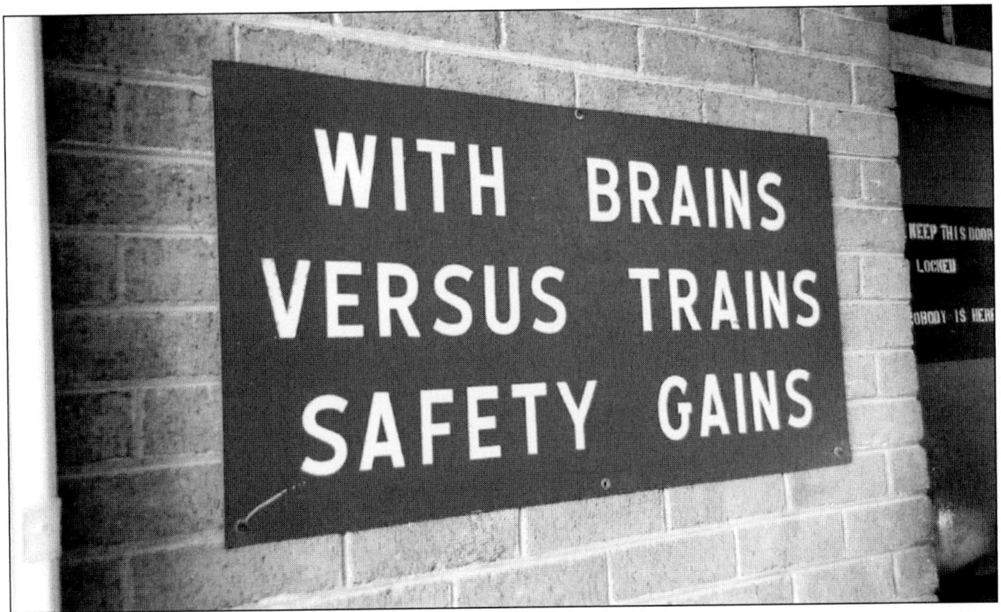

RAILROAD SAFETY. Railroad safety was always an issue. The extremely heavy steel equipment that laborers worked with was often a disaster waiting to happen. Accidents can happen suddenly, and it is important to pay attention to the task at hand, as this Illinois Central sign, from Centralia, Illinois, states quite well. It hangs outside on the dockside of the French Lick freight house to the north of the passenger depot.

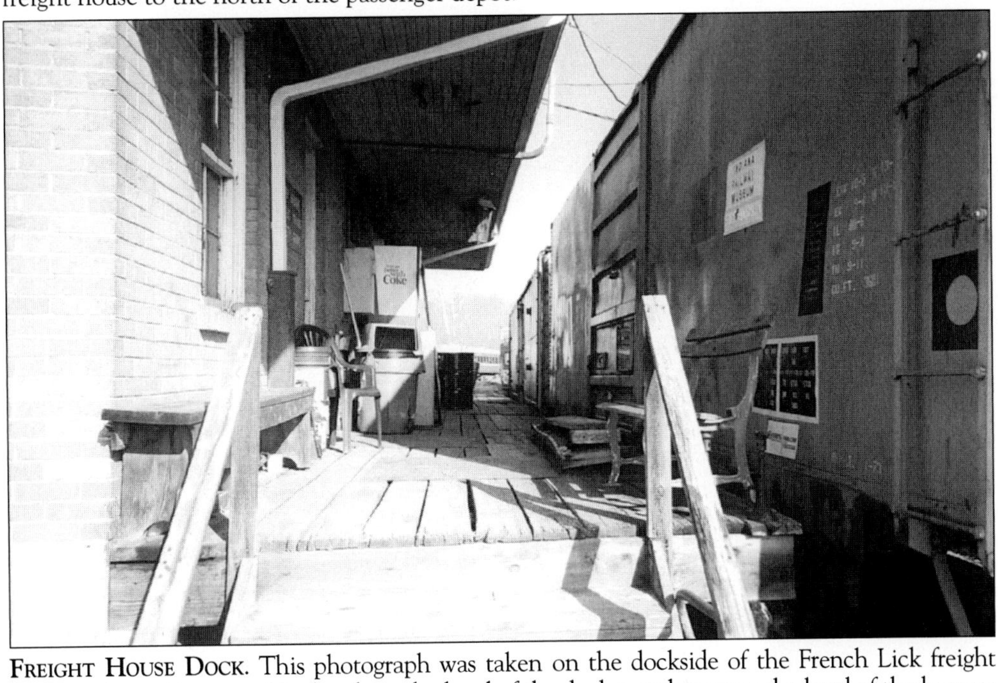

FREIGHT HOUSE DOCK. This photograph was taken on the dockside of the French Lick freight house and provides a good look at how the level of the dock matches up to the level of the boxcars or other rolling stock. Steel plates could be moved into position, allowing a forklift to drive from the dock into the boxcar and remove a pallet loaded with shipped goods. If this freight house was working as it did years ago, there would not be as much "clutter" as is seen here.

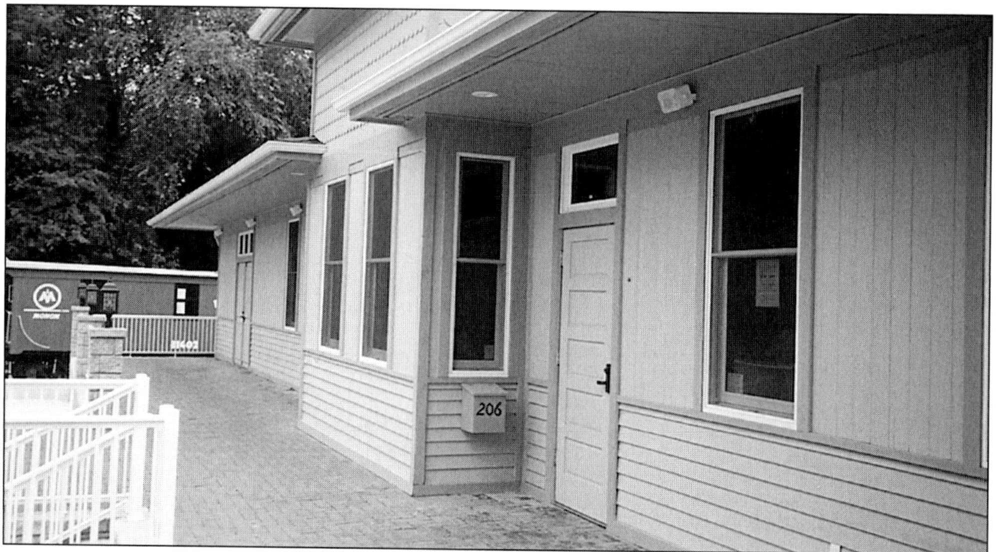

The Depot at Salem. While in Salem, visit The Depot, a railroad museum, which replicates the most recent Salem Monon depot. The last Monon depot was demolished in 1982. While at the museum, look up Cecil Smith, a guiding force behind the planning of this fine structure. Cecil and others helped to acquire the funds needed to finance the depot. It was constructed by students from local high schools who were members of the building trades class at New Albany's Prosser School of Technology. Many antiques dealing with the history of the Monon and other railroads can be found here. The museum is located on the property of the John Hay Center, south of the main museum.

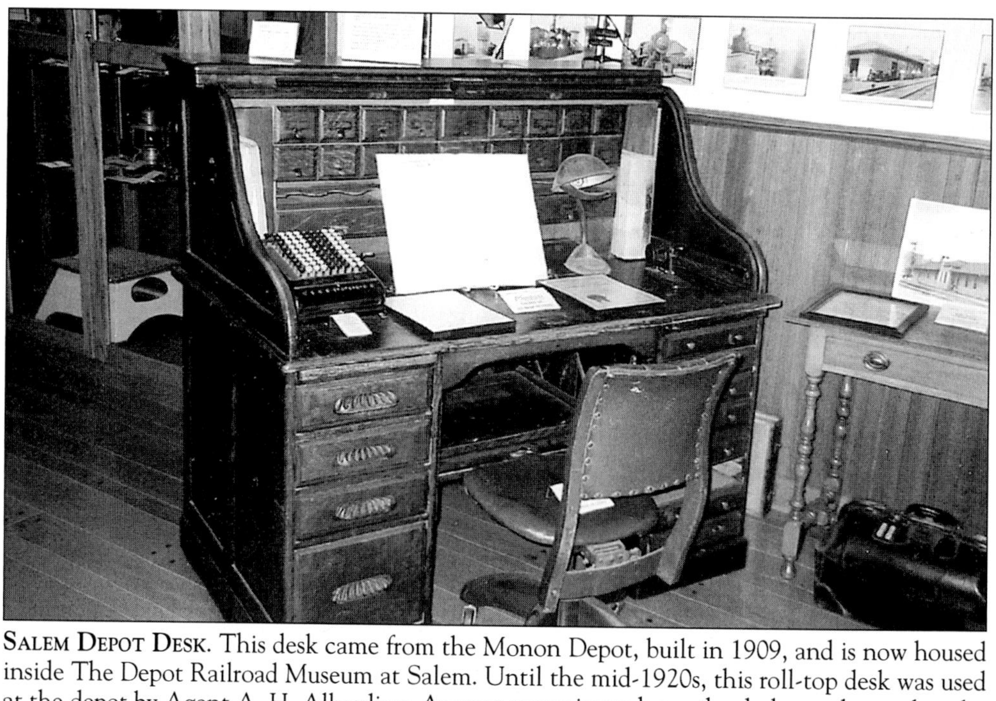

Salem Depot Desk. This desk came from the Monon Depot, built in 1909, and is now housed inside The Depot Railroad Museum at Salem. Until the mid-1920s, this roll-top desk was used at the depot by Agent A. H. Alberding. As were many items here, the desk was donated to the museum by John and Julie Campbell of Louisville and Cecil and Martha Smith of Salem.

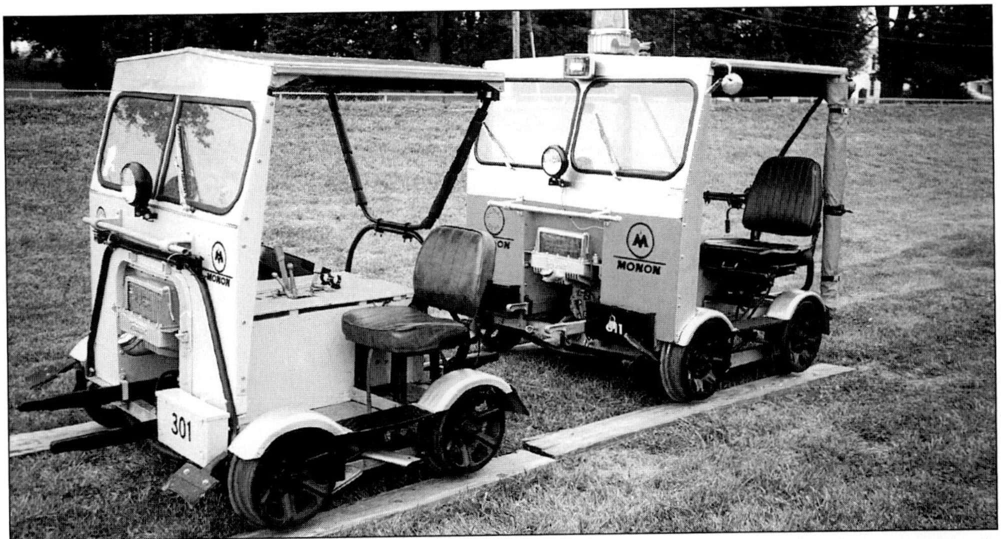

Rail Inspection Motor Car. A Fairmont motor car is displayed at The Depot, but was difficult to capture on film in its current setting. These two cars were photographed while on display at the Linden Depot during a Monon Society meeting. They were used by workers to inspect track and travel to work sites along the railroad's trackage. Today, rail workers use trucks of various sizes with special rail attachments (Hy-rail vehicles) that allow the driver to go from road to rail with ease. The Fairmont Gas Engine and Railway Motor Car Co. began in 1911, and by 1949, offered 19 models of motorcars to customers.

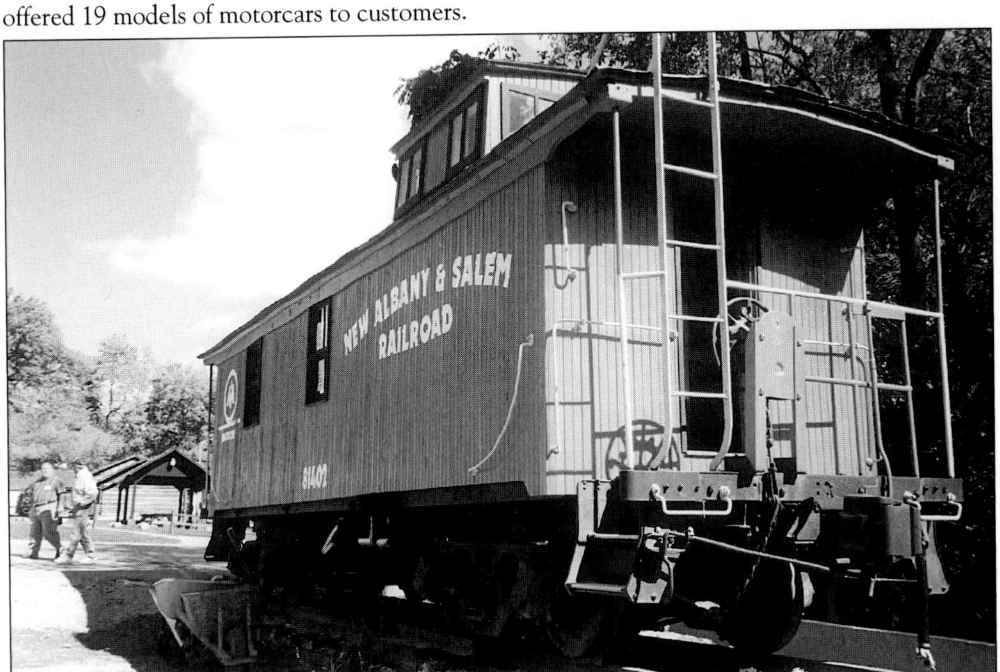

New Albany & Salem Railroad Caboose. This Monon caboose, built in 1929 by the American Car and Foundry Co., is now located at the John Hay Center. It is at the east end of the depot and has been restored to the specifications of the Monon. Notice the lettering and the numbering, #81402. This caboose has a wooden exterior.

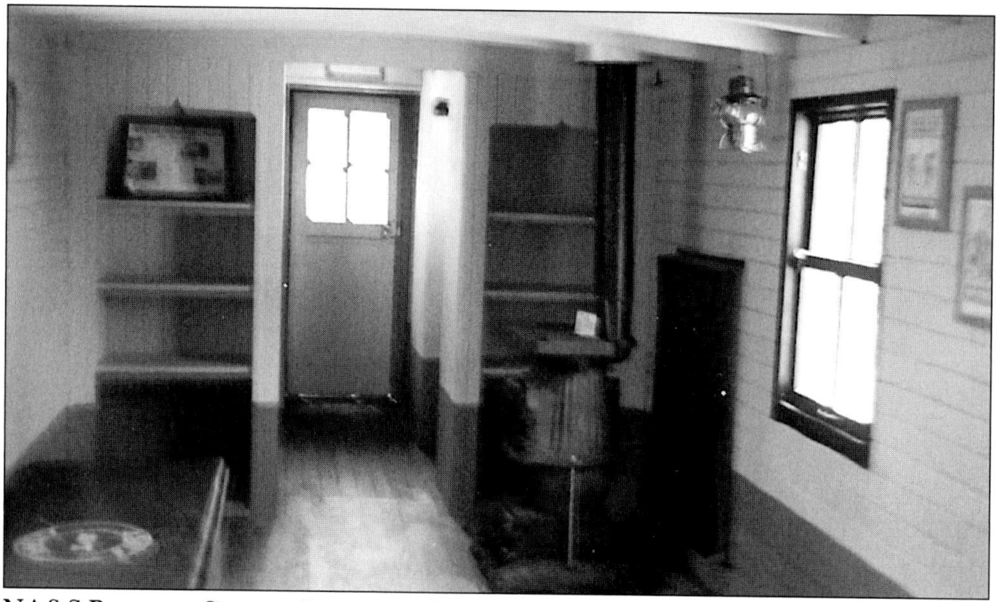

NA&S Railroad Caboose Interior. This photograph shows the interior of Monon Caboose #81402. Note the heating stove to the right. (And you always wondered why they had that small chimney.) The benches/beds are to the left. Toward the doorway are the stairs leading to the cupola, which gave a visual advantage to the conductor, who could notify the engineer of a problem.

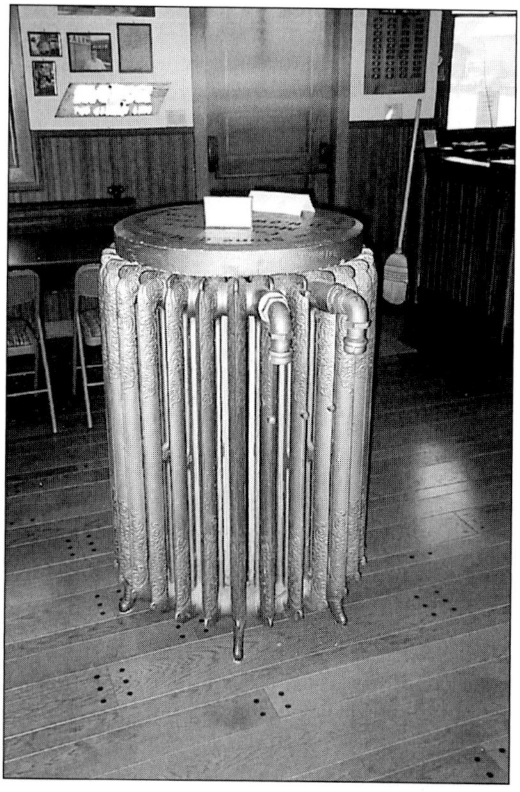

Steam Radiator. On cold Indiana mornings, Monon railroad crews looked forward to the stop at the Salem Depot. This gave them opportunity to huddle around the steam radiator located in the center of the depot's waiting room. The stone top diffuses the heat.

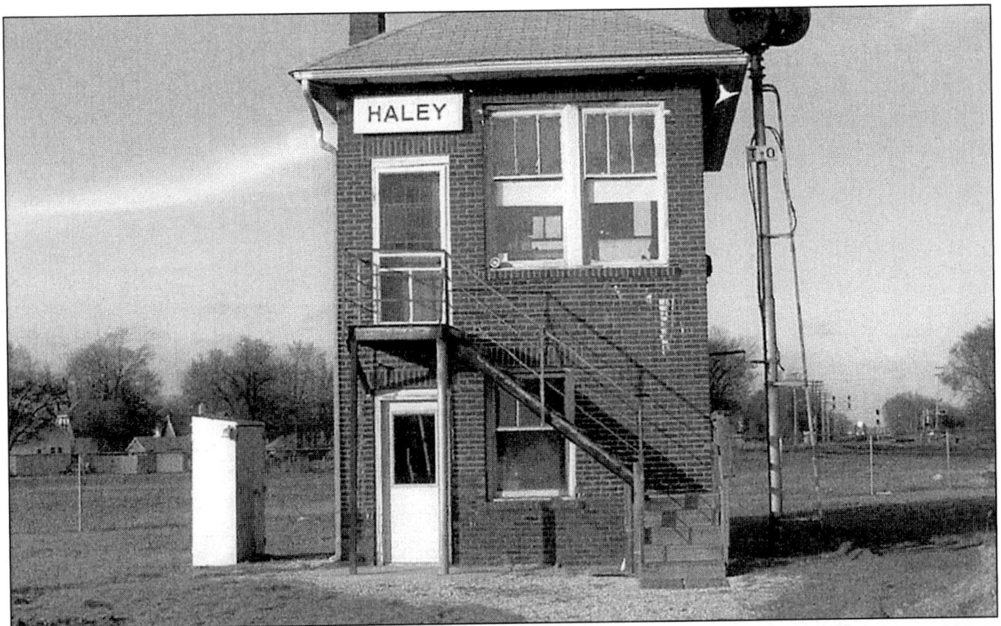

HALEY TOWER. This Haley Tower was built in 1904, replacing an older wooden tower. With few depots remaining in Terre Haute, a railroad group in the Wabash Valley area is moving in a different direction with efforts to preserve the local railroad heritage. Haley Tower was located in Terre Haute and was one of the very last manned interlocking towers in the Midwest. The Haley Tower Historical and Technical Society has been quite successful in acquiring and relocating the brick tower to their property. (Courtesy Bob Mount.)

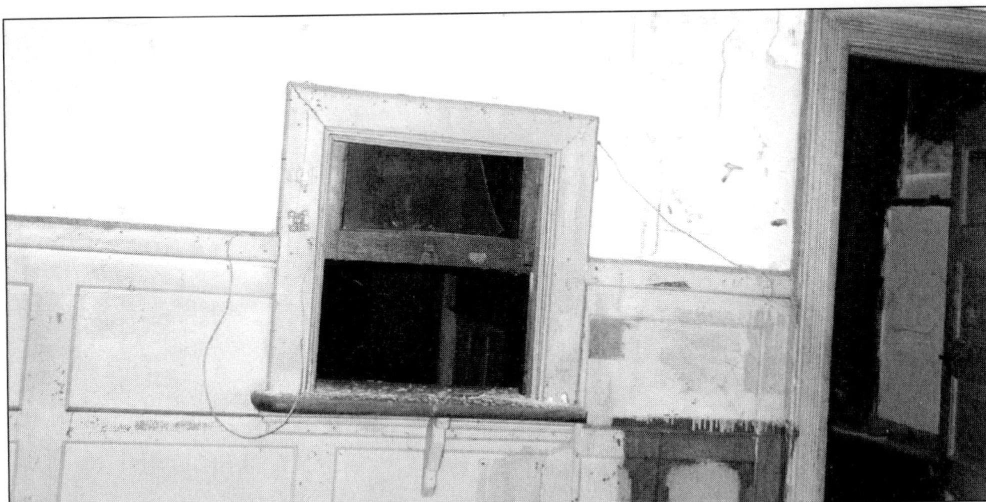

BEDFORD MILWAUKEE PASSENGER. Jamie Harris, director of Bedford Urban Enterprise, kindly allowed entrance to view the interior of two depots in Bedford. This group now owns both the Monon Passenger depot with its recycling operation and the Milwaukee (CMStP&P) Passenger depot. A grant of $260,000 was acquired for repair of the custom-made, Italian-tile roof at the Milwaukee depot. The roof leaks have allowed areas of the depot to incur further damage. Though work on the roof has not begun yet, an application has been made for $800,000 for its future repair. The photograph shows one of the rooms, with a window, possibly for selling tickets.

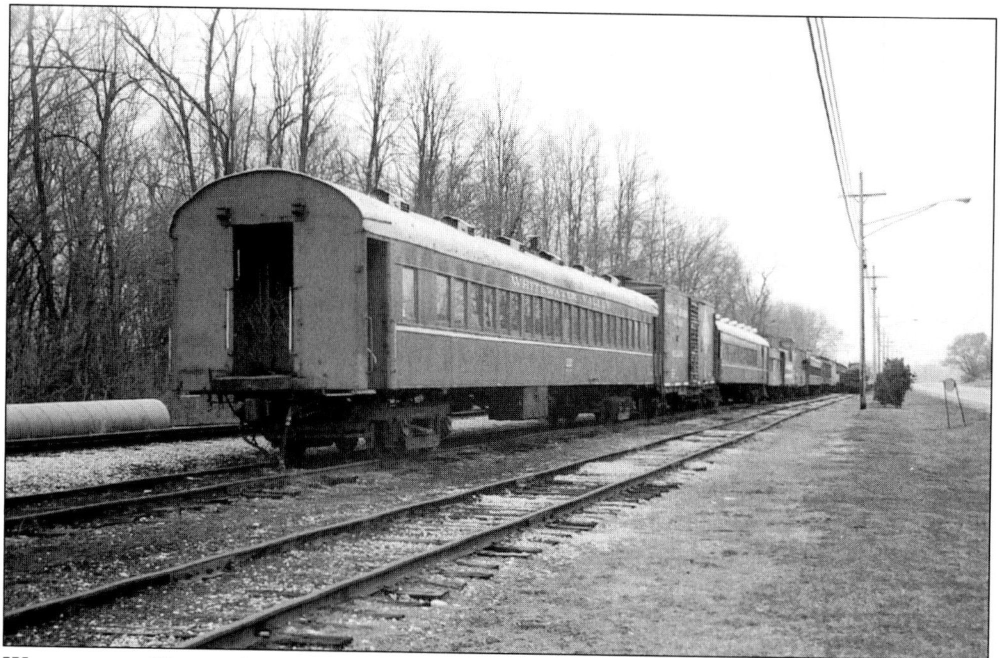

WHITEWATER VALLEY RAILROAD. The Whitewater Valley Railroad (WVRR) is an operating railroad museum dedicated to preserving an historic branch line. It is based in Connersville, where the Grand Central Station stands at Grande Avenue and Fifth Street. Its train yard and maintenance buildings are on Highway 121. One of its missions is to conduct educational programs for the surrounding areas. This photograph shows the train yard.

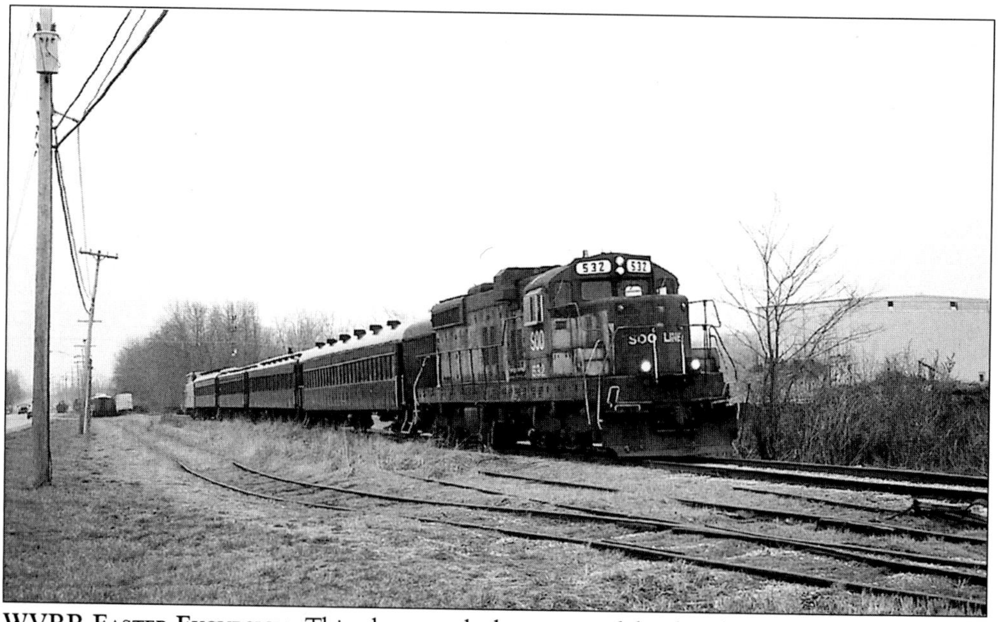

WVRR EASTER EXCURSION. This photograph shows one of the diesel locomotives pulling four coaches full of excited children south of Connersville to hunt and collect Easter eggs. Unlike most passenger trains, this train has a caboose at the end where the Easter Bunny was allowed to ride and find some peace.

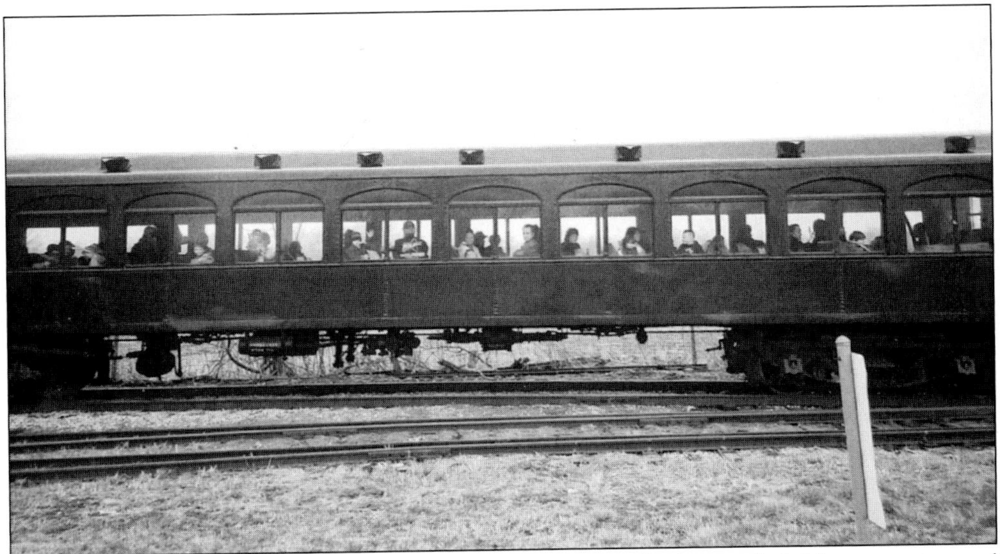

WVRR COACH. Like the other three coaches, this one is full of excited children, parents, and grandparents. The Easter excursion allows kids to experience a train ride. Preservation groups like Whitewater River Valley Railroad, the Carthage, Knightstown & Shirley Tourist Railroad, and the Indiana Railway Museum are doing a marvelous job educating our youth about the railroad experience.

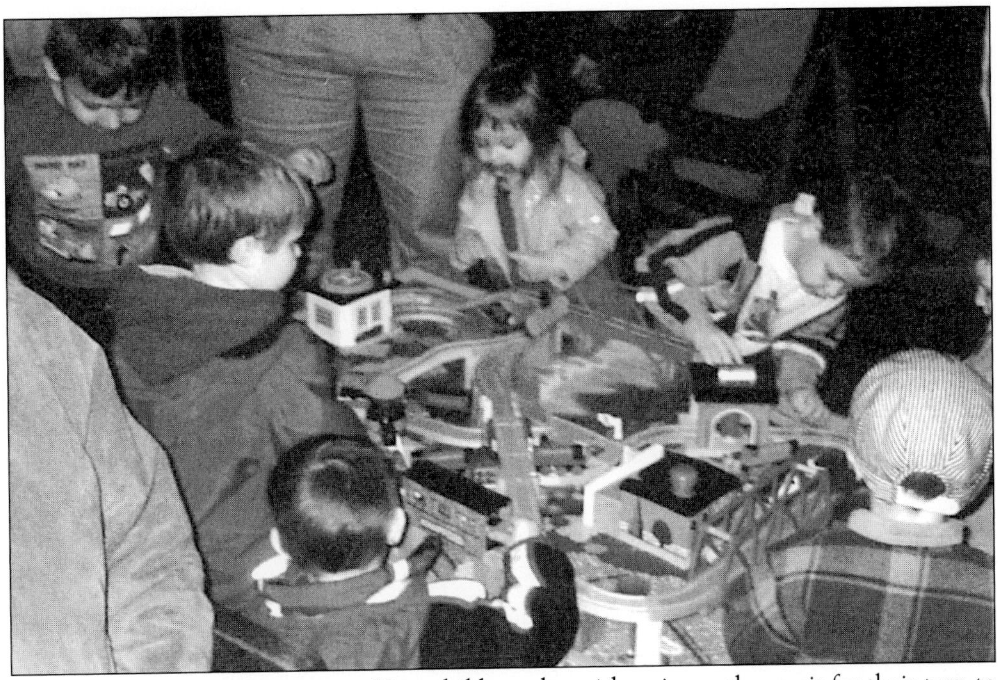

TOY TRAINS . . . THE BEGINNING. Here children play with trains as they wait for their turn to ride the real passenger train. The WVRR train station has several of these popular play areas that keep young children entertained and educated. The station also has an excellent souvenir shop. It has railroad magazines and collectibles for adults and numerous railroad toys for youth.

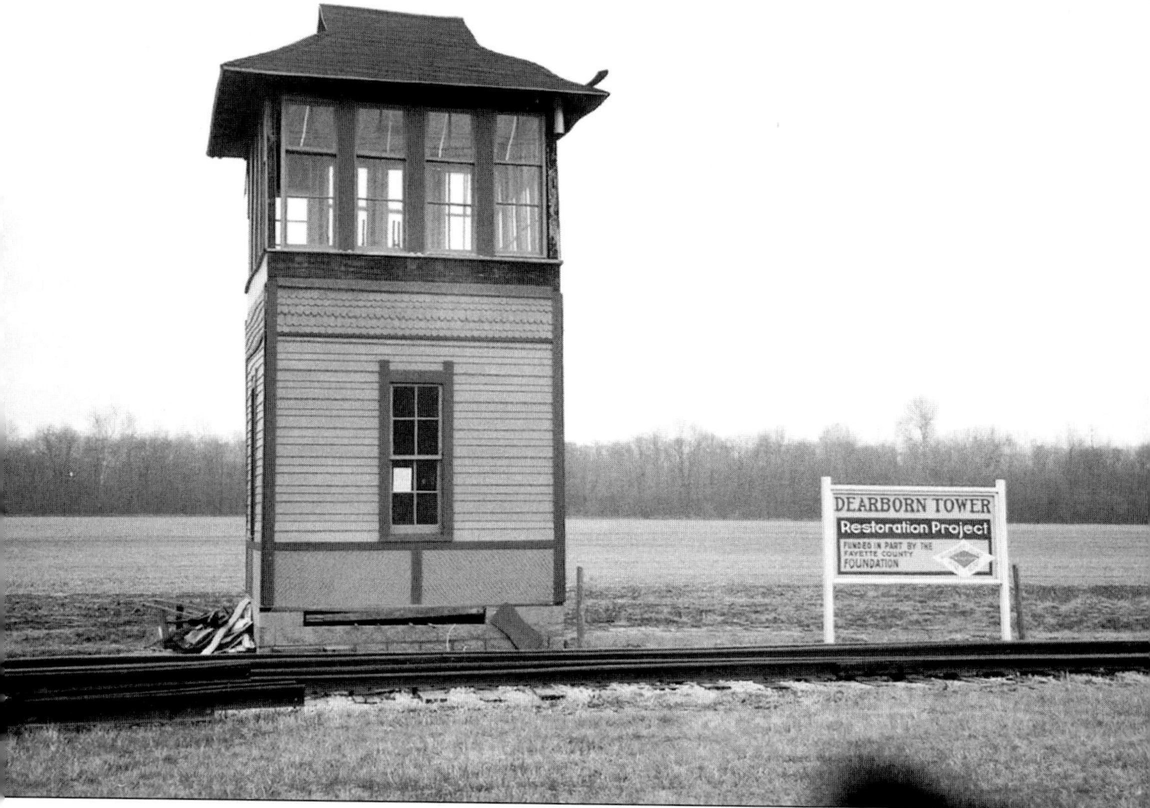

DEARBORN TOWER. One of the current restoration projects of the Whitewater Valley Railroad is the restoration of the Dearborn Tower. This preservation effort is supported by the Fayette County Foundation and CSX Transportation. The tower is now located on Highway 121, just south of the rail yard. It was disassembled and moved from Lawrenceburg, Indiana, in July 2003. When completed, it will serve the WVRR as an artifact interpretation and display center. Built in 1886, the signal tower was used by CSX until 1986.

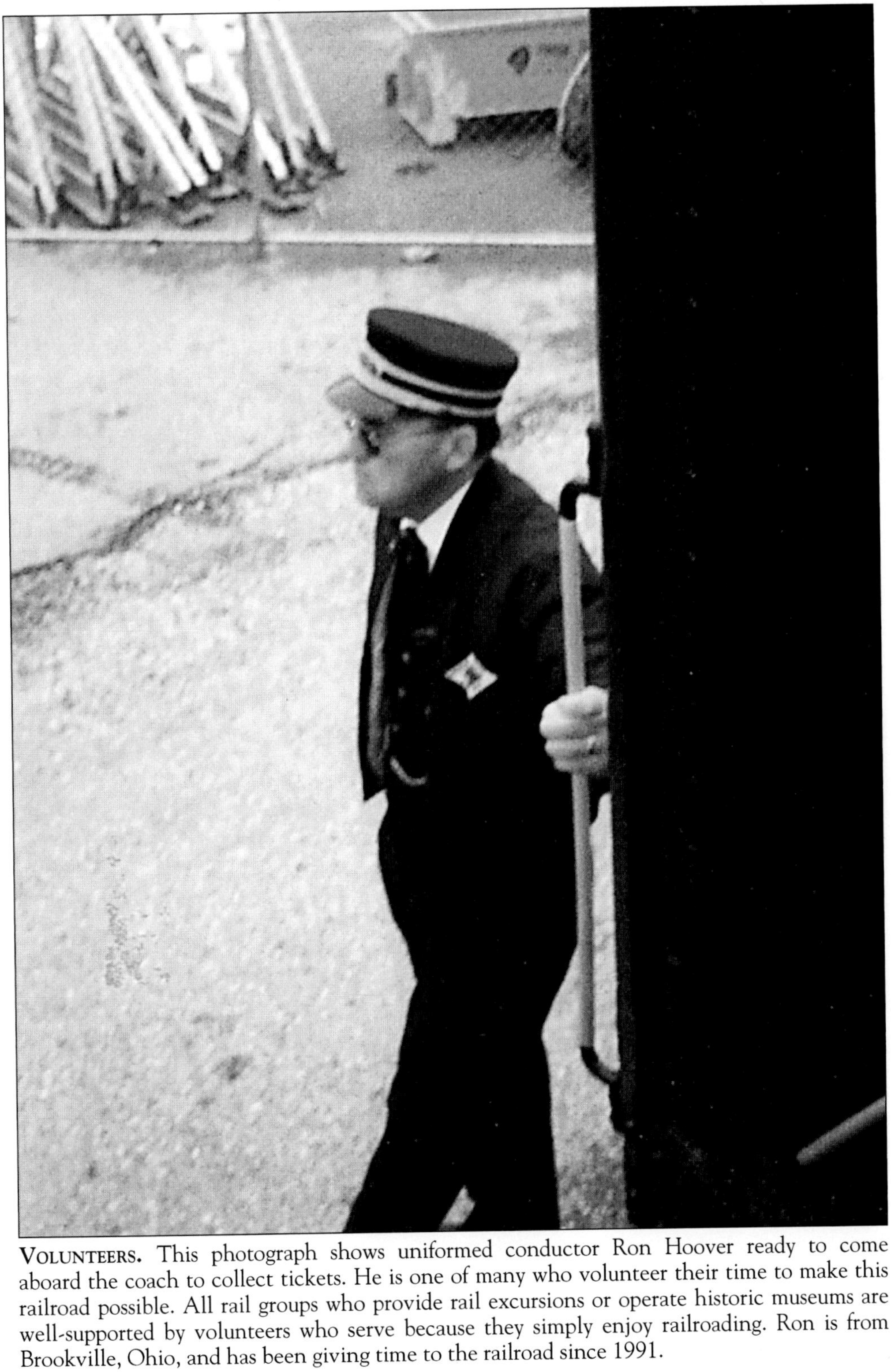

Volunteers. This photograph shows uniformed conductor Ron Hoover ready to come aboard the coach to collect tickets. He is one of many who volunteer their time to make this railroad possible. All rail groups who provide rail excursions or operate historic museums are well-supported by volunteers who serve because they simply enjoy railroading. Ron is from Brookville, Ohio, and has been giving time to the railroad since 1991.

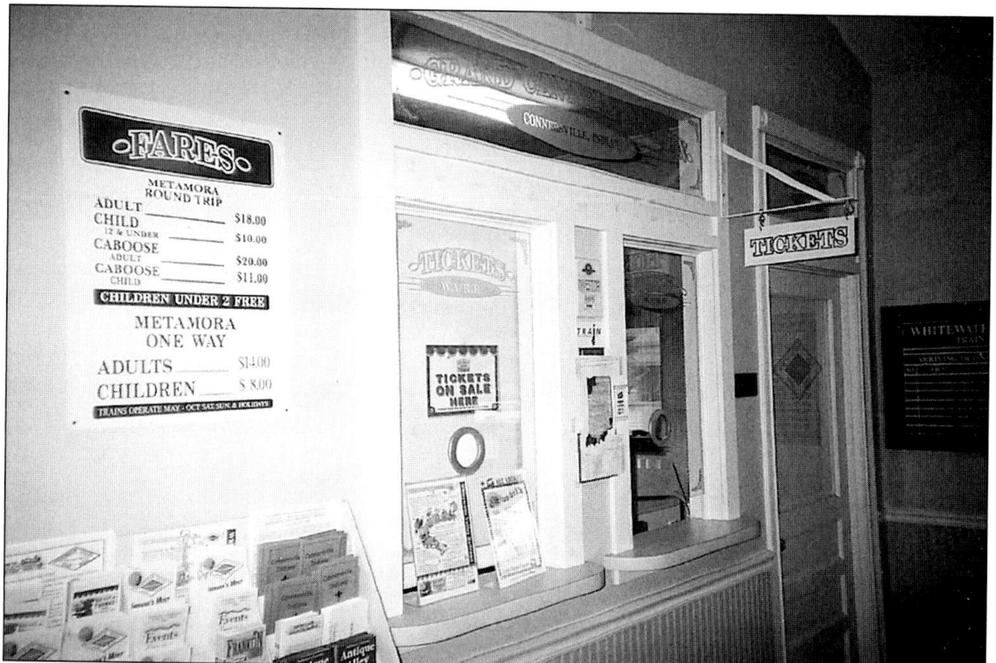

WVRR Ticket Window. The Whitewater Valley Railroad depot was built for the railroad and has no historical significance. The excursions are quite popular in the Connersville area, and tickets can be purchased at this window, by telephone, and online. The ticket booth is located in the waiting room.

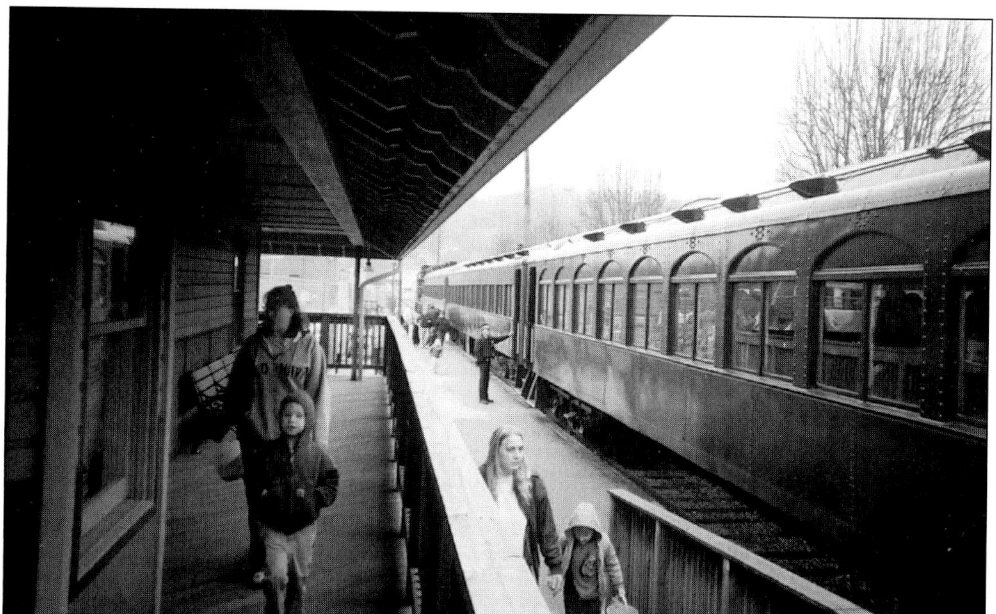

A Nice Time. Passengers disembark the coaches at the end of the Easter Egg Excursion, intended for children and adult chaperones, who may be left holding the egg bucket. The trip provided an excellent opportunity to share the history of railroading with youth and for parents to build their relationships with their children.

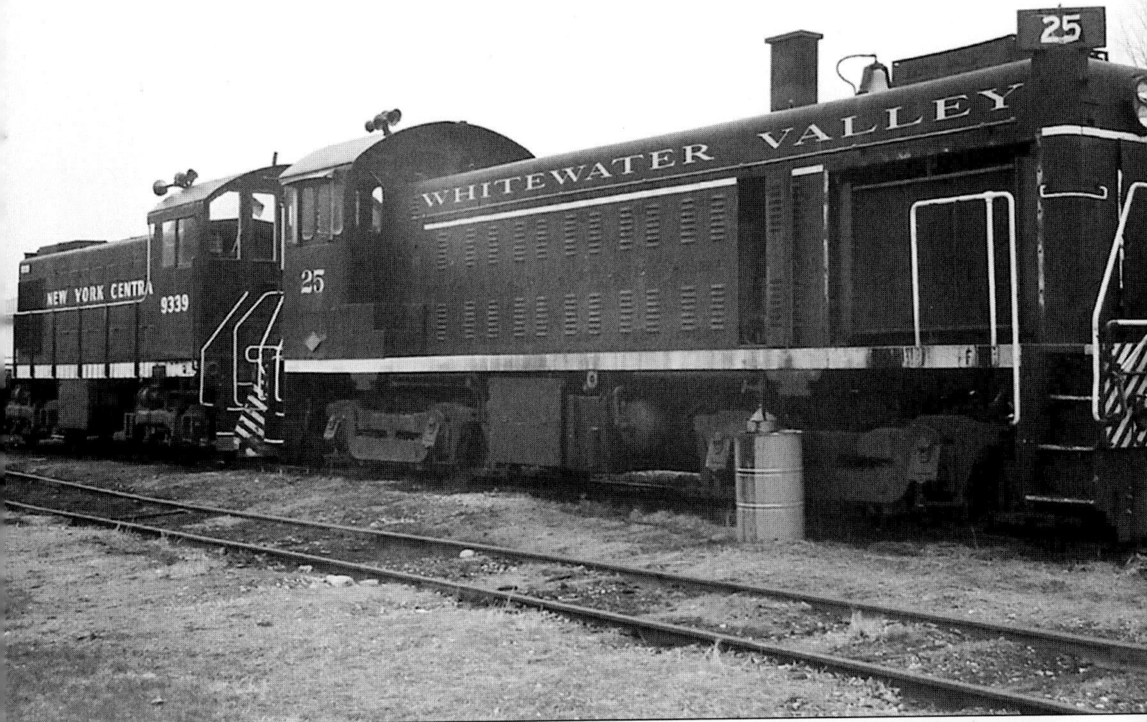

WHITEWATER VALLEY LOCOMOTIVES. This photograph shows two of the railroad's ten engines currently listed on their web page. On the left is the New York Central #9339, a switcher built by Alco GE in 1948. The other engine, #25, is also a switcher built by Lima Hamilton and has 750 HP. It was constructed as a passenger switcher for the Cincinnati Union Terminal in 1951. Aficionados who wish to operate some of the equipment at the railroad, have a chance to do so. The WVRR holds free training classes in the early spring for volunteers who may choose to get into authentic train operation for this railroad. The classes allow them to learn about railroad safety, operating rules, train operations, signaling, switching, and dispatching. Volunteers may also train to be a brakeman, fireman, engineer, or depot agent.

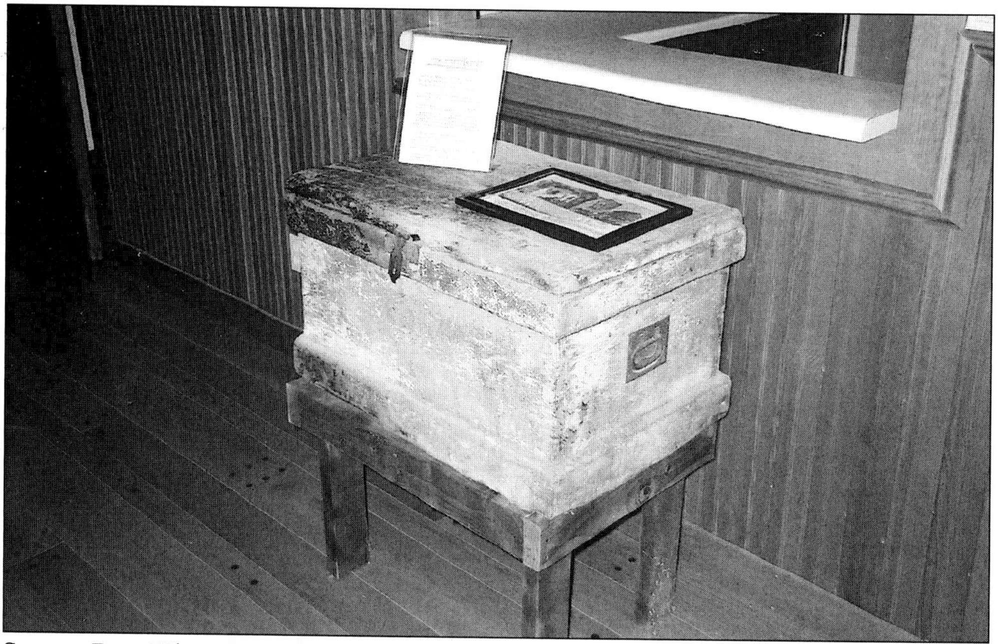

STRONG BOX. When General John Hunt Morgan was raiding in the Hoosier state, he stopped at Salem on July 10, 1863, after raiding Corydon. Before Morgan arrived, the station agent removed all of the valuables and filled the box with tools. He then had the valuables taken to another site. When Morgan arrived, he ordered his men to open the box, which they did by shooting off the lock. When he found the strong box had only tools, he had his men torch the depot, burn some boxcars, and tear up track. The strong box is at the Depot Railroad Museum in Salem.

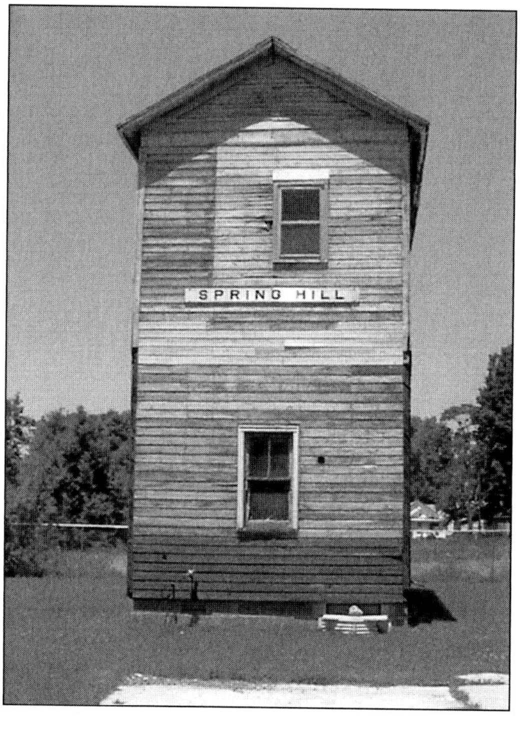

SPRING HILL TOWER. The Haley Tower Historical and Technical Society (HTHTS) recently gained a second tower, the wooden Spring Hill Tower, built in 1910. Spring Hill Tower controlled rail lines belonging to the Evansville & Terre Haute (E&TH), the Evansville & Indianapolis (E&I), and the Chicago, Terre Haute & Southeastern (CTH&SE), which eventually became the Milwaukee Road. It was last used in January 1999, and the HTHTS bought it from the Canadian Pacific a year later. Their current efforts are in restoring this tower. (Courtesy Bob Mount.)

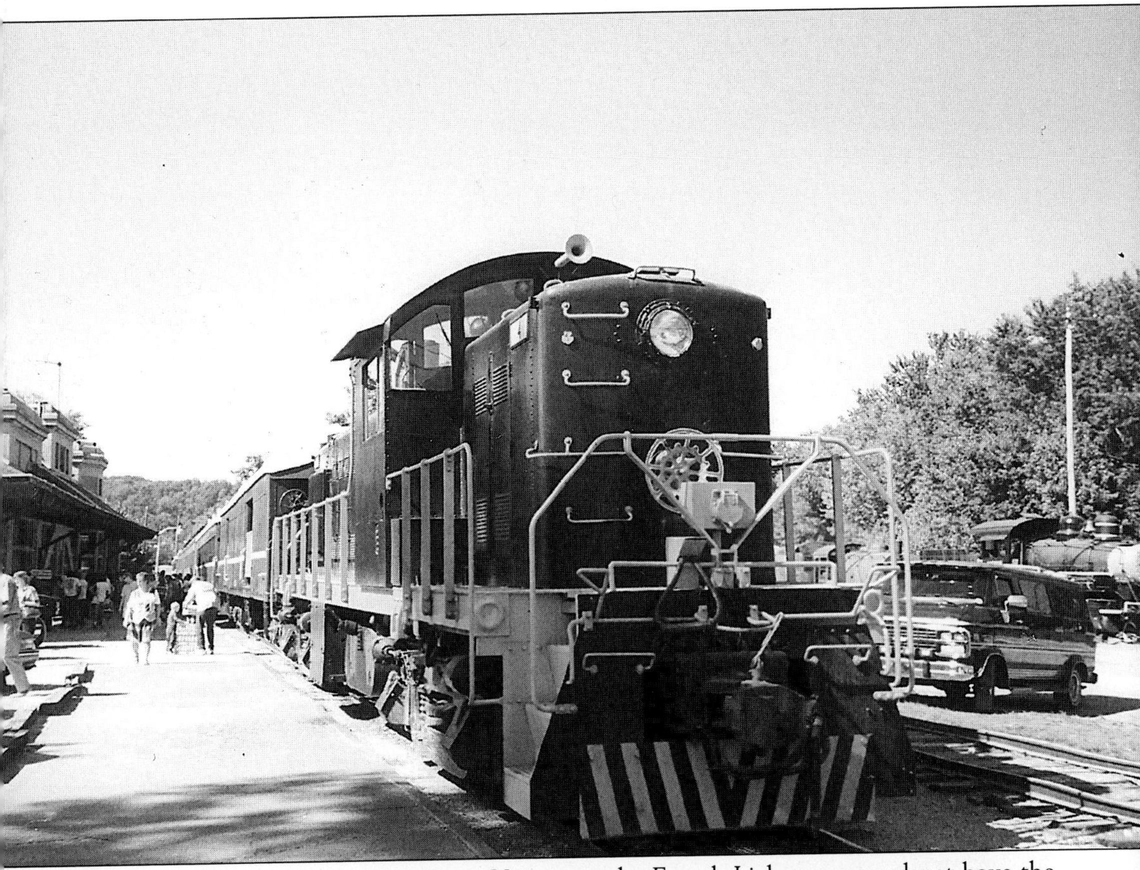

DIESEL AT INDIANA RAILWAY MUSEUM. Visitors to the French Lick passenger depot have the opportunity to ride the tourist train shown here. The diesel locomotive in this photograph is an Alco RS-1, built in 1947, which was in use during 2000. The museum railroad has continued to grow and currently boasts a roster of over 65 pieces of rolling stock and locomotives. In 2004, the railroad had a ridership of over 23,000 passengers.

ACKNOWLEDGMENTS

Books

Art Work of New Albany. Chicago: West H. Parish Publishing Co, 1893.
Dolzall, Gary W. and Stephen F. Dolzall. *Monon, The Hoosier Line*. Bloomington: Indiana University Press, 1987.
Parker, Francis H. *Indiana Railroad Depots*. Muncie, IN: Ball State University, 1989.
Simons, Richard S. and Francis H. Parker. *Railroads of Indiana*. Bloomington: Indiana University Press, 1997.

Web Sites

Bloomfield State Bank/Greene County HomeFinder. http://www.eurekaboy.com/viaduct/viaduct.htm
Carr, Joseph D. "Madison Incline." http://www.jeffersoncountyhistoricalsociety.com
"Funds Freeze Stalls Plans." *Indianapolis Star*, July 14, 2001.
Goodman, Wayne, "PRR Depot Richmond." www.historiclandmarks.org
Kipshire, Tom. "Bygone Places of the Monon." http://www.chrispy.net/~monon/bygone/main.
Owen, Charles. "Louisville, New Albany & Corydon Railroad." http://www.lnacrr.com
Parsons. "Short Lines Indiana Rail Plan." http://www.in.gov/dot/pubs/train_plan/
PRR Station Richmond. http://www.historiclandmarks.org

Newspapers, Journals, Magazines, Documents

"End of New Albany Depot." *The Hoosier Line*, Sept. 1995.
Hall, Gregory. "Charlestown May Tear Down . . ." *Courier-Journal*, April 24, 2001.
Hetherington, James A. "In the Van of Progress." *Traces*, Summer 2001.
Lortz, George. "The K&I Bridge, Part 1" *The Hoosier Line*, May 2001 (20).
"Elliston's Triple Crossing." *The Hoosier Line*, May 2003 (22).
McFeely, Dan. "Historical Old Depot Needs Aid." *Indianapolis Star*, January 6, 1999.
New Albany Chamber of Commerce. *Monon Centennial Celebration*. 1947.
Powers, Jack. "Monon to Establish General Offices Here." *New Albany Tribune*, May 9, 1963.
"New Monon Freight House." *New Albany Tribune*, November 21, 1962.
"Project to Transform Depot Wins Award." *Indianapolis Star*, September 2, 2004.
Sandusky, Dale. "Historic Train Station Faces its Final Stop." *New Albany Tribune*, August 27, 1995.
Simons, Parker. "On Track." *Traces*, Summer 2001.
Smith, Cecil. "Caboose 81402." *The Hoosier Line*, (17) 1, March 1998.
Watson, Thomas. "Forty-two Lost in the Building of the Big Four Rail Span." Associated Press.
Watt, Bill. "Passenger Trains Fade." *Courier-Journal*, July 21, 1968.
Wozniczka, Denny. *Hoosier Line*. (7) 1, March 1987.